Understanding public attitudes to criminal justice

CRIME AND JUSTICE
Series editor: Mike Maguire
Cardiff University

Crime and Justice is a series of short introductory texts on central topics in criminology. The books in this series are written for students by internationally renowned authors. Each book tackles a key area within criminology, providing a concise and up-to-date overview of the principal concepts, theories, methods and findings relating to the area. Taken as a whole, the *Crime and Justice* series will cover all the core components of an undergraduate criminology course.

Understanding public attitudes to criminal justice

Julian V. Roberts and Michael J. Hough

Open University Press

Open University Press
McGraw-Hill Education
McGraw-Hill House
Shoppenhangers Road
Maidenhead
Berkshire
SL6 2QL

email: enquiries@openup.co.uk
world wide web: www.openup.co.uk

and Two Penn Plaza, New York, NY 10121-2289, USA

First published 2005

A catalogue record of this book is available from the British Library

ISBN-10: 0 335 21536 X (pb)
          0 335 21537 8 (hb)
ISBN-13: 978 0335 21536 2 (pb)
          978 0335 21537 9 (hb)

Library of Congress Cataloging-in-Publication Data
CIP data has been applied for

Typeset by RefineCatch Ltd, Bungay, Suffolk
Printed in Great Britain by Bell & Bain Ltd., Glasgow

Dedicated to Second Officer Kay Ducker of the Women's Royal Naval
Service
(1917–2005)

The oldest have borne most; we that are young
Shall never see so much or live so long.

Contents

Series editors foreword

This book by Julian Roberts and Mike Hough is the fourteenth in the *Crime and Justice* series published by Open University Press/McGraw Hill. The series is well established as a key resource in universities teaching criminology or criminal justice, especially in the UK but increasingly also overseas. The aim from the outset has been to give undergraduates and graduates both a solid grounding in the relevant area and a taste to explore it further. Although aimed primarily at students new to the field, and written as far as possible in plain language, the books are not oversimplified. On the contrary, the authors set out to 'stretch' readers and to encourage them to approach criminological knowledge and theory in a critical and questioning frame of mind.

The editors of this volume are among the leading experts in the area of public opinion and crime. Mike Hough was one of the original designers of the British Crime Survey, and Julian Roberts has written widely on public attitudes to crime and justice in an international context. The topic has been attracting increasing academic attention in the light of populist trends in policy-making and a growing governmental discourse around the idea of 'empowering' or 're-connecting with' communities. Such policies clearly demand some form of knowledge about what 'the public' or 'the community' thinks about crime and the agencies which respond to it. As the book shows, this raises all kinds of problematic conceptual and methodological issues, and despite the plethora of public surveys and focus groups that claim to reflect 'public attitudes', there remains a considerable lack of clarity in the area. The authors address these issues in accessible language and give strong warnings about the misinterpretations of findings that can arise. However, the book is focused less on methodology than on discussing key empirical research findings and their implications. One of its central themes is the importance of knowledge about public trust and confidence in criminal justice which, the authors conclude, are at critically low levels not only in England and Wales but 'almost everywhere'. There are specific chapters on attitudes towards – and, importantly, knowledge about – each of three major components of the criminal process (the police, the courts, and the prison system) and another on youth justice. Attention is also drawn to recent research on important topics that have received less academic and media attention, such as attitudes towards restorative justice. The book concludes with a discussion about the role that public views should play in the evolution of criminal justice policies, as well as how the state of public knowledge might be improved.

Other books previously published in the *Crime and Justice* series – all of whose titles begin with the word 'Understanding' – have covered criminological theory (Sandra Walklate), penal theory (Barbara Hudson), crime data and statistics (Clive Coleman and Jenny Moynihan), crime prevention (Gordon Hughes), violent crime (Stephen Jones), community penalties (Peter Raynor and Maurice Vanstone), white collar crime (Hazel Croall), risk and crime (Hazel Kemshall), youth and crime (Sheila Brown), social control (Martin Innes), psychology and crime (James McGuire), victims and restorative justice (James Dignan) and drugs and crime (Trevor Bennett and Katy Holloway). Three are already in second editions and other second editions are planned. Other new books in the pipeline include texts on prisons, policing, criminological research methods, race and crime, 'cybercrime' and political violence. All are topics which are either already widely taught or are growing in prominence in university degree courses on crime and criminal justice, and each book should make an ideal foundation text for a relevant module. As an aid to understanding, clear summaries are provided at regular intervals, and a glossary of key terms and concepts is a feature of every book. In addition, to help students expand their knowledge, recommendations for further reading are given at the end of each chapter.

Mike Maguire
September 2005

Acknowledgements

We would like to thank Mark Barratt from McGraw-Hill and the Series Editor (Mike Maguire) for helping to bring this volume to press. We are grateful to Brandon Applegate for comments on the prison chapter, and Sherri Matta for research assistance throughout the project.

Julian V. Roberts[1]
Mike Hough[2]
Oxford and London, July 2005

[1] Centre for Criminology, University of Oxford; julian.roberts@crim.ox.ac.uk
[2] Institute for Criminal Policy Research, King's College London; mike.hough@kcl.ac.uk

chapter one

Introduction to public opinion and criminal justice

Introduction

Public opinion has always played a significant role in the administration of criminal justice, and information about public attitudes is clearly important to politicians and criminal justice professionals (see Sundt 1994). At the beginning of the twenty-first century, governments in most Western nations routinely conduct opinion polls to track the nature of public attitudes to important issues in criminal justice. More recently, many countries have conducted surveys to measure levels of public confidence in the system. The results of these surveys – revealing low levels of public confidence – have led to attempts to promote public confidence in criminal justice, and to ensure that the justice system does not drift too far away from the views of the community that it serves (see Hough and Roberts 2004a).

To a degree, this heightened sensitivity to the views of the public reflects an element of *penal populism* – where politicians promote policies simply because they are judged to be attractive to the electorate, regardless of their actual value in reducing crime rates or promoting justice. In recent years, penal populism has led to the emergence of many punitive policies, including mandatory sentences of imprisonment. A number of scholars have explored and explained the rise of penal populism across Western nations (e.g. Garland 2001; Roberts *et al.* 2003; Hutton 2005; Pratt and Clark 2005), and we return to the issue later in this chapter.

However, populism is not the whole story; it is perfectly proper for politicians to ensure that the justice system does not fall totally out of step with public opinion. The existence of a wide discrepancy between the views of the public and the practice of the justice system will undermine the legitimacy of the institutions of criminal justice. It will also undermine the administration of justice; disenchanted or alienated members of the public will be less likely to report crimes to the police, and less willing to participate in the criminal process as witnesses or jurors. There is also evidence that people who have little faith in their justice system tend to be less committed to the society in which they live:[1] promoting confidence in criminal justice may well promote social cohesion. So politicians ought to be responsive to public opinion – but only to the extent that this responsiveness will serve the public interest.

Most countries have also conducted public opinion research not simply to gauge levels of confidence in justice but also to find ways of reducing the mismatch between public opinion and criminal justice practices. This has occurred principally in the area of sentencing. For example, the Sentencing Advisory Panel in England and Wales has commissioned several studies to identify the factors that people feel should be considered at sentencing (e.g. Russell and Morgan 2001; Clarke *et al.* 2002; for discussion of the role of public opinion in criminal justice policy, see Morgan 2002). In the words of the Panel's chairman, this research 'proved to be of great assistance to the Panel in formulating its advice to the Court of Appeal' (Wasik 2002). The Home Office Review of Sentencing in England and Wales commissioned studies to assess public opinion on several aspects of sentencing (see Home Office 2001: Appendix 5); the findings clearly had an impact on the review's recommendations (for discussion see Roberts 2002c).

Other jurisdictions have also undertaken extensive public consultations of this sort. The US Sentencing Guidelines Commission funded a major study that compared guideline sentences with public views of the appropriate punishments for such crimes (Rossi and Berk 1997). In Canada, a Royal Commission into sentencing mounted three extensive national opinion surveys to guide its deliberations about the future of sentencing in that country (see Roberts 1988b). It is perhaps no coincidence that all of these government-funded explorations of public attitudes focused on sentencing. This aspect of the criminal justice system attracts more attention than any other, and it is with respect to sentencing that the debates about criminal law reform become most heated.

Since the early 1990s, there has been a dramatic increase in the volume of research upon public attitudes to criminal justice, and over this period our understanding of public opinion in this field has greatly improved. There is now a body of research that shows how specific methodologies influence findings. We have a much clearer idea of the commonalities in attitudes in different countries and cultures – and of the differences. But understanding public opinion about justice is not simply a question of summarizing the findings from surveys and polls. We need to determine which factors shape public opinion, and we need to consider the impact of public opinion on the functioning of the justice system. How do the views of the public influence criminal justice policy and practice? This latter question is hard to research, and few studies have undertaken the task.[2]

The focus of the volume

This volume in the 'Understanding' series explores the knowledge and opinions of the public in the area of criminal justice. This may seem a near-impossible task: how can the complexity and diversity of public opinion in a modern industrialized state be captured by surveys or even by more sophisticated methodologies such as 'Deliberative Polls'? (This research technique is described later in this chapter; see also Fishkin 1995; Hough and Park 2002.) The views of the public are ever changing, ever evolving, as the following examples show:

- In 1960, four out of five respondents to a nationwide poll in Britain supported the use of corporal punishment as a sentencing option (Silvey 1961). Today, few members of the public in Britain would find this to be an acceptable legal punishment.

- Just 30 years ago, when Americans were asked to identify the major contributors to violence in their country, two of the most popular options (endorsed by over half the sample) were 'communists' and 'radical revolutionary groups' (Harris 1975). Public perceptions of the sources of violence have evolved considerably since this survey was conducted.
- Only 17 per cent of respondents to a 1974 survey believed that female police officers are as effective as their male counterparts in all situations (cited in Knowles 1985). Here too, public attitudes have changed; there is little evidence that the public see female officers as being less effective.

Moreover, there is no such single entity as the British public, or 'Americans', but a multitude of publics, broken down by gender, age, race, ethnicity and many other variables, several of which are linked in important ways to opinions about crime and justice (see Wood and Viki 2004 for a review). The best that can be achieved, and what we seek to achieve, is to paint a broad-brush picture of public views regarding criminal justice. Describing public attitudes to any topic inevitably involves generalization, and this generalization will by definition do some injustice to the diversity of individual viewpoints.

The field of public opinion and criminal justice has yet to develop a truly international foundation. Comparative research remains rare (for an early, limited investigation see Scott and Al-Thakeb 1977). While researchers have explored several issues in different jurisdictions, no public opinion database collects public attitude data using standardized questions and uniform sampling strategies across different countries.[3] The International Crime Victimization Survey (ICVS) comes close to this. The survey has been conducted on four occasions now and currently includes over 50 countries. It employs a broadly comparable methodology across all sites. However, it contains only one question measuring attitudes to punishment: respondents are asked to 'sentence' an offender described in a brief scenario. This single question allows only limited international comparisons of public attitudes to punishment (see Kury 2002; Mayhew and van Kesteren 2002). What is needed is an annual, standardized survey instrument that explores a wide range of issues within the area of criminal justice, particularly those relevant to all countries (such as confidence in the justice system).[4]

Much of the discussion in this book is policy-related. We may not be able to represent fully the views of 55 million people by summarizing findings from opinion surveys, but we can speak of the broad community reaction to specific policies (or policy directions). To take one example of great current interest, youth justice remains a priority for all Western nations. Most countries – and in particular Britain, Canada and the USA – have introduced major reforms to their youth justice systems in recent years in response to rising youth crime rates and public concern about juvenile offending (see Roberts 2004 and Tonry and Doob 2004 for a review of public opinion research). Some politicians in the USA have urged the elim-ination of the youth justice system, and the adoption of a unified criminal justice system that processes all offenders, regardless of their age. Where does the public stand on this issue? Having reviewed the literature across jurisdictions, we feel that we can provide an answer to questions such as these.

The research that we review in this book derives largely from the United Kingdom, the United States and Canada. Many of the findings apply across jurisdictions, and when this is the case we introduce research from other countries. One example of a finding that emerges in all juris-dictions concerns public ratings of different branches of criminal justice. Whenever the public are asked to rate the performance of different branches of the justice system, the police always receive the most posi-tive ratings, the courts the most negative. (This material is reviewed in Chapter 2.)

Outline of the volume

The scope of the book and issues excluded from the review

The focus of this book is on recent research in the field. We do not review in great detail issues that have been summarized elsewhere; for reviews of earlier studies, the reader is directed to a number of publications (e.g. Walker and Hough 1988; Roberts 1992; Flanagan and Longmire 1996; Roberts and Stalans 1997; Cullen *et al.* 2000). In order to keep the volume to a manageable length, we have explicitly excluded a number of important (and related) issues from our inquiry. Other than the summary provided earlier in this chapter, we do not review public knowledge or opinion about crime trends and offender characteristics; this material is available in earlier publications (e.g. Roberts 1992, 1995; Roberts and Stalans 1997).

Rather than describing the state of public knowledge with respect to criminal justice, each chapter begins with a summary of findings related to the specific issue being examined. We do not explore public fear of crime, or reactions to criminal victimization; a number of recent publications deal with these topics. No discussion is provided of attitudes to capital punish-ment, as this sentencing option is relevant only to a single jurisdiction in the Western world (see Longmire 1996 for a review of research on Ameri-can attitudes to the death penalty). Finally, we have attempted to explore some areas that to date have been neglected by researchers. Two such examples are public opinion regarding imprisonment and attitudes to restorative justice. As well, we review the numerous polls that have been conducted in recent years on the critical issue of public trust or confidence in criminal justice.

The book does not address theoretical aspects of public opinion – the focus is upon the empirical literature. We draw heavily upon two extensive surveys of British attitudes to criminal justice, both which were conducted in 2003. One of these examined all principal components of the justice system, the second focused on youth crime and youth justice. Taken together, they provide the most comprehensive examination of public opinion in British history. We also review findings from repeated administrations of the British Crime Survey, and research from a number of other jurisdictions, such as Scotland, Northern Ireland, South Africa, New Zealand and Canada, where surveys have recently been conducted.

Most of the research that we review is quantitative in nature, simply because qualitative studies (such as focus groups) account for a relatively small proportion of all published material. The research we include was almost exclusively conducted in English-speaking countries, although there is a growing and very significant body of research emerging from continental Europe (e.g. Kury and Ferdinand 1999; Kury *et al.* 2002; Parmentier *et al.* 2004a, b). One of the goals of public opinion research in the future is clearly to integrate findings from across a wider range of jurisdictions and legal systems.

The contents of the volume

Chapter 2 explores what has been described as the 'crisis of confidence in criminal justice'. Most Western nations have now conducted surveys of public confidence or trust in criminal justice, and the results suggest that low levels of public confidence exist almost everywhere (Hough and Roberts 2004a). This chapter places this problem in context, and identifies the specific criminal justice agencies in which the public reposes least confidence. Chapters 3 to 5 summarize findings relating to public attitudes to the three principal components of the criminal process: the police, the courts and the prison system. As we demonstrate, there is a considerable degree of consistency in the responses of members of the public in different countries with respect to these branches of the justice system.

Chapter 6 explores the issue of youth justice. All Western nations employ a separate system of justice – which incorporates less severe penalties than those imposed on adult offenders – to respond to young offenders. We explore the nature of public reaction to youth justice, drawing on a wealth of surveys. Chapter 7 explores public attitudes to restorative justice programmes and initiatives. Restorative justice has emerged as an important alternative to conventional criminal justice processing in recent years (Braithwaite 1999), and this chapter summarizes public reaction to this new way of responding to crime. Finally, Chapter 8 draws some conclusions about the nature of public opinion, and the role that public views should play in the evolution of criminal justice policies. We also review and evaluate a number of experimental attempts to change attitudes by improving the state of public knowledge of criminal justice.

For the remainder of this introductory chapter we review a number of issues that provide the context for the findings and discussion that follow.

Public interest in criminal justice is high; levels of knowledge are low

Hutton (2005) reports findings from a survey of Scottish respondents that capture one of the central paradoxes in the area: interest in criminal justice is very high but knowledge levels are low. Respondents were asked about their *level of interest*, as well as their *level of knowledge* of criminal justice. When asked about their level of interest in criminal justice, 88 per cent of the Scottish respondents were fairly or very interested in the subject, but levels of knowledge were low (well over half the sample acknowledged knowing little about courts or prisons). Crime news attracts more public interest than any other subject, as can be seen in Table 1.1. While these data come from the USA, and the ordering of issues may vary somewhat in Europe, it seems likely that crime stories would emerge at or near the top of such rankings in other countries as well.

Public interest in criminal justice manifests itself in other ways. Most people follow criminal cases covered by the news media closely, and feel confident enough to make judgements about guilt and innocence. Consider the case of the singer Michael Jackson, facing criminal charges as this volume was being written. An American poll asked members of the public whether they had a view about Jackson's guilt or innocence. The results – shown in Figure 1.1 – are interesting from two perspectives. First, over

Table 1.1 Public interest in news categories, USA

Issue	Percentage of respondents who report following issue 'very closely'
Crime	30
Health	29
Sports	27
Community	26
Religion	21
Local government	20
Science and technology	18
Washington news	17
Entertainment stories	14
International affairs	14
Business and finance	14
Consumer news	12
Culture and the arts	10

Source: adapted from Pew Research Centre (2000).

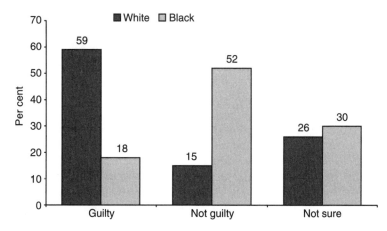

Figure 1.1 American perceptions of the Michael Jackson case (*source*: Taylor 2004)

two-thirds of respondents held an opinion about Jackson's guilt or innocence without having seen a shred of evidence. Second, perceptions of guilt or innocence were highly dependent on the ethnic origin of the respondent. Fifty-nine per cent of white respondents believed that Jackson was guilty; almost as high a percentage of black respondents believed he was not guilty (Taylor 2004). We now know that Jackson was found not guilty on all charges.

Attitudes are dependent upon knowledge; and levels of public knowledge vary greatly across the different branches of the criminal justice system. People admit knowing little about a number of stages of criminal justice. Table 1.2 summarizes responses to a 2003 MORI poll[5] that asked British respondents how much they knew about various components of the justice system. As can be seen, police and courts aside, people report having little familiarity with most branches of criminal justice. Over one-quarter of the respondents admitted that they knew 'nothing at all' about youth

Table 1.2 Self-reported level of knowledge about criminal justice agencies in Britain (percentages)

	A great deal/fair amount	Not very much	Hardly anything/ nothing at all
Police	74	19	7
Courts	51	32	17
Prisons	30	38	31
Probation service	23	40	37
Crown Prosecution Service	27	41	33
Youth courts	18	38	45
Youth offending teams	13	28	59

Source: MORI (2003). Question: 'How much, if anything, do you know about each of the following . . .'

courts; one Briton in five acknowledged they know nothing about an organization as large and important as the probation service. In addition, as will be seen throughout this volume, even for the courts or the prison system, when asked specific questions about the justice system, many people are misinformed about current practices.

Functions of the criminal justice system: public rankings of importance

The criminal justice system attempts to perform many functions, including preventing crime, prosecuting and punishing offenders and protecting the public. Within these general objectives there are many more specific goals. Prosecuting offenders includes protecting the rights of accused persons, and providing services for crime victims who testify in court. The MORI survey mentioned above conducted a unique exploration of public perceptions of the importance of different criminal justice functions. Respondents were provided with a list of 20 functions, and were asked to rate each function using a ten-point importance scale, with ten being the score assigned to a function that is 'absolutely essential'. Some of these functions were utilitarian in nature (e.g. 'reducing the level of crime'), while others invoked normative considerations, such as 'treating people fairly'.

Table 1.3 lists the seven most important functions of criminal justice from the public's perspective.[6] This table provides invaluable insight into the criminal justice priorities of the general public. As can be seen, the list is composed of two kinds of objectives. Some of these are utilitarian in nature – they aim to prevent offending. Other objectives relate to the principles that should guide the justice system. One of these principles (equality of treatment) attracted the highest percentage of 'absolutely essential' ratings. Thereafter, the objectives relate to public safety, and invoke preventing

Table 1.3 Public importance ratings of criminal justice system functions

	Percentage of sample rating function as 'absolutely essential'
Treating all people fairly, regardless of race	72
Creating a society where people feel safe	69
Bringing people who commit crimes to justice	68
Dealing effectively with sex offenders	68
Dealing effectively with violent crime	67
Reducing the level of crime	63
Stopping offenders from committing more crimes	60

Source: MORI (2003). Question: 'How important, if at all, do you regard each of the following aspects of the criminal justice system? For each, please give me a number from 1 to 10 where 1 is not at all important and 10 is absolutely essential.'

crime and reducing re-offending. The strong utilitarian character of the functions listed in Table 1.3 suggests that it is important to know more about public knowledge of crime trends.

Perceptions of crime trends

In many respects the criminal justice system is unlike most other public services. Media coverage of crime and justice is often sensationalized and frequently promotes a negative view of the criminal justice system (e.g. O'Connell 1999). In addition, although this literature is not exhaustively reviewed in this volume, attitudes to criminal justice must be considered in the light of public knowledge of the problem to which the system is a response. Studies in numerous countries have demonstrated that public perceptions of crime rates have been at odds with statistical trends for many years. Most of this research has been conducted in North America or Britain. However, recent research has generated the same finding in other countries, such as Australia (Weatherburn and Indermaur 2004) and South Africa (Monograph 2000). This body of literature demonstrates that there has often been a discrepancy between public perceptions of crime trends and reality.

For example, although rates of both violent and property crimes in Britain declined from 2000 to 2002 – continuing a trend that began in the mid-1990s – almost three-quarters of the British public believed crime had increased over this two-year period (Finney 2004). Perceptions of rising crime rates translate into concern about crime. When the British public were asked in 2000 to express their level of concern about crime, almost half responded that their concern had 'increased a lot' in the past few years (MORI 2000). Almost three-quarters of the sample said that their concern had increased to some degree, despite the decrease in crime rates in the preceding few years.

This discrepancy between public perception and reality has emerged from studies conducted in many countries since the 1980s (e.g. Knowles 1985) and 1990s (US Department of Justice 1997).[7] As recently as 2004, a survey in Australia also found that the majority of the public believed that crime rates had been increasing when in fact rates had been stable or falling over the period in question (Weatherburn and Indermaur 2004).[8] Similarly, although the volume of serious crime declined in South Africa between 1994 and 1999, most South Africans held the opposite view (Monograph 2000). Recent surveys of New Zealanders and residents of Northern Ireland found the same result. The overwhelming majority of the sample (83 per cent) in New Zealand believed (erroneously) that crime rates had increased over the previous two years (Paulin et al. 2003; see also Amelin et al. 2000).

Americans, too, have continually responded to polls by stating that crime rates are increasing, even though in the 1990s this was no longer the case. In 2001, over half the respondents to a national poll believed that crime rates were increasing, although in reality they had been declining (Taylor 1999). In one of the few studies conducted outside Western industrialized countries, Nuttall *et al.* (2003) found that residents of Barbados also held inaccurate perceptions of crime trends. Although crime rates on the island had increased only slightly in the five years preceding the survey, 69 per cent of respondents believed that there was a 'lot more' crime.

This consistent pattern of findings across diverse publics suggests that the source of the public's perception of ever-rising crime rates is the media. Evidence pointing the finger at the media has accumulated for years now. Indeed, the public acknowledges the importance of the media as a source of information about crime. In 1967, a nationwide US survey found that people were more likely to believe crime rates were increasing rather than stable or falling. Respondents to that poll were asked why they thought the crime rate had increased, and the most frequent response was 'what I read and see on television' (American Correctional Association 1968).

Explaining misperceptions of crime trends

It is unclear why the public is so pessimistic with respect to crime trends. Of course crime rates *did* rise steeply in most industrialized countries in the four decades after the Second World War. There may simply be a long lag between changes in crime trends and changes in the public mindset about crime. But this is clearly not the whole explanation. Surveys exploring other issues reveal similar misperceptions. For example, when Americans were asked about employment trends, or the number of teen pregnancies every year – two other important social issues covered by the media – a similar pattern emerged. People held more pessimistic views of the number of jobs created and the trends with respect to teen pregnancies than was justified by statistics (Taylor 1999). Job creation was booming and teen pregnancies had been declining at the time. Taken together these findings suggest that 'good news' – for example, declining crime or unemployment rates – is seldom conveyed by the news media, and accordingly is less likely to be assimilated by the public. In short, bad news sells better than good news, so bad news is what people get.

The entrenched public misperception of increasing crime rates helps to explain why criminal justice remains such a salient public policy issue: in 2003, over half the respondents to a national survey in Britain agreed that 'crime levels are a top priority issue for the government' (*Observer* 2003). This finding demonstrates an association between two attitudes – it does not prove that perceptions of crime determine evaluations of the system. However, it is significant that the people who perceive crime to be increasing also hold the most negative views of the justice system, as can be seen in Table 1.4.

Table 1.4 Perceptions of crime trends by ratings of criminal justice agencies in Britain (percentages)

	Lot more crime	About the same amount of crime	Little less or lot less crime
Police are doing			
Excellent job	37	25	6
Very poor job	71	10	1
Judges are doing			
Excellent job	33	19	12
Very poor job	62	14	1
Prisons are doing			
Excellent job	34	21	11
Very poor job	60	15	2

Source: adapted from Finney (2004).

Systematic research in a number of countries has demonstrated other public misperceptions about crime and offenders.[9] Since these are not explored in detail in this volume, we summarize the principal findings, drawn from representative surveys of the public in many countries over the past 20 years:

- the public over-estimate the proportion of crime that involves violence (Indermaur 1987; Doob and Roberts 1988; Hough and Roberts 1999; Amelin *et al.* 2000; Nuttall *et al.* 2003; Paulin *et al.* 2003);
- the public believe that the homicide rate has increased since the abolition of the death penalty, when in reality homicide rates have declined in countries such as Canada since capital punishment was abolished (Roberts 1995; Nuttall *et al.* 2003; Weatherburn and Indermaur 2004);
- the public see offenders as a group apart from society, and wrongly attribute most offences to a small proportion of the population (e.g. Simmons 1965);[10]
- people over-estimate the volume of offending committed by people on bail (Paulin *et al.* 2003);
- people over-estimate the recidivism rates of offenders released from prison (Doob and Roberts 1988; Roberts 1988a; Redondo *et al.* 1996;[11] Paulin *et al.* 2003);
- people assume that offenders 'specialize', and that clear profiles exist for property offenders, violent offenders and drug offenders (Roberts and White 1986) when in reality most offenders with criminal histories have previous convictions in a number of offence categories.

Members of the public hold strong views about criminal justice issues, and these opinions are often picked up by polls that pose deceptively simple questions. In its 2003 survey of public attitudes to crime and criminal justice in Britain, the *Observer* newspaper found that four out five respondents were of the opinion that an influx of asylum seekers would lead to higher crime rates (*Observer* 2003). When Canadians were asked this question about immigrants in 1990, about half the sample held the same view (Palmer 1990). This association between asylum seekers or immigrants and crime is a good example of an attitude formed in the total absence of any systematic supporting evidence. Indeed, if a subsequent question had asked people to cite the source of this perceived link between immigration and crime, the responses would surely have made interesting reading.

There are many issues within the field of criminal justice on which the public hold strong opinions that were conceived on the basis of weak or faulty evidence. Of course, we all hold opinions that are based on less than scientific examination of relevant evidence. British attitudes to the National Health Service or American views of Medicare are likely to be founded more on the occasional interminable wait in an emergency ward than a comparative analysis of health delivery indicators across countries. But at least direct experience plays a role in the area of health care; most people have occasion to visit a clinic, hospital or physician several times a year. In contrast, far fewer people have recent, direct experience of a criminal court.

With respect to criminal justice, then, we form opinions about sentencing or the criminal process in the absence of careful study or direct or indirect experience. A good example concerns the provisions in the Criminal Justice Act 2003 that permit, under certain circumstances, the retrial of a person acquitted of a charge. When an *Observer* poll asked the public about this issue, four out of five respondents expressed agreement with the proposed reform (*Observer* 2003). It is quite likely, however, that few of the respondents had even considered the issue (let alone the implications of the reform) until they responded to the survey. Their response was based on their ideological perspective with respect to criminal justice; in no way could it be described as 'evidence based'. While the public's direct knowledge of the courts, probation and prison is limited, many more people have direct experience of the police in the course of a year, and as we shall see in a later chapter, their views are more clearly linked to experience.

Perceptions of justice

Perceptions of leniency to offenders

One of the leitmotifs of public attitudes to criminal justice is the desire for a harsher response to crime. Most people believe that the justice system is too lenient towards offenders. This perception goes back many years (see Roberts 1992; Cullen *et al.* 2000), and has persisted despite many changes to the criminal justice environment, including the introduction of tougher sentencing reforms in the USA and the UK, which resulted in record numbers of prisoners by the end of the 1990s in both jurisdictions. Thus in 1974, 30 years before the present volume was written, a survey found that three-quarters of the US public agreed that 'one of the major problems in preventing crime today is that we are making it too easy on convicted offenders' (Duffee and Ritti 1977).

Since then, criminal justice systems have evolved considerably in all countries. In the USA, the sentencing system has become much tougher as a result of sentencing reforms such as 'three strikes' laws, mandatory sentences of imprisonment for drug offenders and legislation that ensures that prisoners spend at least 85 per cent of their sentences in prison. Mandatory sentencing laws have been enacted in England and Wales as well. By the turn of the century, the numbers of prisoners in the UK and the USA had reached record proportions (see, for example, Hough *et al.* 2003 for an analysis of trends in England and Wales). Yet the public still answers questions about sentence severity with the same response: sentences are too lenient.

To some extent this perception of leniency reflects a lack of awareness of the 'get tough' sentencing reforms, or of the mounting numbers of people in prison. A survey conducted by the Esmée Fairbairn Foundation (2003) found that although the British public knew that the prison population had been increasing, most people under-estimated the increase by a substantial margin. Similarly, with the exception of the widely publicized 'three strikes' legislation in the USA, most people are unaware of the severe mandatory minimum penalties introduced over the past decade (see Roberts 2003a). Once again, public reaction appears to be based on preconception rather than a reasoned evaluation of the evidence. This 'get tough' attitude typically emerges from polls that simply ask respondents whether court sentences are tough enough, or ask them to agree or disagree with the view that sentences are too soft. An impression of a punitive American public also emerges from a 1991 survey in which respondents were asked whether they supported or opposed restricting the rights of convicted murderers 'so that they can be executed more promptly': two-thirds were in favour (Cole 1991).

The British public is equally intolerant of obstacles to prosecuting (and convicting) defendants. The aphorism is well engrained in legal thinking that it is better to acquit ten guilty individuals than allow an innocent person to be convicted. The desire to ensure that the innocent are acquitted explains the many criminal procedures designed to avoid such a judicial mistake. The public, however, appears to be less concerned about the occurrence of wrongful convictions. A British Attitudes Survey asked people whether it was worse to convict an innocent person or let a guilty person go free. If asked this question, lawyers would respond that the first kind of judicial error was far worse. However, almost half (42 per cent) of the public felt that letting a guilty person go free was worse (Dowds 1995: Table B.3). This finding reflects the 'crime control' orientation of the public. Most people are more interested in a justice system that allows police and prosecutors significant powers than in a system that follows procedural safeguards to ensure that due process is maintained.

The lopsided scales of justice?

When reviewing polls conducted over the past 40 years, it is hard not to notice clear evidence of 'penal impatience' on the part of the public. People often want a simple solution to the complex problem of offending, and they frequently see little merit in a justice system that goes to some lengths to protect the rights of defendants and to ensure that punishment, when inflicted, is principled in nature. One manifestation of this impatience is a public perception that the scales of justice are skewed in favour of the suspect, accused or offender, at the expense of the victim. According to the public, 'criminals' are treated better, and have more rights, than crime victims. The following examples are illustrative of this perspective:

- 70 per cent of Americans polled on the issue agreed that the laws and the courts are more concerned with protecting the rights of criminals than they are with protecting the rights of victims (Cole 1991);
- more than four out of five Americans supported a number of reforms to increase victims' rights in the criminal justice system (National Victim Centre 1991);
- almost three-quarters of respondents to a MORI poll in Britain agreed that 'the law works to the advantage of the criminal and not victims' (MORI 2000);
- when respondents in Britain were asked to rate the importance of 20 functions of the criminal justice system, the function attracting the least support was 'respecting the rights of people accused of crime' (MORI 2003).

Penal populism

This overview of key findings in attitudes to crime and justice has pointed to some consistent findings across several developed industrialized countries. People tend to be overly pessimistic about the extent of crime problems and markedly impatient with criminal justice responses to these problems. Not surprisingly, these features of public opinion tend to evoke characteristic responses from politicians. In several industrialized democracies, the principal political parties have increasingly vied with each other to offer tough 'no nonsense' policies that 'crack down' on crime. At the start of this chapter we touched on the emergence of penal populism. Now is the time to discuss this issue in a little more depth.

Defining penal populism

The term penal populism, or variants on it such as 'populist punitiveness', has gained considerable currency in recent years in analysis of the politics of law and order (see Bottoms 1995; Roberts *et al.* 2003). Populism is a value-laden term: nobody approves of populist politicians. The nuances of populism can be drawn out by contrasting populist policies to ones that are *responsive*, on the one hand, and to those that are merely *popular*, on the other.

It would be naive or unfair to complain about politicians being responsive to public opinion. Such responsiveness is a central feature of representative democracy: the whole point of an electoral system is to ensure that politicians do not stray too far from the wishes of their electorate. In other words, elected politicians are always to an extent mandated; they do not, and should not, have unfettered freedom to interpret the best interests of those whom they represent. Politics is the art of the possible, and public opinion is one of the factors that define the limits of possibility. If some degree of responsiveness to public opinion is desirable, it is equally unreasonable to attack a politician for pursuing *popular* policies. Indeed, it would be a cause for some concern if elected political parties failed consistently to have broad-based support for their policies. On the other hand, few people are comfortable with the idea of an election manifesto that is constructed solely to secure as many votes as possible.

In other words, representative democracies in the early twenty-first century are characterized by an uneasy tension between the politics of principle and consumer-driven politics. The former involves the promotion of policies that are thought to be in the country's best interests; the latter are those that are reckoned to secure public support and are promoted simply on this account. Any political party that is serious about gaining power will have one eye on the marketability of its policies. However, marketability can take precedence over principle, and it is at this point that politicians can reasonably be accused of populism. Penal populism consists of the pursuit of a set of penal policies to win votes rather than to reduce crime rates or to promote justice. *Penal populists allow the electoral advantage of a policy to take precedence over its contribution to justice and its penal effectiveness.*

Clearly it is a matter of judgement whether politicians are acting in a populist way. One has to assess their – usually well hidden – intentions. It is important to draw a distinction between the negligent disregard for evidence about fairness and effectiveness inherent in penal populism and the sincere and thoughtful belief in effectiveness and justice that underlies some politicians' advocacy of some harsh policies. In principle at least, one can also distinguish between what we might term 'benign' and 'malign' populism. Benign populism – a rare phenomenon in penal politics – involves the pursuit of the right policies (fair and effective crime policies), but for the wrong reasons (simply to get elected). Malign populism by contrast involves the promotion of policies that are electorally attractive, but unfair or ineffective or both. Penal populism also promotes simplistic solutions to complex problems – such as mandatory sentencing as a solution to rising crime rates – and represents penal reforms along a false dichotomy of offenders versus victims. All potential reforms are seen as being offender- or victim-oriented, whereas in reality treating victims with more respect and understanding does not have to result in adverse consequences for offenders.

Advocates of tough punishment might argue that we are simply using penal populism as a pejorative term for policies with which we disagree. This is not the place to argue the merits of the case for controlling crime by introducing harsher sentencing. We shall simply refer the reader to the relevant sources[12] and assert our views on the matter: the evidence in support of measures such as lengthy mandatory terms of imprisonment is flimsy but their electoral appeal remains strong. Our strong suspicion is that many politicians have reached the same conclusions – but promoted the measures, notwithstanding. In other words, we think that populist motives often lie behind harsh penal policies.

The emergence of penal populism

It is only in the past 25 years that crime control has emerged in Britain as a contentious electoral issue – and more recently still that penal politics have acquired their current populist quality. Similar developments have occurred over the past quarter century in North America, in some European countries and in Australia and New Zealand. Why should this tendency to populism emerge across several countries over this period?

The first point to make is that for much of the second half of the twentieth century most forms of crime were rising in most industrialized countries, and it would be strange if crime had *not* emerged as a political priority. However, a common trend over the past decades – or longer in some countries – has been a clear decline in crime rates. A sense of insecurity about crime and popular and political enthusiasm for 'getting tough' have nevertheless remained. The reasons for this are complex, and are discussed in more detail in Garland (2001) and Roberts *et al.* (2003). The key factors include:

- the increasing uncertainties of 'late modern' societies, associated with economic insecurity, less stable and cohesive communities and families and the decline of religious beliefs;
- the consequent public responsiveness to politicians who formulate the threats to security in clear and simple terms, and offer equally clear and simple responses to these threats;
- declining trust in professional expertise in tackling social problems, and the resulting withdrawal of support, especially among the middle

classes, for the complex and technical solutions to crime advocated by liberal professionals;
• the increasing exposure of the print and broadcast mass media to commercial competition, and the subsequent emergence of contemporary news values that privilege dramatic material involving conflict, threat and reports of violent or sexual offending;
• the consequent systematic distortions in public – and political – understanding about crime;
• an increasingly personalized form of politics, whereby individual politicians rather than political parties are 'held to account' by the media for their performance.

While all these factors are implicated in the emergence of penal populism, the interplay between the media and politicians is of particular importance. This can take several forms. In some circumstances the electoral system serves to select politicians whose understanding of complex social issues is about as subtle as the coverage of these issues in tabloid newspapers. This can and does occur,[13] but to date it remains the exception rather than the rule in the politics of developed industrialized societies. Sometimes politicians exploit the possibilities offered by the mass media to frame policy issues in ways that suit their political agenda (see Beckett 1997). In other words, politicians lead the mass media to present policy issues in particular ways.[14] The third is that the media exert such power in the politics of late-modern societies that politicians have little alternative except to engage publicly with complex social issues in media-defined terms.

We would argue that Anglo-American penal politics over the past decade have been characterized by a growing preoccupation with public opinion, coupled with a consistent tendency to misread the true nature and complexity of public opinion and its formation. Politicians and the press have 'talked tough' about sentencing. To a degree, sentencers in Britain and the USA have responded, handing down tougher sentences. The public remains dissatisfied at the supposed leniency of the criminal process, however, and will remain dissatisfied as long as sources of information about crime and punishment systematically distort public understanding and knowledge. Penal populism is likely to continue unchecked if those who are complicit in the process have only a partial understanding of what people actually think about crime and punishment.

Measuring public attitudes

This volume is not a methodological text that explores ways of measuring public opinion. Many such texts and readings exist (e.g. Ferguson 2000; Manza *et al.* 2002; Stalans 2002; Asher 2004). However, it is important to consider some issues relating to methodology, if only because different methodologies reveal differing portraits of public attitudes. Throughout the remainder of the book, we also provide concrete illustrations of specific studies that have utilized different methodologies.

The principal decision confronting a researcher working in the area of public attitudes concerns the category of research tool: qualitative or quantitative. Both have their advantages and disadvantages, although quantitative research accounts for the vast majority of studies conducted. Quantitative surveys have a number of limitations that we shall shortly discuss, but with respect to policy-driven research they are to be preferred over qualitative designs. If policy-makers want to know where the public stands with respect to a particular policy question – for example, the purposes of sentencing, or whether young offenders should be sentenced according to different criteria from adults – there is no substitute for a representative survey, from which inferences about the population response can be reasonably drawn from the responses from a small sample. When a polling company reports a finding based upon a sample of known characteristics, we know, within the limits of probability, how the population would respond to the same question.

A specific example will illustrate what we mean. In a recent survey of public attitudes to youth justice, we included a question that was asked of a sub-sample of 558 people: 'A 16-year-old has been convicted of assault. He has two previous convictions for assault and selling stolen property. Choosing your answer from this card, what sentence do you think he should receive?' Sixty-two per cent of our sub-sample opted for 'detention followed by community supervision'. This percentage represents simply an *estimate* of how the overall population in the country would answer this question. The degree of precision of the estimate – or its 'sampling error' – can be calculated, however. In this case, the small sample size means that the estimate is actually quite imprecise: allowing for the way in which the sample was constructed, one can say with 95 per cent certainty that if the entire adult population were asked this question, between 57 and 67 per cent would have opted for detention and community supervision. Had the sample been larger – say, 2000 – the margin of error would have been much smaller, with the estimate falling within 2.5 percentage points of the 'true' figure.

The clear advantage of representative polls is their demonstrable *replicability*. If two properly executed sample surveys are carried out on the same population at the same time, they will come up with very similar findings. The implication of this is that well conducted polls repeated over time can yield reliable trends over time. For many issues in the field of criminal justice – particularly confidence in justice (see Chapter 2) – policy-makers are interested in trends. Although polls have their limitations, these are generally constant. If the wording is the same, repeating a question year after year does permit pollsters to track changes in public confidence in the police, for example, or support for capital punishment. In addition, politicians and policy-makers are sometimes interested in making international comparisons: how do levels of confidence in criminal justice compare across jurisdictions? A number of polls have been conducted using the same question across different countries. This material is reviewed in a later chapter. At this point we simply make the point that this kind of information could not be gleaned from a series of focus groups in the various countries.

Limitations on polls

Despite their primacy as a tool for public opinion researchers, polls are subject to a number of weaknesses. We have already mentioned that sample surveys produce estimates, and these are subject to imprecision as a result of sampling error. But factors apart from sampling procedures can also impose limitations on the value of surveys. The most important of these relates to the quantification of attitudes, which can do injustice to the subtlety of people's viewpoints. Typically, surveys offer respondents structured responses to simple questions. Thus they might have only five options from which to choose when asked if court sentences are tough enough: much too tough; a little too tough; about right; a little too lenient; or much too lenient. A thoughtful person might well be reluctant to generalize, feeling that some sentencers in some courts were far too tough on some crimes, and others were too soft on others. But the interviewer will push the respondent to make a single choice from a limited range of options. In this way, an attitude to the court is shaped or, some might say, created by the measuring instrument.

The importance of providing adequate response alternatives

A sound sampling technique is essential to the integrity of any public opinion survey. However, the most carefully constructed and conducted survey will provide a false reading of public attitudes if the response options are inappropriate or insufficient. Most polls employ a fixed-choice format in which respondents are asked to choose from among a limited number of alternatives. When this method is used, researchers have to ensure that the options represent a range of possibilities. Otherwise public support will simply reflect the alternatives favoured by researchers. Consider a poll conducted for the *Mail on Sunday* in 2000. Respondents were asked to identify the strategies that would do the most to reduce the level of crime in Britain. Table 1.5 summarizes the options provided and the percentage of respondents who supported each proposal.

The problem with this 'forced choice' methodology is that respondents have no way of expressing their support for other crime prevention strategies, such as social prevention or situational crime prevention. Since respondents are encouraged to make a choice, and are discouraged from refusing to answer, responses to this list will convey a false sense of the degree of public support for the limited range of strategies among which

Table 1.5 Public support for ways of reducing crime in Britain

	Percentage of respondents
More police	54
National identity card	31
Fine parents for children's crimes	27
Speed up court proceedings	27
Tougher prisons for young offenders	25
Capital punishment for murder	25
Longer prison sentences	18
Genetic fingerprint all citizens	17
Improve Crown Prosecution Service	15
Put more offenders in prison	6
More vigilante groups	1

Source: MORI (2000). Question: 'I am going to read out some different suggestions for ways in which crime levels can be reduced in Britain. Which two or three, if any, do you think would do most to reduce the level of crime in Britain?'

they have been asked to choose. When measuring public attitudes to an issue such as crime prevention, it is essential to develop appropriate lists of options that actually include all the main categories that most people are likely to want to select. Developing such a list usually requires piloting, and often benefits from prior qualitative work.

Inappropriate wording

Polls are often used by politicians to bolster a particular position or penal policy. The tool to measure public opinion becomes a means of manipulating public attitudes. Many examples of misleading or manipulative polls exist. A typical example concerns parole. Opponents of conditional release from prison often cite surveys in which respondents are asked whether they support 'early release' for violent offenders. When no mention is made of the conditions imposed on parolees (reporting requirements, non-association conditions etc.), the public is encouraged to see parole as simply 'time off' the sentence, rather than as a tool to promote the safe reintegration of prisoners (see Roberts *et al.* 2003 for examples of manipulative questions).

Categorical judgements

We describe another weakness with crime polls as the 'categorical error'. By this we refer to the tendency to ask the public to arrive at a decision about issues such as capital punishment, sentencing or parole in terms of a category, rather than individual cases. For example, polls examining attitudes to parole often ask respondents whether they support or oppose parole for prisoners serving terms for crimes of violence.[15] Parole boards do not make decisions about categories of offending, and it is accordingly inappropriate to ask the public to judge offenders in this way. The best way of understanding the level of public support for an issue such as parole or capital punishment is to ask respondents to make decisions in individual cases.

When this approach is adopted, a far more refined and accurate portrait of public opinion emerges. This has been demonstrated in a number of research projects involving members of the public and crime victims. In one of the earliest demonstrations, Maguire and Bennett (1982) found that when burglary victims were asked to sentence burglars in general, they responded punitively. However, when asked to sentence 'their burglar', these victims were more likely to favour imposition of a non-custodial penalty. Using members of the public as subjects, Cumberland and Zamble (1992) found high levels of support for restricting parole to non-violent offenders when respondents were asked a general question. However, confronted with specific parole applications to review, public attitudes look quite different. For example, approximately four-fifths of the sample supported granting parole to a burglar, and over half the sample favoured parole for an offender convicted of aggravated assault and robbery (see Cumberland and Zamble 1992: Table 1). These findings are inconsistent with the position that parole should be denied prisoners serving time for crimes of violence. Zamble and Kalm (1990) report the same phenomenon with respect to sentencing: when asked the general question, people respond very punitively, but when asked to sentence offenders described in detailed scenarios the resultant sentences were comparable to actual court dispositions (see also Indermaur 1990).

Legitimate indecision?

Another illustration of the importance of the wording of survey questions comes from the United States. In the only Western nation that retains the death penalty, public opinion polls routinely address the issue of capital punishment. The standard question posed by the Gallup organization is the following: 'Are you in favour of the death penalty for a person convicted of murder?' (Gallup 2004). People are allowed to respond negatively or affirmatively. If they respond 'don't know', or refuse to answer, their responses are ignored, or they are classified as respondents with 'no opinion'. In all probability, few people have no opinion about this issue; but many are undecided or conflicted about their opinion (see Unnever *et al.* 2005). Attitudes to the death penalty are far more nuanced and complex than this simple question would suggest.

This wording prevents the respondent from expressing the degree to which he or she supports or opposes capital punishment. Nor does the question permit people to give contingent answers such as 'I support the death penalty, but only for certain categories of murder.' Finally, the question fails to allow people to express an *agnostic* view, to state that they are 'undecided'. In reality, few proponents of capital punishment favour the death penalty for all cases, in all contexts. Even the wording used by Gallup – which doesn't permit people to be 'undecided' – generates a significant number of respondents who appear undecided. Thus, in 1995, fully 10 per cent of the population responded 'don't know'; this corresponds to approximately 30 million Americans. Question wording is therefore important. Consider the issue of the 'undecided' or ambivalent respondent with respect to capital punishment. Jones (1994) examined different ways of posing the question about death penalty attitudes. He found that if you simply ask the respondent whether he or she is in favour of the death penalty, 20 per cent spontaneously respond 'depends' or 'don't know'. If people are first asked whether they have an opinion, and then asked to express that opinion, this percentage rises to 38 per cent, a very significant shift.

Limited time

Another limiting factor is that surveys often allocate respondents limited time for the consideration of the complex issues in the field of criminal justice. Attitudes to issues such as capital punishment, mandatory sentencing or sex offender registries must be captured within the space of a few minutes using a few simple questions. The consequence is that polls oversimplify both the issue under examination and the nature of public opinion with respect to the issue. To say that two-thirds of the public believe that sentences should be harsher or that capital punishment should be reinstated fails to reflect the complexities of public attitudes to these issues. One solution is to ask follow-up questions – for example, first to ask people whether they are in favour of or opposed to the death penalty, and then to follow this up by asking them to consider a list of offences. When this method is adopted, it reveals that most advocates of capital punishment favour the death penalty only for the most serious forms of murder.

Limited information

The process of rapid quantification of attitudes is by no means the only limitation to polls and surveys. Arguably, a more insidious limitation concerns the paucity of information available to the respondent. Again, attitudes to punishment represent a good illustration of the problem. Asking people whether sentences are severe enough yields large majorities in favour of tougher punishment whenever and wherever the question is posed (see Chapter 4). The problem with this approach is that pollsters cannot control the images of offences and offenders in the respondent's mind when he or she answers the question. Since some researchers have asked people to state the kinds of offender that they had in mind when responding to such a question, we know that most people think about serious crime committed by repeat offenders (Doob and Roberts 1988).

These images 'drive' the response offered. This is why it is important, wherever possible, to specify a particular case before asking members of the public about the appropriateness of sentencing patterns. Simple questions, posed at a high level of generality, tend to elicit a punitive response from respondents. When people are provided with more time, more questions or more information about the topic, their reactions become less punitive – and more in line with the practice of the criminal justice system. This is perhaps the best documented – and most important – lesson from public opinion research.[16]

This finding is not restricted to English-speaking countries; it reflects the phenomenology of criminal punishment. We tend to want to act tough and to strike out at offenders when we have only the bare facts of the crime in front of us; when the complicated interplay of background factors is made clear to us, we moderate our punitive reaction. On hearing about a serious crime, our initial reaction is often to 'get tough' – this usually means imprisoning the offender, often for a significant period. When we learn more about the offence and the offender, imprisonment seems to many of us less necessary, and community penalties more plausible, more appropriate (e.g. Hough and Roberts 2004b). There is also a basic human tendency to recognize that actions, even serious criminal acts, can arise from factors beyond the actor's control. When people are told about an offender's history of childhood abuse, for example, their desire for severe punishment diminishes. Throughout this book we provide a number of illustrations of this proposition, drawing upon research from several different countries.

The importance of qualitative work

Focus groups – the tool that accounts for most qualitative studies in the field – have an important role to play in the field. They can help in developing understanding of a field, and in producing an appreciation of the dynamics of attitude formation. Focus groups permit researchers to explore the general environment before settling on specific questions for use in a representative survey. For example, prior to conducting a poll on public attitudes to the police, it would be prudent to carry out some focus groups to understand better the issues that people are 'talking about' (see Hough 1996). Or, if researchers are interested in a specific question that they have determined to place on a poll, focus groups can be useful in establishing the options that will be offered to respondents, since most polls use close-ended questions. However, qualitative work does not allow reliable generalizations to be made about the population at large; nor can it shed light on trends. In an ideal world, one would want to see a judicious mix of qualitative and quantitative research methods. In reality, one rarely gets both.

Deliberative polls

Finally, mention should be made of deliberative polls. We have suggested that the survey method can sometimes prove crude and reductionist. The deliberative poll is designed to give people the time, space and information to develop *considered* views on a topic. As such, it carries much promise, but at a considerable cost. This technique marries the advantages of qualitative research with those of quantitative approaches. Here, in a nutshell, is how it works. Researchers conduct a representative survey to measure public attitudes regarding a wide range of issues. Respondents are also asked if they will participate in a weekend seminar. Such an event is subsequently held, and attitudes are measured at the beginning of the event (to ensure that the sample has not been biased or skewed by the 'volunteer' effect) and at the end. In between, participants hear presentations on the issues.

The participants constitute a representative sample, so inferences may be drawn about the attitudes of the population. At the same time, the experience lasts more than just a few minutes; this gives researchers the opportunity to provide information to the participants, who can then deliberate (hence the title) before responding. Only a couple of deliberative polls have been conducted in criminal justice (e.g. Hough and Park 2002), for the simple reason that they are very expensive. However, there is no reason why a deliberative poll may not be mounted for a single evening, rather than a weekend. This would dramatically reduce the costs, and at the same time increase the proportion of the original sample attending.

Summary

To summarize, public attitudes to issues as complex as criminal justice can only be understood by considering findings from a variety of methodologies. The principal tool is the representative survey, but findings from this approach must be regarded with caution. Qualitative methods of exploring public opinion are also important, and the ideal approach is to combine different methods within the same research project. A good example of this can be found in the research reported by Hutton (2005) using Scottish respondents, which contained three components: a large, representative survey; a series of focus groups; and a form of 'deliberative poll' in which participants were asked to complete sentencing exercises after having been exposed to presentations on crime and punishment by experts in the field.

Further reading

Asher, H. (2004) *Polling and the Public. What Every Citizen Should Know.* Washington, DC: Congressional Quarterly.

Bottoms, A. (1995) The politics of sentencing reform, in C. Clarkson and R. Morgan (eds) *The Philosophy and Politics of Punishment and Sentencing.* Oxford: Oxford University Press.

Bottoms, A., Rex, S. and Robinson, G. (2005) *Alternative to Prison: Options for an Insecure Society.* Cullompton: Willan Publishing.

Cullen, F. T., Fisher, B. and Applegate, B. (2000) Public opinion about punishment and corrections, in M. Tonry (ed.) *Crime and Justice, Volume 27.* Chicago: University of Chicago Press.

Hough, M. (2003) Modernisation and public opinion: some criminal justice paradoxes, *Contemporary Politics*, 9: 143–55.

Hough, M., Jacobson, J. and Millie, A. (2003) *The Decision to Imprison: Sentencing and The Prison Population.* London: Prison Reform Trust.

Hough, M. and Park, A. (2002) How malleable are public attitudes to crime and punishment?, in J. V. Roberts and M. Hough (eds) *Changing Attitudes to Punishment: Public Opinion around the Globe.* Cullompton: Willan Publishing.

Hough, M. and Roberts, J. (2004) *Youth Crime and Youth Justice: Public Opinion in England and Wales.* Bristol: Policy Press.

Hutton, N. (2005) Beyond populist punitiveness?, *Punishment and Society*, in press.

Kury, H. and Ferdinand, T. (1999) Public opinion and punitivity, *International Journal of Law and Psychiatry*, 22: 373–92.

Kury, H., Oberfell-Fuchs, J. and Smartt, U. (2002) The evolution of public attitudes to punishment in Western and Eastern Europe, in J. V. Roberts and M. Hough (eds) *Changing Attitudes to Punishment.* Cullompton: Willan Publishing.

Parmentier, S., Vervaeke, G., Doutrelepont, R. and Kellens, G. (eds) (2004) *Popular Perceptions and Their Implications for Policy-making in Western Countries.* Brussels: Politeia Press.

Roberts, J. V. and Hough, M. (2002) *Changing Attitudes to Punishment.* Cullompton: Willan Publishing.

Roberts, J. V. and Stalans, L. S. (1997) *Public Opinion, Crime, and Criminal Justice.* Boulder, CO: Westview Press.

Roberts, J. V., Stalans, L. S., Indermaur, D. and Hough, M. (2003) *Penal Populism and Public Opinion. Findings from Five Countries.* New York: Oxford University Press.

Stalans, L. S. (2002) Measuring attitudes to sentencing, in J. V. Roberts and M. Hough (eds) *Changing Attitudes to Punishment.* Cullompton: Willan Publishing.

Wood, J. and Tendavi Viki, G. (2004) Public perceptions of crime and punishment, in J. Adler (ed.) *Forensic Psychology. Concepts, Debates and Practice.* Cullompton: Willan Publishing.

Notes

---

1 This finding emerges from the latest, as yet unpublished, administration of the General Social Survey in Canada.

2 An exception, in England and Wales, is a study conducted by one of the authors and his colleagues (Hough *et al.* 2003).

3 Two international surveys – the World Values Survey and the European Values Survey – collect data pertaining to public confidence in the justice system; see, for example, www.worldvaluessurvey.org.

4 The European Values Study is an example of this approach (see Halman 2001).

5 This is the first reference in our volume to the MORI poll that explored public confidence in criminal justice (and related issues) in 2003. Hereafter, unless indicated otherwise, all citations to MORI polls refer to this particular survey (see Hough and Roberts 2004a for further information).

6 We have not included one item in the list ('All of the parts of the criminal justice system working together to tackle crime'). Unlike all the other items, it is not as much a specific function as a characteristic of the justice system, and something of a 'motherhood' statement. Sixty-one per cent of respondents ascribed it a 'ten'.

7 Knowles (1985) reports a survey conducted in Ohio in which nearly one-third of respondents estimated the violent crime rate to be at least six times higher than was actually the case.

8 Respondents were asked about six offences or offence categories. Although rates had been stable or falling over the previous two years, a majority of respondents believed that rates had been rising (see Weatherburn and Indermaur 2004).

9 It is perhaps unreasonable to expect the public to have accurate perceptions of crime trends. In addition, the public has quite inaccurate views on a wide range of social issues. For example, a survey conducted in 2000 for the Cancer Research Campaign found that more than half of men and a third of women in Britain subscribe to misperceptions about cancer, such as the myth that cancer can be 'caught' like a cold.

10 The prevalence of criminal behaviour has been demonstrated by self-report studies, and also research on the proportion of the public with a criminal conviction. By the time that they reach 40, just under half the male population of Britain will have acquired a criminal conviction for a non-motoring offence. The public is unaware of this, as demonstrated by responses to the 1996 BCS and a MORI poll conducted in 2003: over half the sample under-estimated this statistic (Hough and Roberts 1998; Esmée Fairbairn Foundation 2003).

11 In the study involving Spanish respondents Redondo *et al.* (1996) found that public estimates of recidivism rates for drug offenders were six times higher than reality.

12 A number of recent reviews of the empirical research on deterrence, for example, have shown that harsher sentencing does little to lower overall crime rates; see von Hirsch *et al.* (1999) and Doob and Webster (2004).

13 The One Nation party in Australia under Pauline Hanson's leadership is a possible example.

14 Katherine Beckett's thesis is that the US political rhetoric about criminals as outsiders was politically led, and served to support a separate policy agenda of paring down public expenditure on social security and welfare programmes. More recently, it has been argued that it was in the Bush administration's interest to exaggerate the extent of organization and the degree of threat posed by those using terrorist tactics against the USA.

15 The error is frequently compounded by asking people whether they support

parole for 'violent offenders', which summons to the respondent's mind images of dangerous individuals with lengthy criminal records involving exclusively violent offences.

16 Many demonstrations of this effect exist, going back at least 40 years (e.g. Knight 1965; Doob and Roberts 1983; Hough and Roberts 1998; Monograph 2000; Roberts and Hough 2002b).

chapter two

Public confidence in the criminal justice system

Introduction

There are a number of reasons why public trust or confidence is critical to the functioning of the criminal justice system. First, almost all crimes come to the attention of the police as a result of a report from the victim or a witness – members of the public, in other words. If a charge is laid against a suspect, the Crown Prosecution Service (CPS) will build the case against the accused. This is generally only possible if the victim (now a complainant) cooperates and agrees to offer evidence in the event that the matter proceeds to trial. Victim participation may directly influence developments in the case, as many defendants plead guilty once they know that the victim is going to testify. In addition, in many cases, other witnesses must come forward if the state is going to secure a conviction. Britain has seen a number of high-profile trials in which the prosecution has failed to obtain a conviction (or even launch a prosecution) because witnesses were unwilling to cooperate. Victims and witnesses will cooperate with the police and the CPS only if they have confidence in the justice system as a whole, and if they trust the specific criminal justice professionals with whom they have contact.

So far, we have considered the importance of retaining public confidence in straightforwardly instrumental terms: if people lack confidence in the system, they will be unprepared to report crimes, to present evidence in court, to act as jurors and so on. There are additional, more abstract, reasons for ensuring that the justice system commands public confidence. Whatever effectiveness the criminal justice system achieves, this is largely because most people consent to the rule of law most of the time. They do so because the component parts of the system command legitimacy, and thus authority. To the extent that people comply with the requirements of the system, they do so at least in part because they trust the police and the courts, and think them fair.

This can be seen most clearly in respect of the police, who have the capacity to use coercive force, but rarely do so in practice. Instead, they secure compliance by drawing on the authority of their office – or on their institutional legitimacy, an issue to which we shall return in Chapter 3. The main building blocks of police legitimacy are integrity, fairness and civility – though competence is also likely to be an important factor, an issue to which we shall return in Chapter 3. Legitimacy is equally important to other parts of the criminal justice system. If prosecutors are regarded as incompetent, or sentencers thought to be capricious and unfair, or if the justice system is thought to discriminate against particular groups, its legitimacy will suffer, and the authority of the rule of law will diminish as a consequence. Increasingly, 'retaining confidence in justice' – confidence in its fairness and its effectiveness – is used in policy debate as a sort of shorthand to refer to concerns about institutional legitimacy.

Finally, politicians have sought to maintain public confidence in the criminal justice system for the very simple reason that if they are seen to fail in their obligations to control crime and maintain order, they may well pay an electoral price. Even if they are not voted out of office, they will come under pressure to overhaul the justice system: a survey conducted in the USA found that more than four out of five respondents favoured the idea of 'totally revamping the way that the [criminal justice] system works' (see Sherman 2002).

Confidence in justice is not a unidimensional concept. It is important to distinguish between confidence in the integrity and fairness of the system, on the one hand, and confidence in its effectiveness, on the other. It is also useful to distinguish between someone's expectation that they *personally* will receive effective and fair treatment from the system and their belief that *overall* the system is effective and fair. Some people – articulate, self-confident professionals, for example – may rightly or wrongly anticipate better than average treatment when they use the system, while believing that others are treated worse than themselves. Most people are likely to generalize from their own experience at the hands of the justice system, though some may distinguish between personal satisfaction with services received and overall confidence in the system's operation.

Anyone who is concerned to increase public confidence in justice needs to understand the dynamics of public confidence in justice. People's trust in the criminal justice system is by no means a function simply of its objective performance. There are important links between public knowledge of the system, attitudes to it and confidence in it. Confidence reflects positive attitudes to the system. If people *believe* that sentences are too lenient, or that the police discriminate against particular groups or take bribes, then regardless of the reality, confidence will suffer. Thus knowledge – or ignorance – plays a role in influencing opinion and confidence levels. The final chapter of this book summarizes the results of experiments that show the effect of information on public attitudes to crime (Chapman *et al.* 2002; Hough and Park 2002). The British Crime Survey has demonstrated that most people under-estimate the severity of sentences imposed,[1] and this contributes to the opinion that judges are too lenient towards convicted offenders (see Hough and Roberts 1998). This in turn undermines public confidence in the courts.

Public trust or confidence has become, at the beginning of this century, one of the most researched issues in the field of public opinion and justice. Recognizing the importance of maintaining public faith in justice, almost all Western nations have conducted surveys to measure levels of public confidence in criminal justice (see Hough and Roberts 2004a for a review). As will be seen over the course of this chapter, these polls have revealed low levels of public confidence in justice across many countries. As a result, a number of jurisdictions have also launched initiatives to promote public confidence in the administration of justice.

In England and Wales, increasing public confidence in the justice system has recently become a government priority. The three main government criminal justice departments share a formal stated objective, 'To improve public confidence in the criminal justice system'. This goal manifests itself in specific reform initiatives. Thus the 2002 White Paper, which gave rise to the Criminal Justice Act 2003, sets out a series of reforms 'to create a system that meets the needs of society and wins the trust of citizens' (Secretary of State 2002: 13). A year earlier, the report of the Home Office review of sentencing set out a framework that in the words of its authors 'should increase the contribution of sentencing to crime reduction and public confidence' (Home Office 2001: i). Other countries (in particular the USA[2]) have created programmes designed to promote public confidence in the administration of justice (Hough and Roberts 2004a). Unfortunately, none of these initiatives has to date been subject to scientific evaluation.[3]

Measuring public confidence and interpreting survey findings

Confidence or trust has been measured using a number of different questions. Pollsters have asked questions that address issues of fairness and integrity, and ones that address issues of competence or effectiveness. These include:

- global questions about how much confidence or satisfaction people express with respect to the criminal justice system as a whole;
- questions about confidence or trust in the specific branches of the system, including police, courts and prisons;
- questions about the perceived performance of these agencies (or the system as a whole);
- levels of satisfaction with personal contacts.

No single question will be sufficient to capture the complex concept of 'confidence'. The word means different things to different people within and across countries. It is important, therefore, to consider the findings from surveys that have approached the issue in different ways. In general, the more precise the question the better. For this reason, specifying the branch of the system (e.g. the prison system) and the specific function being considered (e.g. 'rehabilitating prisoners') represents the best way to understand the nature of public reaction. Pollsters do not always specify whether the respondent should consider the local or national level, and public reactions differ greatly when this distinction is made.

The problem of threshold: what constitutes an acceptable level of confidence?

Interpreting survey findings measuring confidence can be problematic. For example, what survey outcome constitutes an acceptable level of public confidence in the criminal justice system? Although the question is subjective, it is surely unreasonable to expect 95 per cent of the public to have a high degree of confidence in the justice system when crime rates are perceived to be constantly rising,[4] and when media coverage of criminal justice emphasizes violent crime, lenient sentencing and cases in which the system has failed. In addition, most people in Britain see crime occurring on a regular basis, as the following statistics demonstrate:

- one-quarter of British households experiences some criminal victimization each year;
- approximately one person in five reported having witnessed a violent assault within the past two years (MORI 2003);
- almost one-third of respondents had witnessed an incident of criminal damage or vandalism;
- one person in five reports having been the victim of theft within the previous two years.

In the light of trends such as these, it is unlikely that people will consider the system to be working well. The public probably concludes that if the system were working well, there would be less crime.

Many of the crime stories with the highest media profile in recent years deal with cases such as the murder of two schoolgirls in Soham by Ian Huntley, and the failed prosecution with respect to Damilola Taylor – instances where the justice system failed. In Belgium, the case of a notorious serial killer who escaped from custody precipitated a crisis in confidence in the justice system: a survey conducted after intense media coverage of the case found that over half of the polled public lacked confidence in the justice system (Parmentier *et al.* 2004a). News media broadcasts of the videotaped assaults by police officers in the USA appear to have had a similar effect on public perceptions of the police in that country. There is also little doubt that the acquittal of O. J. Simpson had a powerful effect on American perceptions of the administration of justice. Cases such as these[5] are the ones that people talk about, and that undermine confidence in the administration of justice.[6]

It is tempting to imbue single attitudinal statistics with more meaning than they actually have. Surveys often ask people whether the system (or its constituent parts) is doing a 'very good', 'fairly good', 'fairly poor' or 'very poor' job. Combining the first two categories, around four out of five people in Britain think their police are doing a good job. Is this a clear vote of confidence? Not necessarily. The majority of those who give this rating actually say 'fairly good'. Some analysts would argue that 'fairly good' should be taken at face value. Others would regard it more as a neutral rating than as a positive one. Certainly it is the option that people are most likely to select if they have no strong feelings on the matter. The point to bear in mind here is that the strength of the survey method is that it enables comparisons between groups, and comparisons over time. Its weakness is that a single survey statistic presented in isolation can be hard to interpret with any confidence.[7]

Effect of mandate of the justice system on public confidence

The final factor to take into account when interpreting findings on confidence in, or satisfaction with, the criminal justice system concerns the mandate of the system. Speaking of the lack of public confidence in the courts, Kritzer and Voelker (2002: 59) wrote that 'It is not surprising that courts generate dissatisfaction; they are associated with unpleasant things such as criminals, injuries, divorces and the like. Many, perhaps most people are probably as likely to choose voluntarily to go to court as they are to choose to have their wisdom teeth extracted.'

Comparison with the health service is instructive. The patient's well-being is the foremost concern of the National Health Service, and of the professionals who work in the system. However, when crime victims get caught up in the justice process, they are not the exclusive focus of attention; the justice system has many functions besides responding to the needs of victims. For many crime victims, the protracted nature of legal proceedings, the experience of being cross-examined in court and their inability to influence sentencing are sources of frustration. This helps to explain the negative views of the justice system expressed by many victims of crime. Victims' views of the system will undoubtedly be conveyed to family and friends, and this is another way in which public attitudes to the administration of justice are formed.

There is also an ideological component to public evaluations of criminal justice professionals, and this is not the case with respect to other public services, such as the armed forces or the medical profession. Many people have a theory regarding the way that the system should respond to offenders, and when criminal justice practices contradict that theory – for example, when offenders appear to be treated with leniency – ratings of the justice system and its professions suffer. Evaluations of other public services are far more pragmatic, less based on ideology. For example, public evaluations of the health service, for example, are not guided or influenced by any ideological perspective or theory of health care delivery. People want expeditious and effective treatment, and ratings of health professionals simply reflect the extent to which they perceive these goals to have been achieved.

We therefore need to be cautious in our interpretation of findings from surveys in this area. It is unreasonable to expect public confidence in the justice system, or public performance ratings to be as high as for institutions such as the armed forces, the National Health Service or the educational system. Rather than making a subjective judgement about whether the confidence level is high or low, it is probably best to take a 'balance sheet' approach, and ask whether the percentage of the public with confidence in the system exceeds the proportion of respondents without confidence. It is also important to make comparisons (where possible) between confidence ratings in Britain and elsewhere, as well as comparisons within Britain over time. Whatever the *absolute* level of public confidence in criminal justice, if this level has been declining, we would regard this as cause for concern.

This chapter therefore aims to sketch out the contours of public confidence in criminal justice with a particular focus on England and

Wales. Later chapters explore public confidence in specific agencies in greater detail. Here we summarize key findings relating to:

- overall levels of confidence and satisfaction with the response to crime;
- comparisons between different agencies *within* the criminal justice system;
- comparisons *between* the criminal justice system and other groups;
- trends in public confidence levels over time and across jurisdictions.

In exploring the nature of public confidence in criminal justice in Britain we draw upon a survey of the British public conducted by the MORI organization in 2003. This survey represents the most comprehensive examination of public confidence ever undertaken, in Britain or any other country. We summarize the principal findings in this chapter (for a more detailed account, see Hough and Roberts 2004a).

Satisfaction with the local and national response to crime

As noted earlier, the literature in this field includes questions on satisfaction and confidence. The MORI survey posed questions exploring both concepts. Respondents were first asked: *Overall, how satisfied are you with the way crime is dealt with?* This question was asked with respect to the area in which they live as well as the country as a whole. Unlike some other questions (discussed later in the chapter), where respondents are asked about specific functions of specific branches of the system, this question is at once general and somewhat vague. Some people may interpret the question in terms of the crime preventive function of the justice system; others may have in mind the treatment of people accused or convicted of criminal acts. This rather amorphous nature of the question should be borne in mind when evaluating public responses.

The response options included: very satisfied; fairly satisfied; neutral; fairly dissatisfied; or very dissatisfied ('no opinion' and 'don't know' were also accepted as responses). The proportion of respondents reporting that they were satisfied with the local response to crime was significantly higher than the proportion reporting that they were dissatisfied: 56 per cent were satisfied, 27 per cent dissatisfied and 12 per cent neutral. However, this positive 'balance' did not emerge when respondents were asked about the response to crime at the national level: now only 34 per cent of respondents were satisfied, 15 per cent neutral and fully 48 per cent dissatisfied (see Figure 2.1).

Confidence in the local and national response to crime

Respondents were asked about their confidence in the justice system, as follows: *Overall, how confident are you about the way crime is dealt with?* As before, the question was posed with respect to the respondent's area and the country as a whole. There were four response options: very

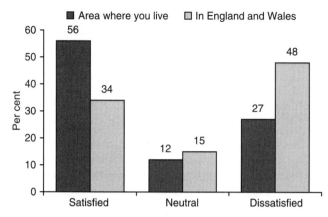

Figure 2.1 Public satisfaction with criminal justice in Britain. Question: 'Overall, how satisfied or dissatisfied are you with the way crime is dealt with . . . [in the area where you live/in England and Wales]?' (*source:* MORI 2003)

confident; fairly confident; not very confident; and not confident at all. In the analysis that follows, we have combined the response categories to define 'confident' and 'not confident' groups.

When the question asked about confidence in the local response, the results were the same as the 'satisfaction' question: significantly more people were confident than not confident with the way that the justice system is dealing with crime. Almost two-thirds (63 per cent) had confidence in the response to crime at the local level, compared to 34 per cent who lacked confidence. Moreover, the same reversal seen with respect to the satisfaction question occurred when the confidence question shifted to the national level: 47 per cent expressed confidence, 51 per cent lacked confidence. The contrast is very marked if we compare respondents who chose 'very confident' with those who chose 'not at all confident'; only 3 per cent of the sample was very confident in the way that crime is dealt with at the national level, compared to 12 per cent who were not at all confident.

These findings constitute further evidence that different factors affect public confidence in justice at the local and national levels. Conclusions about levels of confidence in criminal justice can therefore only be drawn having first made a distinction between the local and national levels. At the local level, a strong majority of the public has confidence in the criminal justice response to crime. At the national level, a slim majority *lacks* confidence. Finally, the fact that the same pattern of responses emerged whether people were asked about 'satisfaction' or 'confidence' suggests that the two questions are capturing the same general concept.

Which evaluation reflects the true state of public confidence in criminal justice? We are inclined to the view that public attitudes to the local response are more important. Knowledge about crime across the country, and the nature of the criminal justice response, comes from the news media, and is indirect in nature. Public confidence in local authorities' response to crime is far more likely to reflect direct experience with individuals and programmes. Moreover, feelings of personal safety are determined more by perceptions of crime in the neighbourhood, rather than views on the national crime trends. And whether a member of the public reports a crime to the police, or participates in the criminal justice system in some other way, is less likely to be affected by his or her perceptions of how well crime is being confronted on the national level. On the other hand, people may well vote in national elections with the government's *national* performance at the front of their mind. If so, national politicians probably need to take stock of both local and national ratings.

Finally, it is important to note that the measure of confidence employed by the MORI poll focuses on the crime reduction function of the criminal justice system. People were asked how much confidence they have that the system is 'dealing with crime'. This wording ties the function of the system closely to crime trends. If the confidence question were broader, or focused on other issues such as 'doing justice', responses would be different. Indeed, as we document below with respect to specific branches of criminal justice, confidence levels vary greatly, depending on the specific function of the system that is under scrutiny. We conclude, however, that the balance of public confidence in justice in Britain is more on the positive than the negative side.

Confidence in the justice response to victimization

Another way of approaching the issue of confidence is to ask people how much confidence they have that they would be treated fairly by the justice system in the event that they became a crime victim. This question was posed to respondents in Britain by MORI in 2003. The responses are summarized in Table 2.1. Two trends are important in this table. First, adopting the 'balance sheet' approach to which we referred at the beginning of this chapter, people appear to be more positive than negative.

Table 2.1 British public's confidence in response of justice system to victimization (percentages)

	Very or fairly confident	Not very or not at all confident	Don't know
Car theft	51	43	5
Domestic violence	59	30	11
Burglary	50	46	3
Rape	57	29	14
Grievous bodily harm	64	31	6

Source: adapted from MORI (2004a). Question: 'How confident, if at all, are you that you would be treated fairly in the criminal justice system if you were a victim of . . .?'

If we assume that 'very confident' and 'fairly confident' options constitute a positive response and the other options a negative response, the balance is positive, particularly for the more serious offences of rape and grievous bodily harm, where the positive/negative ratio is approximately two to one. The second trend, however, is that significant minorities of respondents have little confidence in the justice response to victimization for certain crimes. Thus almost half (46 per cent) of the sample had little confidence that they would be treated appropriately in the event that they became victims of burglary.

Confidence in specific functions of justice

Considerable variability exists in public levels of confidence with respect to specific functions of the criminal justice system. The MORI poll asked the public how much confidence they had in a number of specific functions of the justice system. As can be seen in Figure 2.2, confidence levels are much higher for some functions than for others. Over three-quarters of the public have confidence that the system respects the rights of accused persons and treats them fairly, but less than one-quarter of the polled public are confident that the system is effective in dealing with young people accused of a crime.[8] Once again, some of these questions are somewhat vague, and without follow-up probes (or qualitative research in which researchers have the time to explore respondents' interpretations of the questions) we are left unsure of what people had in mind. For example, being effective in

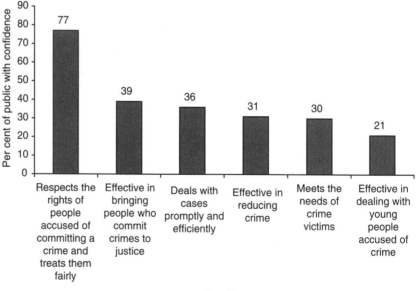

Figure 2.2 Confidence levels for specific functions of criminal justice, 2002/3 (*source:* Simmons and Dodd 2003)

dealing with young people accused of crime may mean being tough (rather than lenient), or it may mean something quite different, such as using official sanctions only when absolutely necessary.

A more detailed picture of the functions that attract the lowest levels of public confidence may be derived from the 2003 MORI survey. Respondents were asked to express how much confidence they had in 20 specific functions of the criminal justice system 'as a whole'. Table 2.2 lists the functions for which at least half the sample stated they were not very, or not at all, confident. The fact that half the functions meet our 'low confidence' threshold of 50 per cent is cause for concern. The nature of the functions on the list is also revelatory. It suggests that much of the public's lack of confidence springs from concern about public safety. People appear to have the least amount of confidence that the system is dealing with crimes of high visibility: mugging, burglary and drug dealing, for example. It is also interesting that the lowest confidence rating occurs for the issue of preventing re-offending. This finding is consistent with a number of other polls that have found that people believe re-offending rates are high, and that the system is incapable of addressing the problem. This has implications for public confidence in, and attitudes to, the sentencing stage of the criminal process, to which we return in Chapter 4.

Comparisons within the criminal justice system

Most countries have now conducted surveys in which people are asked to rate their level of confidence or trust in specific branches of the justice

Table 2.2 Functions of criminal justice system that attract lowest levels of public confidence

	Percentage of sample responding 'not very' or 'not at all' confident
Stopping offenders from committing more crime	73
Dealing effectively with drug-related crime	60
Dealing effectively with street robbery (including mugging)	60
Dealing effectively with burglary	59
Creating a society in which people feel safe	59
Reducing the level of crime	58
Tackling the causes of crime	57
Dealing effectively with young offenders	53
Dealing with crime promptly and efficiently	51
Dealing effectively with public disorder, anti-social behaviour and vandalism	50

Source: MORI (2003). Question: 'Thinking about the criminal justice system as a whole, that is, the police, the Crown Prosecution Service, the courts, prison and probation services, please tell me how confident you are that it is . . .?'

system. Respondents to the 2003 MORI poll were asked how much confidence they had that different branches of the criminal justice system were doing a good job.[9] This wording fuses the concepts of confidence and evaluation in a single question, but the hierarchy of professions that emerges is the same as when respondents are asked to rate the job that various professions are doing.

Table 2.3 shows that the public has most confidence in the police, least in the courts and prisons. This is consistent with responses to previous administrations of the British Crime Survey (see Nicholas and Walker 2004). As can be seen, there is a 30 per cent range in the confidence ratings. Although confidence ratings are significantly lower for some parts of the justice system than others, the confidence 'balance' is positive even for the branch that attracts the lowest confidence ratings: the youth courts.

Variation also emerges in terms of public levels of confidence with respect to the functions of specific criminal justice agencies. People seem to have an intuitive sense of the extent to which these agencies are capable of achieving specific goals. For example, with respect to the prison system, 25 per cent of the public are very confident that prisons 'maintain security' – a relatively high confidence rating (for this particular branch of justice). However, only 5 per cent of the public has this level of confidence in the ability of the prison system to help to prepare prisoners to live law-abiding lives. (These findings are explored in more detail in subsequent chapters devoted to the principal criminal justice agencies.)

Perceptions of visible minorities

Research into ethnic differences in confidence in criminal justice yields a rather contradictory pattern of results. Most research on minority

Table 2.3 Public confidence in branches of the criminal justice system in Britain

	Percentage of respondents very or fairly confident	Percentage of respondents not very or not at all confident
Local police	76	22
Police in England and Wales	73	25
Probation service	59	29
Crown Prosecution Service	57	36
Magistrates	55	38
Judges	54	43
Courts	51	44
Prisons	48	43
Youth courts	46	38

Source: MORI (2003). Question: 'We would like to know how confident you are that each of the groups of people who make up the criminal justice system are doing a good job. How confident are you that . . . are doing a good job? Is that very/fairly/not very/not at all confident?'

perceptions of justice has focused on the police, as they are the justice professionals with whom the public has most contact. A survey conducted for the BBC in 2002 asked respondents how well the police do their job, and the responses can be seen in Table 2.4. As can be seen, overall, the police received a quite positive response from all categories of respondents. Although White respondents assigned more positive ratings to the police than did Black or Asians, the differences between groups are far from great: the proportion of Black respondents giving a negative rating was 19 per cent compared to 13 per cent of the White sample (BBC 2002). These findings are consistent with research drawing upon responses to the British Crime Survey. Clancy *et al.* (2001) report findings from the 2000 British Crime Survey in which respondents were asked the following question: *Would you say the police in this area do a good or a poor job?* Satisfaction rates were 74 per cent for Black respondents, 74 per cent for Asian respondents and 79 per cent for White respondents.[10]

However, with respect to other areas of criminal justice, much larger differences emerge between White and Black respondents. For example, regarding courts, 77 per cent of White but only 53 per cent of Black respondents believed that they would receive a fair trial. Half the Black respondents but only a quarter of the Whites stated that they would be concerned about the racial make-up of the jury. Finally, 60 per cent of White but only 43 per cent of Black respondents believed that the courts treat people from ethnic minorities fairly (BBC 2002).

Minorities in other countries express even less confidence in criminal justice agencies, particularly the police. The gap between White and Black respondents with respect to confidence in the police appears to be significantly greater in the USA. For example, 24 per cent of White respondents but 38 per cent of Black Americans expressed little or no confidence in the criminal justice system. Similarly, two-thirds of White Americans but only one-third of Black respondents had a great deal of confidence in the police (Sourcebook of Criminal Justice Statistics 2004). This has led one leading researcher to describe the discrepancies in confidence levels as a 'racial divide' (Sherman 2002: 23).

Table 2.4 Public performance ratings of police in Britain (percentages)

	White	Black	Asian
Good job	83	74	71
Bad job	13	19	18
Don't know	4	7	11

Source: adapted from BBC (2002). Question: 'How well do the police do their job?'

Trends in British confidence in justice

Has the level of confidence in the British justice system *as a whole*
declined in recent years? Without a series of annual polls addressing the
question it is hard to come to a definitive conclusion. Nevertheless, there
seems more cause for optimism than pessimism. A decade ago a MORI
poll found that only 29 per cent of the sample agreed that 'you can have
confidence in the legal system'; over half the sample disagreed. While far
from uniformly positive, the state of confidence in justice as a whole in
2003 reflected in the MORI poll would appear to be an improvement on
levels of a decade before. A similar trend is found in the USA, the only
other jurisdiction in which confidence has been repeatedly measured over a
number of years. In 2003, 29 per cent of the polled public expressed a great
deal or quite a lot of confidence in the justice system; although this may not
be a very high proportion of the public, the percentage of Americans
expressing this level of confidence in criminal justice has risen steadily in
recent years, from 17 per cent a decade before (Sourcebook of Criminal
Justice Statistics 2004).

This positive conclusion must be modified by the fact that there does
seem to have been some decline with respect to *specific components* of the
system. Although the police attract the best performance ratings from the
public in Britain, there is clear evidence of a decline in these ratings over
time. A generation ago (in 1982), 43 per cent of respondents expressed the
view that the police were doing a very good job. The percentage of
respondents holding this view has declined systematically since then, drop-
ping to 34 per cent in 1984 and then 24 per cent in 1994. By 2001/2, only
14 per cent of respondents rated the police as doing a very good job
(Brown 2003).

There is additional independent evidence that public confidence or trust
in the police has been declining. Dowds (1995) reports findings from
repeated administrations of the British Social Attitudes Survey. In 1983, 75
per cent of male respondents and 82 per cent of female respondents
expressed satisfaction with 'the way that the police do their job'. These
percentages fell to 66 and 75 per cent respectively by 1990. Similar declines
were observed regarding the percentage of respondents who had had contact with the police and who reported that the police had been very helpful.
Another manifestation of this decline in approval of the police concerns the
question of professional integrity. Respondents were also asked whether
the police could be trusted 'not to bend the rules'. In 1987, over half stated
that the police could be trusted always or most of the time in this respect;
the percentage with this view declined over the next few years to 45 per
cent in 1994.

The reasons for the decline in public confidence in the police are discussed in more detail in the next chapter. For the present, however, it is
worth noting that the police alone within the criminal justice system have
had significant 'headroom' to allow for a decline in confidence levels. With

the exception of prisons there has been no corresponding erosion in confidence ratings for other criminal justice agencies.

The percentage of the public rating the prisons as doing a good job fell
from 38 per cent in 1996, to 32 per cent in 1998, 30 per cent in 2000 and
26 per cent in 2001 (Whitehead and Taylor 2003). In contrast, public
performance ratings of the courts, the Crown Prosecution Service and sentencers have been stable. In 1996, 27 per cent of the public rated magistrates as doing a good job, almost the same percentage as in 2001 (29 per
cent). Similarly, 26 per cent of respondents held this view of the probation
service in 1996 and 25 per cent in 2001. Table 2.5 summarizes trends with
respect to public perceptions of different branches of the criminal justice
system in Britain. Despite the decline in ratings of the police over time, the
public still assign more positive ratings to this branch than any other
agency: approval ratings are approximately twice as high for the police (see
Table 2.5).

Comparisons with public confidence levels in other jurisdictions

How do levels of confidence in Britain compare with findings from surveys
in other countries? Inconsistencies in the wording of specific questions in
different countries make it hard to make direct comparisons. Nevertheless,
some conclusions may be drawn. Confidence levels seem no lower in
Britain than other countries, and may well be higher, as the following
examples suggest.

• A Gallup survey conducted in the USA in 2003 (the same year as the
  MORI poll) found that 29 per cent of respondents expressed a 'great
  deal' or 'quite a lot of confidence' in the criminal justice system – considerably lower than the 47 per cent of British respondents who were
  very or fairly confident in the way that crime is dealt with here. The US
  public also have less confidence in their criminal justice system than in
  other public institutions. Thus 29 per cent of Americans expressed con-

Table 2.5 Percentage of respondents rating criminal justice agencies as doing an excellent or good job, 1996–2003

	1996	1998	2000	2001/2	2002/3
Police	64	60	53	47	48
Prisons	38	32	30	26	25
Magistrates	27	29	26	29	26
Judges	20	23	21	29	25
Crown Prosecution Service	23	n.a.	23	27	23
Probation service	26	26	23	25	24
Youth courts	n.a.	14	12	16	14

Source: Nicholas and Walker (2004).

fidence in the criminal justice system, compared to 82 per cent who expressed confidence in the military, 55 per cent in the presidency, 50 per cent in banks and 44 per cent in the medical system (Sourcebook of Criminal Justice Statistics 2003, 2004).

- Over half the respondents to a survey in Belgium expressed dissatisfaction with the current functioning of the criminal justice system (Parmentier *et al.* 2004a). Almost six of ten respondents stated that they lacked confidence in the Belgian judiciary.
- A survey of the public in South Africa found that almost 40 per cent of the sample expressed 'not much' or no confidence at all in the criminal justice system (Kotze 2003).
- The Social Values Survey is conducted across 32 European countries. Respondents in 1999 were asked how much confidence they had in a range of public institutions. Consistent with other polls in North America, the justice system attracted lower confidence ratings than many other institutions. Averaged across all countries, 45 per cent of respondents had a great deal or quite a lot of confidence in the justice system – compared to 60 per cent who had this level of confidence in the health care system and 71 per cent in the education system (Halman 2001). Confidence levels were quite variable. The percentage expressing a great deal of confidence in the justice system ranged from 3 per cent in Slovakia to 18 per cent in Iceland (10 per cent held this view in Britain).[11] In relative terms, confidence levels in Britain were higher than in most other countries. Only 14 per cent of British respondents expressed no confidence at all; considerably higher percentages expressed this view in some other countries.[12]

The hierarchy of confidence – with the police at the top and the courts at the bottom – is found in all other countries in which people have been asked their reaction to specific branches of the system. For example, when Canadians were asked how much confidence they had in various agencies of the criminal justice system, 37 per cent were very confident in the police, but only 7 per cent expressed this level of confidence in the courts. The lowest confidence levels emerged with respect to the prison and parole systems; even fewer respondents (3 per cent) had this much confidence in these institutions (Roberts 2004). Public performance ratings in other countries produce the same result. Thus three-quarters of the New Zealand public gave the police as excellent or good ratings. Only 45 per cent of New Zealanders rated the courts in such a positive way (Paulin *et al.* 2003).

Table 2.6 provides a comparison between evaluations of criminal justice professions in three jurisdictions, Britain, Canada and New Zealand. This table confirms that the police are viewed most positively in all three countries; however, evaluations of prosecutors and judges are less positive in Britain, probably as a result of adverse media coverage of failed prosecutions and lenient sentencing in that country.

Explaining the high levels of confidence in the police

Why are ratings of the police so much more positive than those for the other branches of criminal justice? The fact that this finding emerges in different countries may provide an answer. Police practices vary considerably from country to country. It is therefore probably not the professional competence or conduct of the police but some explanation common to all jurisdictions. One such explanation has to do with mere familiarity. People are generally more familiar with the police than any of the other criminal justice professions. When people think of criminal justice professionals or agencies, the police are most likely to come to mind. The MORI (2003) survey found that just over half the sample thought about the police, compared to 15 per cent for probation, 14 per cent for the Crown Prosecution Service and 12 per cent for judges.

As noted in Chapter 1, the public report knowing much more about the police than any other branch of criminal justice (see Table 1.2). This familiarity derives in part from contact: Almost everyone has stopped, or been stopped by, a police officer somewhere at some time – even if only to ask the officer for directions. Survey results confirm this degree of familiarity; people report having more contact with police officers than any other criminal justice professional. According to the 2002–3 British Crime Survey, just under half the population had had some contact with the police in the previous year (Nicholas and Walker 2004). Most of these contacts were

Table 2.6 Public evaluations of criminal justice professions in Canada, Britain and New Zealand (percentages)

	Excellent or good	Average	Poor or very poor
Canada			
Police	67	25	7
Defence counsel	56	36	6
Prosecutors	53	40	5
Judges	50	31	17
Britain			
Police	53	30	6
Defence counsel	n.a.	n.a.	n.a.
Prosecutors	23	53	24
Judges	21	49	32
New Zealand			
Police	74	19	7
Defence counsel	45	42	13
Prosecutors	n.a.	n.a.	n.a.
Judges	42	37	22

Source: Mirrlees-Black (2001), Roberts (2002d), Paulin *et al.* (2003).

perceived by the public as positive in nature: almost two-thirds of the MORI poll respondents who reporting having contact with police in the previous 12 months expressed satisfaction with this contact; fewer than a quarter were dissatisfied. We have far less direct contact with judges or parole boards. This degree of familiarity with the police is likely to enhance public approval ratings. In addition, by their presence on the streets, the police are seen to be 'on the job' – unlike other criminal justice professionals, who work out of the public eye. One obvious reason why the public might not be confident in the work of probation officers or prosecutors is that most people have little concrete idea what these professionals do.

Related to familiarity is the level of knowledge people have about different branches of criminal justice. People know far less about the courts and the prison system than about the police. A nationwide survey of Americans found that three-quarters of respondents acknowledged that they knew either very little or almost nothing about the courts (National Centre for State Courts 1978). Similarly, almost half the respondents in a more recent survey conducted in South Australia stated that they knew 'just a little' about the courts, and 13 per cent responded that they knew nothing at all (see Hough and Roberts 2004a). Knowledge of the operation of criminal justice agencies is often correlated with approval.

On the other hand – and as we shall in Chapter 3 – one of the consistent findings of surveys that examine public experience of police contact is that being a recipient of police services is a predictor of dissatisfaction. This is true, unsurprisingly, for those whose contact arose from police suspicions about them; more worryingly, it is also true for those who ask for police help (Fitzgerald *et al.* 2002; Skogan 2005). It seems likely, therefore, that the overall support for the police derives from a variety of sources, including positive representations in films and television dramas, and that direct experience of the police plays a somewhat ambiguous role in shaping public attitudes to them. People seem comforted by the sight of police officers on the streets, and this affects their general attitudes; however, when they become embroiled in an incident and have to avail themselves of police services, the experience is not always positive.

Crime control versus due process

Another reason for the high degree of public confidence in the police pertains to the mandate of different criminal justice agencies. The public may have more faith in the police – and assign them higher approval ratings – because the police are seen to be on the public's 'side' in the fight against crime. Packer (1968) identified two competing models of criminal justice. The 'crime control' model favours placing emphasis on police powers, and opposes granting many rights to suspects or defendants. In contrast, the 'due process' model emphasizes the importance of providing procedural rights to people suspected of or charged with committing a crime.

Although in practice the criminal justice system attempts to strike a balance between the two models, the public is more supportive of crime control than due process.

In the popular mind,[13] the mandate of the police is closer to the crime control model of justice. Judges, on the other hand, must strive to protect the rights of the accused during a trial, and the Crown Prosecution Service must consider the interests of justice, not just pursue the conviction of the defendant. In some cases, prosecutors may decide that it is not in the public interest to initiate or continue a prosecution. The public is seldom aware of this prosecutorial duty. Members of the public are less familiar with, and also have less sympathy with, these elements of justice, and this may be reflected in the perceptions that people have of the courts and the Crown Prosecution Service.

This point has a more general application to public evaluations of different professions. Medical professionals receive very positive evaluations from the public: fully 96 per cent of respondents to a MORI poll in 2000 expressed satisfaction with nurses, significantly higher than the percentage who were satisfied with judges (69 per cent). This discrepancy surely reflects the fact that the profession of nursing has an exclusive mandate to help members of the public, whereas judges are paid to discharge a number of functions, some of which may conflict with the views of the public.

Influences upon public confidence in criminal justice

It is hard to make general statements about the factors that influence public confidence in justice; these vary from issue to issue, and country to country. Nevertheless, some common elements have emerged from the literature. Sherman (2002) identifies three domains affecting public confidence in justice: (a) the practice of the justice system, and of criminal justice professionals; (b) changing values and expectations of the culture the system serves; (c) the images of criminal justice projected by the media. He argues that changes in modern society have left the procedures and behaviour of criminal justice officials out of tune with popular values. To this list we would add public knowledge of crime and criminal justice statistics, and experience with the system as a witness, juror or crime victim.

Perceptions of crime trends and criminal justice statistics

Findings relating to public knowledge of crime and justice statistics were summarized in Chapter 1. For the present we simply note that a number of beliefs are associated with low confidence ratings or poor performance ratings, including the following:

- crime rates increasing, particularly violent crime;

- re-offending rates perceived to be high;
- sentencing patterns lenient, and parole rates high.

These perceptions contribute to the global view that the criminal justice system is insufficiently harsh.

Low levels of knowledge and unrealistic expectations of justice

The public subscribes to myths about the criminal justice system, and these create unrealistic expectations that cannot be met. For example, many people believe that there is a fairly direct relationship between the severity of the system and crime rates. When they see (or believe) crime rates to be rising, these individuals blame judges for failing to control crime (see Chapter 4). However, most sentencing experts agree that increasing the custody rate or the average length of imprisonment imposed for an offence such as robbery is unlikely to lower the crime rate for this offence by a large margin. The factors affecting rising (or falling) crime rates lie largely outside the reach of sentencers. The public also have unrealistic expectations about the roles and responsibilities of various criminal justice professionals. For example, many people believe that the prosecutor 'represents' the crime victim, the way that a barrister represents an accused person (Roberts 2002d). This leads to unrealistic expectations about the extent to which the CPS can take the victim's opinions into account when making decisions pertaining to plea bargaining or a possible appeal. One of the frequent criticisms of the justice system is that it is insufficiently attentive to the interests of victims, and this view diminishes public faith in the administration of justice.

Experience with the criminal justice system

It would be overly simplistic to say that experience always increases or decreases confidence in criminal justice. Instead, it is necessary to establish whether a specific individual's treatment by the system was positive or negative, and whether they had expectations about the system that remained unfulfilled. Some findings are clear. Criminal victimization generally lowers confidence in the justice system, particularly if the crime involved violence (National Institute of Justice 2003). If victims, witnesses and other members of the public who are involved in the system (such as jurors) are treated with respect, their expressed satisfaction with the justice system increases. Further, satisfaction is higher when victims are informed about developments in their case and when they have (or perceive they have) some input into the process. Victims left in the dark about court dates, or who are informed after the date has passed, tend to be very dissatisfied with the justice system. In many contexts perceptions are the fairness of procedures are more important than the nature of the outcomes (e.g. Tyler 1990).

Conclusion

A number of researchers have referred to the 'crisis' of public confidence in the criminal justice system (e.g. Mattinson and Mirrlees-Black 2000: 47). Has the lack of public confidence reached crisis levels? As we noted at the beginning of this chapter, establishing whether confidence levels are acceptable or not is a tricky and subjective enterprise. However, there appears to be a clear consensus among researchers and policy-makers in many countries that current trends are a cause for concern. The 2003 MORI survey in Britain found that only 4 per cent of respondents were very confident that the justice system was reducing the level of crime. An even smaller percentage was very confident that this criminal justice system was 'stopping offenders from committing more crime'. Much higher percentages had no confidence at all that the system was achieving these basic goals. Fully one respondent in five had no confidence at all that the system was stopping offenders from re-offending. Public levels of confidence in criminal justice will probably never achieve those attained by the health service, the armed forces or the education system. Nevertheless, statistics such as these suggest that efforts to improve the public image of criminal justice are necessary.

Summary

In this chapter we have reviewed (and placed in comparative context) findings from a recent representative poll that explored public confidence in criminal justice in Britain. The results suggest that people are more positive than negative about the response to crime at the local level, but that this trend reverses itself when people are asked about the national response to crime. When people are asked to express confidence in, or rate the performance of, different branches of the criminal justice system, a clear hierarchy emerges. People express far more confidence in the police than the other branches of the criminal justice system. The courts (in particular the youth courts) and prison system receive the most negative ratings. Since this finding emerges in all other countries in which people have been asked to rate different components of the justice system, we would conclude that part of the reason is that people are more aligned to the crime control function of the police, and have less time for the due process considerations that must be taken into account by courts.

Further reading

Mirrlees-Black, C. (2001) *Confidence in the Criminal Justice System: Findings from the 2000 British Crime Survey*. London: Home Office, Research, Development and Statistics Directorate.

Hough, M. and Roberts, J. V. (2004) *Confidence in Criminal Justice. An International Review*. ICPR Research Paper No. 3. London: King's College.

Sherman, L. (2002) Trust and confidence in criminal justice. *National Institute of Justice Journal*, 248: 22–31.

Tyler, T. (2002). *Trust in the Law: Encouraging Public Co-operation with the Police and the Courts*. New York: Russell Sage Foundation.

Notes

1 For example, 62 per cent of the 1996 British Crime Survey respondents underestimated the custody rate for mugging by a significant margin.

2 For example, in the USA, many states have created citizen advisory committees or public awareness programmes to promote public knowledge of justice, and thereby to increase public confidence. A number of countries, such as the USA, Belgium, Canada and Australia, have held national or international conferences to draw public and media attention to the issue of public confidence in justice.

3 A considerable amount of evaluation research has been conducted on the effect of specific policing strategies upon public perceptions of safety, a related yet conceptually distinct issue.

4 Repeated administrations of the British Crime Survey (as well as polls in other countries) have shown that most people believe crime rates are rising, regardless of actual trends in crime statistics. For example, Hough and Roberts (1998) report that three-quarters of the polled public in Britain believed that crime rates had risen within the previous two years; in reality these rates had declined.

5 The media have also provided considerable coverage of cases involving wrongful conviction, in which the state has convicted an innocent person. These cases should also undermine public confidence in the administration of justice, although we suspect that apparently erroneous acquittals or failed prosecutions exercise far more influence over public opinion.

6 Of course, the effect of the media is not restricted to the justice system. Widespread coverage of the mistreatment of prisoners surely undermined public confidence in the US military.

7 And even where comparisons between groups are made, there may be systematic differences, for example, in the preparedness to criticize institutions' performance – or simply differences in the use of language. For example, a British 'quite good' is arguably less positive than an American one, where 'quite' is used less to qualify and more for the sake of emphasis.

8 The youth justice system often receives the lowest ratings from members of the public. Why this is so is unclear. In all likelihood it reflects a public perception that youth crime rates are constantly escalating, and at a faster rate than adult crime rates. This appears to be true in other countries as well as Britain (see

Roberts 2004 for a review). This perception – which is at odds with reality – is likely to fuel dissatisfaction with the youth justice system.

9 The exact wording was the following: 'How confident are you that . . . are doing a good job? Is that very/fairly/not very/not at all confident?'

10 One explanation for these trends is that visible minority respondents do not report being stopped and searched more frequently than White respondents. Differential stop rates are a major cause of negative perceptions of the police in North America (see Wortley *et al.* 1997).

11 The percentage expressing no confidence varied even more, from 2 per cent in Denmark to 29 per cent in Ukraine (Halman 2001).

12 In general, public confidence was highest in the Scandinavian countries, and lowest in the countries that composed the former Soviet Union. Over two-thirds of respondents in Russia and Ukraine stated that they had not very much or no confidence at all in their justice system (Halman 2001).

13 We say 'in the popular mind' because the police are (or should be) as concerned as judges about due process considerations such as whether suspects are advised of their rights.

chapter three

Attitudes to the police

Introduction

There is an extensive international literature on public attitudes to the police. This is hardly surprising. The police absorb the lion's share of criminal justice budgets in all industrialized societies, and people are more likely to have contact with the police than with other professionals working in the criminal justice system. Governments and police managers are understandably keen to discover:

- what sort of policing people want;
- what sort of policing they receive, and how they rate this contact;
- whether people trust the police as an institution.

At their simplest, polls and surveys have set out to conduct a form of market research exercise, to assess the extent to which 'consumers' of police services are satisfied with the 'product'. Although government increasingly applies business concepts to public sector management, the social goods delivered by the police have important differences from those commodities delivered in the market place. In the first place, although there are areas at the margins of police function where the police compete for business directly with private sector security organizations, the public police exercise – by and large – a monopoly. As Egon Bittner (1970) famously observed, the police alone are 'equipped to deal with every exigency in which force may have to be used'. People who seek the assistance of the police obviously have a choice about whether or not to do so, but in most situations there is no real choice about the service providers. This stands in marked contrast to decisions about education or health.

Second, it is questionable, to say the least, to think in terms of a monopoly *service*. The core function of the police is to maintain public order by ensuring compliance with the rule of law. When someone fails to comply with the law, the result is often a crime victim who requires the assistance of the police. However, society cannot be neatly divided into 'offenders' and 'victims'. Few people are entirely compliant with the law, and most of us are routinely subject to police *control* in some or other form. While the police provide a public service, they do not provide a service to individuals in quite the same way as the education or health services. At heart, the job of the police involves social control.

The relevance of this point to research on attitudes to the police becomes obvious when one recognizes that compliance with those who wield authority is crucially dependent on whether their authority is regarded as legitimate. While their *capacity* to use physical force may define the scope of police work, only the most inept police officer would actually have to deploy physical force on a daily basis. Instead, the police secure compliance by drawing on the authority of their office – or on their institutional legitimacy. Without this legitimacy, the police wield power but command no authority; without authority they must police by force rather than by consent. This proposition is hardly contentious; it has been a fundamental principle of British policing since the establishment of the Metropolitan Police.[1]

Traditionally, the compliance with authority that flows from institutional legitimacy has been contrasted with compliance that results from self-interest.[2] On the one hand people may choose to obey the law because they judge that the system works, and that it is in their best interests both to obey and to support the system. On the other, they may defer to the authority of an institution because they think it is a fair one. The balance between self-interest and legitimacy as drivers of compliance with the law is probably unknowable. But it seems unarguable that those whose job is to manage the criminal justice system need to pay due regard to public views about both the system's fairness and its effectiveness. Public views about the fairness and effectiveness of current police practice are inevitably formed against some benchmark of a policing ideal. People compare the policing they receive to the policing that they would like to see, and their views about fairness and effectiveness are the product of this comparison.

The material presented in this chapter focuses mainly on the recent British literature, in particular administrations of the British Crime Survey. We begin by summarizing what people expect of the police, and what priorities they would like them to pursue. We then summarize findings relating to experiences with the police, and satisfaction with this experience. Finally, we examine public ratings of police performance, and explore issues relating to confidence, trust and consent.

Expectations and policing priorities

One approach to assessing people's expectations of the police is to ask them to justify the most important aspects of police work. Table 3.1 summarizes findings from the 2002/3 British Crime Survey. The top priority, by a comfortable margin, is responding to emergency calls. This is an important finding, as political debate tends increasingly to assume that fighting crime is the most important police function. Nevertheless, it is clear that detecting and arresting offenders is also a salient aspect of police work in the eyes of the public, as it is the next most frequently selected option.

Patrolling on foot emerged as the third most important task of a police officer. This is consistent with many surveys that have established a strong public preference to see more 'bobbies on the beat'. A large-scale survey of Londoners (Fitzgerald *et al.* 2002) asked respondents about the activities that the police 'should do more of'. Figure 3.1 shows that foot patrol was by far the most popular option, and that crime detection came quite low down the list. A similar result emerged from the 2003 MORI poll. When

Table 3.1 Perceived importance of different aspects of police work (percentages)

	Main priority	Second priority	Third priority
Responding to emergency calls	40	25	13
Detecting and arresting offenders	31	32	12
Patrolling on foot	17	15	20
Working with schools and young people	4	9	14
Crime prevention advice	3	3	6
Helping/supporting victims	2	8	15
Patrolling in cars	2	5	10
Using CCTV	1	4	7
Policing traffic	0	1	2

Source: Nicholas and Walker (2003). Question: 'On this card are some of the things that the police are asked to do. Which of these do you think is the MOST important thing the police have to do? And which of these do you think is the NEXT most important?'

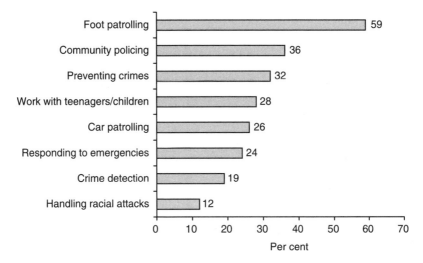

Figure 3.1 Activities the police should spend more time on: percentage choosing each item (only the eight activities that attracted support from more than 10 per cent of the sample are shown; source: Fitzgerald et al. 2002)

respondents were asked to identify the 'two or three things that would most improve the police service', fully two-thirds of the sample chose 'more police on the beat' (MORI 2003); no other proposal came anywhere close to attracting this level of support from the public.[3]

How best to make sense of people's remarkable preference for foot patrol is a matter largely for interpretation. The 'Policing for London' study asked all those who advocated the use of foot patrols to identify the activities that the patrols should engage in, and approximately two-thirds (65 per cent) wanted them to deter or prevent crime, while 49 per cent said they should reassure the community. It seems unlikely that people genuinely believe that foot patrols provide an effective strategy for tackling crime – or at least *serious* crime. The phrase 'more bobbies on the beat' is shorthand in the public mind for a particular style of policing, in which police and community are fully integrated. Certainly this interpretation gains plausibility from the fact that 'community policing' attracted the next highest percentage of preferences in Figure 3.1.

As for the crime problems that people would like the police to tackle most vigorously, in the 2002/3 BCS the highest priority was assigned to drug dealing, followed by burglary and sex crimes, as Table 3.2 shows. It is unsurprising to see burglary near the top of the list, as it poses a threat, at least to some degree, to most households. That drug dealing should be at the top of the list probably reflects the public belief that drug dependency is responsible for much crime. The high priority given to sex offences is somewhat more surprising, in light of the relative rarity of sexual offences – or at least those coming to police attention. It probably reflects women's concerns about their own risk of sexual attack, on the one hand, and, on

Table 3.2 Types of crime local police should give priority to tackling (percentages)

	Three main priorities	Highest priority	Second priority
Drug dealing	54	28	17
Burglary	53	20	18
Sex crime/sexual attacks	41	21	12
Muggings/street robbery	37	10	15
Vehicles being stolen/joyriding	32	5	13
Assault	21	4	9
Taking drugs	18	3	8
Domestic violence	10	1	3
Racial abuse	9	1	3

Source: Nicholas and Walker (2004). Question: 'The police have to deal with a number of different types of crime and the time they have is limited. From the crimes listed on this card which three crimes do you think the police in your local area should give priority to tackling? And which of the crimes you have just mentioned do you think the police in your local area should give highest priority to?'

the other, concern about the activities of paedophiles. Sex offenders have attracted a great deal of attention from the tabloid press since the *News of the World* campaign against paedophilia in 2000. Although sexual offences can be very serious individually, they tend to consume in aggregate only a small proportion of police resources.

Satisfaction with the police

Unlike all other criminal justice agencies, the police have regular contact with a significant proportion of the population. The 2003 MORI poll found that 30 per cent of respondents had contacted the police within the previous 12 months, most often (40 per cent of respondents contacting the police) to report a crime. Taking this group as a whole, we find that a much higher percentage were satisfied than dissatisfied. Thus almost two-thirds of the sample expressed satisfaction with their contact with the police; less than one-quarter were dissatisfied. In fact, the response category attracting the highest percentage of respondents (36 per cent) was 'very satisfied' – a positive outcome by any standards.[4]

The British Crime Survey also reveals that just under a third of the adult population *seeks* contact with the police each year – most frequently to report a crime – and that between a fifth and a quarter are approached by the police for various reasons, most often in relation to a car-stop or foot-stop (Nicholas and Walker 2004). The two groups are partially overlapping – because suspects can be victims of crime and vice versa – so that in the 2003/4 BCS, 44 per cent of respondents reported some kind of contact with the police.

Views of crime victims

In 2002/3, 59 per cent of BCS victims who had reported crimes to the police were very or fairly satisfied with the treatment that they had received. Whether this is a positive or negative result is again a matter for interpretation. Under half of those who were satisfied to some degree selected the 'very satisfied' option – or 25 per cent of all victims with experience of the police. Some survey analysts would regard 'fairly satisfied' as a neutral rather than positive rating, given that the less positive options – 'a bit dissatisfied' and 'very dissatisfied' – are unequivocally negative. What is clear – and of greater concern – is that the proportion of very satisfied victims has declined over the past decade, as Table 3.3 shows (Nicholas and Walker 2004).

Most BCS victims (73 per cent) in 2003/4 expressed satisfaction with police response times; around two-thirds said that the police showed adequate interest and effort in responding to their victimization. However, consistent with several earlier studies, only a minority (34 per cent) felt that they had been kept adequately informed by the police of developments in their case (Ringham and Salisbury 2004). It seems that victims' dissatisfaction with the police usually stems less from actual outcomes, however, and more from the style and manner of the encounter (Fitzgerald *et al.* 2002).

Views of suspects

While a 'consumer orientation' might tend to draw police managers' attention to the satisfaction of those who seek police services, the experiences of suspects are also an important measure of police performance. Unsurprisingly, police suspects tend to include those who are least likely to comply with the rule of law. Within this group, greater compliance is unlikely to be fostered if they have consistently negative experiences with 'the Law' – bearing in mind that the police symbolize the rule of law.

Given the intrinsically unwelcome nature of contact with the police as a suspect, ratings are actually quite high. For example, in the Policing for London study, 37 per cent of those who had been stopped in cars were very

Table 3.3 Trends in victim satisfaction with police, 1992–2002 (percentages)

	1992	1994	1996	1998	2000	2001/2	2002/3
Very satisfied	30	32	28	26	24	24	25
Fairly satisfied	37	36	38	39	35	34	34

Source: Nicholas and Walker (2004). Excludes 'don't know' responses.

satisfied with the way the police handled the incident, and a further 34 per cent said that they were fairly satisfied. Almost half (45 per cent) rated the police as 'very polite', 36 per cent said they were 'fairly polite', 41 per cent felt that the police were 'very fair' and 41 per cent thought they were 'fairly fair'. A similar pattern emerged for foot-stops, but with somewhat lower overall ratings: overall, 54 per cent said that they were satisfied with the way they were dealt with, as against 71 per cent of those stopped in cars. Almost two-thirds (65 per cent) of those stopped on foot found the police to have been polite, and 63 per cent fair. The respective proportions saying 'very polite' and 'very fair' were 29 and 36 per cent (Fitzgerald *et al.* 2002). Equivalent national figures have not been published for some time, but the pattern is likely to be similar. In general, dissatisfaction with experience as a suspect has been found to be correlated with age – young people being more dissatisfied than their elders – and with ethnicity – with Black suspects being more dissatisfied than others.

Public annoyance with the police

The BCS asks respondents whether they have been 'really annoyed' with the police at some point within the previous five years. Around a fifth – 19 per cent in 2002/3 – recall being very annoyed (Nicholas and Walker 2004). Black respondents, those from a mixed ethnic background and younger people were significantly more likely than others to report annoyance. Although there were no gender differences overall, men under 30 were much more likely to report having been annoyed than women of the same age – probably reflecting the fact that young men are more likely than any other group to have had unsought contact with the police.

The Policing for London study identified several demographic factors as significant predictors of annoyance with the police (Fitzgerald *et al.* 2002). Being young was the strongest, followed by being Black. Third was having a higher than average income, fourth was coming from a non-manual household and fifth was car-ownership. Youth and ethnicity can be interpreted as factors that are associated with experience as a police suspect. The counterintuitive correlations between annoyance and income, on the one hand, and social class, on the other, could also be explained in terms of exposure to risk: affluent middle-class people lead lifestyles that may expose them to police contact. But equally the finding could indicate that people who expect deference from the police become very annoyed if and when they do not receive it.

The reasons given for being annoyed varied, but the main ones were related to the manner of the police, or to behaviour that was perceived to be unreasonable or unfair. Lack of friendliness topped the list of complaints, highlighting the importance of the *style* of police behaviour as well as *content*. To put this another way, people are more '*process oriented*' and less '*outcome oriented*' than might be expected (Skogan 2005). This is an important finding, and one that sheds light on the consistent finding across

British and North American surveys that experience with the police is in itself a good predictor of dissatisfaction with the police. Skogan (2005) found that bad experiences with the police had a much stronger impact on attitudes to the police than positive ones.[5] Clearly, if improvements in policing outcomes are achieved at the expense of what might be called 'customer care', the long-term effect on ratings of the police may be negative.

Confidence, trust and consent

At the start of this chapter we suggested that compliance with police authority could flow either from the perceived legitimacy of the police as an institution or from a self-interested belief in the effectiveness of the police. Compliance grounded in institutional legitimacy will be supported by a set of normative beliefs about one's *obligation* to an organization that deserves respect. Compliance grounded in self-interest will be accompanied by beliefs about the personal *benefits* that will accrue from reporting crimes or the *avoidance of costs* that might be incurred by disobeying the law. Surveys have tended to operationalize this distinction by asking questions about respecting the police and about police fairness and probity on the one hand, and about their effectiveness on the other.

Respect, fairness and probity

The British Crime Survey asked respondents whether they themselves respect the police and also whether they think other people do so. The results are paradoxical, in that the *majority* of the population report being respectful themselves, but only a *minority* think that others share their views. Table 3.4 shows that three-quarters of respondents in the 2003/4 BCS said they respected the police, while only 27 per cent thought that

Table 3.4 Degrees of respect for the police (percentages)

	I view police with . . .	Police are viewed by society with . . .
Great respect	16	2
Respect	59	25
Neither respect nor disrespect	22	41
Disrespect	3	30
Great disrespect	1	3

Source: Nicholas and Walker (2004). Questions: 'Overall, which of the statements on this card best describes how you personally view the police?' 'Overall, which of the following statements best describes how you think the police are viewed by society today?'

society at large did so. This finding may reflect a general tendency for the public to see a decline in societal standards, manifested in this case as a loss of respect for the representatives of law and order.[6]

Survey results such as these are hard to make sense of in isolation. At what point should senior police officers – or their political masters – decide that they had maximized the potential for securing respect or trust? Survey findings of this sort become much more useful when they can be benchmarked, allowing comparisons over time, or with other jurisdictions, or with other agencies. A MORI (2003) poll asked a representative sample of adults in England and Wales whether they 'generally trusted' people in a range of occupations to tell the truth. Figure 3.2 shows the results.

The figure provides some – but only some – comfort for the police. They score much higher than politicians and journalists, who are deeply distrusted, and slightly higher than the 'ordinary man or woman in the street'. However, given their central role in a criminal process for which a key function is to establish the truth, one might wish for higher levels of trust among members of the public. It is worth noting that people's views about the trustworthiness of professions are not closely correlated with views on organizational competence; judges come well above the police in Figure 3.2, but, as we shall see, they come well below the police when assessed on their competence.

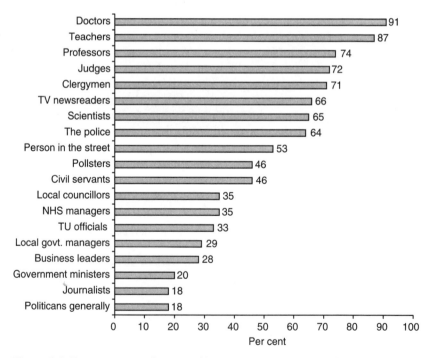

Figure 3.2 Trust in context. Question: 'Now I will read out a list of different people. For each, would you tell me whether you generally trust them to tell the truth or not?' (*source:* MORI 2003)

Government sponsored surveys seldom ask questions about police probity – perhaps because this has not been a very salient political issue, with police *effectiveness* being the perennial political concern. However, the Policing for London study (Fitzgerald *et al.* 2002) did so, replicating questions that had been asked 20 years earlier in the Policy Studies Institute study of the Metropolitan Police (Smith 1983). The questions covered the unnecessary use of force, use of violence in police stations, planting of evidence, taking bribes and extracting favours. The results are shown in Table 3.5.

There appear to be two conflicting trends. On the one hand, the proportion believing that the police *never* act illegally has fallen quite significantly for most items. On the other, the proportion believing that illegal behaviour is common has either remained the same or declined only slightly. There was, however, a statistically significant drop in the proportion thinking that unreasonable force was used in police stations. Two further questions about the prevalence of bribes and other forms of graft showed significant improvements in people's perceptions of police integrity. In 1981, 8 per cent of the sample thought that most or quite a lot of officers took bribes; but by 2000 this had fallen to 4 per cent. In 1981, 14 per cent thought that most or a lot of officers accepted goods or favours from people who wanted to keep on the right side of the police. In 2000 the figure was 7 per cent.

The importance of fairness

Fairness is critical to public perceptions of the police. The MORI survey of 2003 asked respondents to rate a number of police functions on a scale of importance, from one to ten, where ten represented a function that was, in the respondent's opinion, 'absolutely essential'. 'Treating all people fairly' attracted the highest percentage of respondents providing a rating of ten. After the issue of fairness, instrumental concerns predominated. Thus 70

Table 3.5 Beliefs about police malpractice: percentage saying it 'often happens' and 'never happens'

	PSI 1981		PFLS 2000	
	Never	Often	Never	Often
Threats etc. during questioning	30	25	24	23
False recording of interviews	56	11	53	10
Excessive force at arrest	63	13	45	11
Excessive violence in station	53	12	40	7
Fabricating evidence	40	9	29	9

Source: Smith (1983), Fitzgerald *et al.* (2002). 'Don't know' responses included.

per cent of respondents assigned an importance score of ten to 'dealing with violent crime', while 63 per cent assigned this score to 'detecting and arresting offenders'.

Surveys reveal a marked increase in the proportion of the population who think that the police treat minority ethnic groups unfairly. The percentage has risen from under a fifth (22 per cent) to over a third (36 per cent). Interestingly, this change reflects a shift in the responses of White respondents, there being little change among minority groups – perhaps suggesting a growing sensitization among White respondents to minority groups' experience of the police.

A survey conducted by the BBC asked respondents whether they thought that the evidence of Black or Asian suspects would be more or less likely to be believed by police (compared to a White suspect). The results indicated that overall, almost one-third of the sample held the view that visible minority suspects would be less likely to be believed. In addition, Black respondents were significantly more likely than White ones to hold this view (BBC 2002). When asked a more direct question ('Do you think that the police in Britain discriminate on grounds of race?'), over half the Black sample (55 per cent) and almost half the Asian sample (47 per cent) responded affirmatively (BBC 2002).[7] Just over a third of the White respondents held this view.

Ethnicity is a good predictor of public views for several measures of police integrity. For example, Black respondents in the Policing for London study were more likely than others to think that the police used threats, force, false recording and fabrication of evidence than other groups. Other demographic predictors are weak and somewhat counterintuitive. For example, in the Policing for London study, young people, men and people on low incomes tended to think better of the police. One possible explanation for these findings is that older and more affluent people have sharper memories of the corruption scandals and wrongful convictions that frequently made headlines in the 1960s, 1970s and 1980s and affected the image of the police.

Public perceptions of police effectiveness

Many more findings are available on how people rate the competence or effectiveness of the police. Table 3.6 shows BCS findings for the principal criminal justice agencies in 2002/3. Consistent with findings from other industrialized countries, the police head the list of agencies within the criminal justice system. This finding is also very consistent over time.

A similar picture emerges from the MORI (2003) poll. Respondents were asked how much confidence they had that different branches of the criminal justice system were doing a good job. This wording arguably conflates the concepts of probity and competence, but the hierarchy of professions that emerges is similar to that which emerges in response to questions that simply ask respondents to rate the job that various profes-

Table 3.6 Percentage of BCS respondents rating criminal justice agencies as doing a good or excellent job (2002/3)

Police	48
Prisons	25
Magistrates	26
Crown Prosecution Service	23
Probation service	24
Judges	25
Youth courts	14

Source: Nicholas and Walker (2004). Question: 'We would like to know how good a job you think each of the groups of people who make up the criminal justice system are doing. Please give an answer from this card. How good a job do you think [agency] are doing?'

Table 3.7 Public confidence in branches of the criminal justice system in Britain (percentages)

	Very confident	Fairly confident	Not very or not at all confident
Local police	17	59	22
Police in England and Wales	9	64	25
Magistrates	8	47	38
Judges	8	46	43
Crown Prosecution Service	7	50	38
Youth offending teams	7	42	29
Courts	6	45	44
Prisons	6	42	43
Probation service	5	54	29
Youth courts	5	41	38

Source: MORI (2003). Question: 'How confident are you that . . . are doing a good job?'

sions or agencies are doing (see Table 3.7). A noteworthy feature of this table is that confidence in *local* police is higher than for the police *nationally*. This again is a finding that emerges consistently over time and across different jurisdictions.

The MORI poll also asked respondents to compare the performance of criminal justice professionals with that of other professions. Almost the entire sample (95 per cent) was satisfied with the way that nurses performed their job. Doctors scored 91 per cent, teachers 85 per cent and dentists 84 per cent, followed by the police at 70 per cent. While judges commanded more *trust* than the police (see Figure 3.2), a smaller proportion of respondents were satisfied with the way they did their job: 52 per cent, 18 percentage points lower than the police. The Policing for London study asked a similar question, though unusually this included firefighters (Fitzgerald *et al.* 2002). The latter comfortably topped the list of occupations, with 73 per cent saying that they did a 'very good job', and 99.7 per cent saying that they did a 'good' or 'very good' job. Nurses, teachers, doctors and social workers scored more highly than the police (and in that order).

The British Crime Survey can yield a 20-year trend in attitudes to police competence, as the same question about the local police has been used since the survey started. Figure 3.3 shows a marked fall over the 20 years in the proportion of people thinking that their local police did a 'very good job'. This decline is not entirely offset by a growth in the percentage of people thinking that the local police did a 'fairly good job': the proportion offering more negative ratings has also increased.

The issue of confidence in branches of the justice system, including the police, is explored in more detail in the next chapter. For the present, we simply note that this decline in public confidence in the police has not occurred in other jurisdictions. In the USA, for example, the percentage of respondents expressing a positive view of the police has risen over the past 20 years. Thus in 1981, 49 per cent of the American public rated the police performance in positive terms; by 2003, the percentage of respondents with this perception of the police had risen to 60 per cent (Sourcebook of

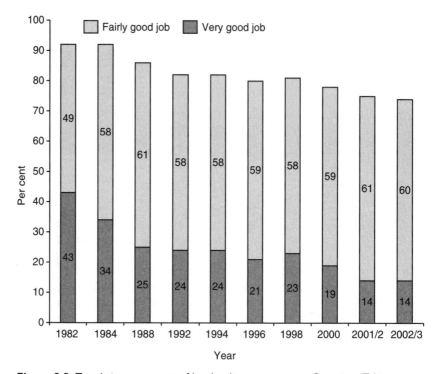

Figure 3.3 Trends in assessment of local police competence. Question: 'Taking every-thing into account, would you say the police in this area do a good job or a poor job?' Interviewer prompt: if good, 'very good or fairly good?'; if poor, 'very poor or fairly poor?' (*source:* Nicholas and Walker 2003)

Criminal Justice Statistics 2004: Table 2.14). Similarly, in Canada, the proportion of Canadians who rated the police as doing a good job remained stable throughout the 1990s (Tufts 2000).

Several factors may explain this – very striking – erosion in public ratings of police competence in Britain. On the one hand, it seems likely that the trend may reflect a broader fall in deference towards a range of institutions that includes the Church, the monarchy and the BBC: people may be more prepared to adopt a sceptical stance towards institutions that previously had enjoyed the status of 'sacred cows'. On the other hand, it should be recognized that crime rates in England and Wales rose consistently throughout most of this period, until the mid-1990s. And although the evidence is fairly clear that crime rates have fallen nationally since then, the majority of the population still believes they are rising: 72 per cent in the 2003/4 BCS. This point suggests that media representations of crime may be an important mediating factor in shaping public confidence in the effectiveness of the police. Crime stories have become a staple of the news media. This in part reflects the news values of a commercial media industry. Crime stories capture the public imagination in a way that is distinctive and more compelling than ones about education or health or other public services.

Other factors are likely to be at work as well. Fitzgerald *et al.* (2002) suggested that the increased focus on crime fighting brought about by a succession of politically set targets may have had perverse effects. In London at least, the focus on crime was achieved in the second part of the 1990s at the expense of the policing of less serious forms of social disorder. Fitzgerald and colleagues argued that this retreat from the policing of low-level disorder was an important factor in the steep decline in public ratings of competence in the second half of the 1990s.[8]

Summary

This chapter has summarized some of the key British findings on expectations about, and attitudes to, the police. It is clear that the British public favour a style of policing in which 'bobbies on the beat' are fully embedded in their local communities, and work in a way that is responsive to community preferences. First and foremost they want a police service that is competent in responding to emergencies, although responding to burglary, drug dealing, sex crimes, vehicle crime and robbery are all high on their list of crime priorities. A large minority of the population has contact with the police each year – unlike the rest of the criminal justice system, where only a small proportion will have direct experience. Satisfaction ratings of victims who reported to the police are generally positive, but the trend is downward. Ratings of those who have experience of the police as suspects are quite high, given the intrinsically unwelcome nature of contact with the police as a suspect. In assessing confidence in the police, it is important to differentiate between ratings of police integrity or trustworthiness and those relating to competence. The police tend to score lower on both counts than doctors. Judges are rated are more trustworthy but less competent. Other agencies within the criminal justice system tend to be rated lower than the police. However, against several measures of confidence police ratings are falling.

In formulating a response to findings of this sort, politicians need to develop much clearer and evidence-based ideas about the relationship between confidence in the police and compliance with police authority. At present, measures of police legitimacy are often conflated with measures that reflect perceived police competence. We do not know whether compliance with police authority is secured more effectively by improving perceptions of legitimacy or beliefs about effectiveness. In an ideal world, of course, one would opt for police services that were both effective and trustworthy. In the less than ideal world inhabited by police managers and politicians, however, choices may have to be made between strategies for enhancing legitimacy, and those for improving effectiveness.

Further reading

FitzGerald, M., Hough, M., Joseph, I. and Qureshi, T. (2002) *Policing for London*. Cullompton: Willan Publishing.

Huang, W. and Vaughn, M. (1996) Support and confidence: public attitudes toward the police, in T. Flanagan and D. Longmire (eds) *Americans View Crime and Justice. A National Public Opinion Survey*. Thousand Oaks, CA: Sage.

Swanton, B., Wilson, P., Walker, J. and Mukherjee, S. (1988) How the public see the police: an Australian survey. *Trends and Issues*, 11. Canberra: Australian Institute of Criminology.

Notes

1 See, for example, the fourth of Rowan and Mayne's nine principles of policing, namely 'To recognise always that the extent to which the co-operation of the public can be secured diminishes proportionately the necessity of the use of physical force and compulsion for achieving police objectives' (quoted in Reith 1956).

2 The idea that institutional legitimacy yields authority can be traced back to Max Weber's discussion of authority.

3 The next most popular option, chosen by only 12 per cent of the sample, was improving 'how quickly the police deal with emergencies'.

4   The breakdown was as follows: 36 per cent very satisfied; 27 per cent satisfied; 13 per cent neutral; 13 per cent dissatisfied; 11 per cent very dissatisfied.

5   The explanation for this asymmetry may lie in expectations of police conduct. People expect the police to be polite and courteous; when this expectation is fulfilled, it has less impact on attitudes. When the police act in an inappropriate fashion, treating members of the public discourteously, public expectations are confounded, and attitudes to the police change as a result.

6   As is often the case, the decline in standards is attributed to other people!

7   In the light of these findings, it is not surprising that the same poll found that fully 84 per cent of Black respondents, but only slightly more than half the White sample, expressed a desire for more visible minority police officers (BBC 2002).

8   There are some consistent differences between demographic groups in ratings of police competence. Men are more sceptical than women, and young people more than their elders. White-collar workers are more positive than those in blue-collar jobs. By the same token, owner-occupiers are more positive than those living in social housing, as are those living in rural areas, relative to city and especially inner-city dwellers.

chapter four

Attitudes to sentencing and the courts

Introduction

This chapter explores public attitudes to the criminal courts. Reviewing this material is no easy task; more research has been conducted on this branch of criminal justice than any other. There are several reasons for this degree of attention. First, the courts have a more visible media profile than many other criminal justice agencies. We may encounter police officers in daily life far more frequently than judges, but the work of the courts attracts more interest from the media. When people follow a high profile case in the media such as Martha Stewart in the USA, Jeffrey Archer in the

UK or the Dutroux trial in Belgium, they are particularly interested in the sentence that is eventually imposed by the courts. When the sentence is announced, the news media often provide adverse commentary and this helps to account for the negative views people hold of the sentencing process, and of judges. The second explanation for the volume of research concerns public expectations of the sentencing process. People appear to have definite expectations about the impact that the courts can have upon crime rates: sentencers are expected to control crime. In this respect, there is a clear divergence between the views of the public and criminal justice researchers about the role that sentencing can play in controlling crime. Most sentencing experts agree that changes to the sentencing process can have only a very limited impact on the overall volume of crime in society (e.g. Ashworth 2000).

In this chapter we review findings in this area and attempt to explain why the public is so critical of sentencers and sentencing. We also attempt to go beyond the level of poll findings; a number of studies have explored public attitudes to sentencing using a variety of different methodologies, with important consequences for understanding public opinion. In light of the volume of research on attitudes to this issue, we generally focus on the latest findings and direct the reader to reviews of earlier research (e.g. Roberts 1992; Roberts and Stalans 1997; Hough and Roberts 1998, 1999, 2002; Cullen *et al.* 2000). First, however, we review findings related to public knowledge of courts and of the sentencing process.

Knowledge of the courts

Public knowledge is generally measured in two ways: by asking people to assess their level of knowledge, or by asking them specific questions to which there is a correct answer. As noted in Chapter 1, fully 49 per cent of respondents to the MORI poll stated that they knew 'not very much', 'hardly anything' or 'nothing at all' about the courts in Britain (see Table 1.2). The public in Britain are not unique in this respect: an earlier survey in the USA found that three out of four Americans acknowledged that they knew 'very little' or 'nothing' about their court system (National Centre for State Courts 1978). The 1978 report of public attitudes to the courts concluded that 'the public appears to be largely uninformed about the courts' (National Centre for State Courts 1978: 4). Comparable levels of self-reported knowledge emerge from a survey of Australians (reported in Hough and Roberts 2004a).

The same lack of awareness emerges when people are asked specific knowledge questions. Although few studies have used this approach, the limited findings reveal that many people fail to answer correctly even some of the most elementary questions about the courts. For example, a survey conducted by the American Bar Association found that one-third of the public in the USA were unaware that the state has to establish the guilt of a person charged with an offence (American Bar Association 1999; see also National Centre for State Courts 1978). Studies of legal knowledge in Canada reach a similar conclusion (see Moore 1985; Roberts 2002d). Although few studies have explored public knowledge of the courts in Britain, the results are the same. One such study found that people were unaware of some obvious features of the court system (see Banks *et al.* 1975).

Functions of the court system

In Chapter 2 we saw that relative to other branches of the criminal justice system, such as the police, the courts do not fare well in terms of public performance ratings. At this point we pursue public confidence in the courts in greater detail, beginning with confidence in the ability of the courts to achieve specific objectives. First, however, it is worth reviewing public ratings of the importance of various court functions.

An ONS survey carried out in 2003 asked respondents to use a ten-point scale to rate the extent to which different functions of the courts were important. The responses provide insight into the model of justice to which the public subscribe. Table 4.1 provides a ranking, based upon the percentage of respondents who assigned a score of ten ('essential') to each specific task of the courts. The public concern for convicting offenders and imposing 'the right sentence' clearly emerges. The public regard protecting the rights of accused persons as being less important than imposing an adequate sentence.

Table 4.2 provides insight into the level of public confidence in differ-

Table 4.1 Importance ratings of court functions in Britain

Specific function	Percentage of respondents rating objective as 'essential'
Ensuring the guilty are convicted and the innocent are acquitted	80
Passing the right sentence	73
Treating all people equally	73
Dealing with cases promptly and efficiently	56
Supporting victims and witnesses	56
Making the right decision whether to grant or deny bail	49
Respecting the rights of accused persons	47

Source: MORI (2003). 'Question: "I'm going to read out some of the different aspects of the work that courts do. For each, please tell me how important it is to you personally. Please give me a number from 1 to 10 where 1 means 'not at all important' and 10 means 'essential'." '

Table 4.2 Confidence ratings of court functions in Britain (percentages)

	Very or fairly confident	Not very or not at all confident	Don't know
Respecting the rights of accused persons	80	14	6
Treating all people equally	74	21	5
Supporting victims and witnesses	66	26	8
Ensuring that the guilty are convicted and the innocent are acquitted	65	26	3
Making the right decision whether to grant or deny bail	64	28	8
Dealing with cases promptly and efficiently	50	45	5
Passing the right sentence	43	54	3

Source: MORI (2003). Question: 'How much confidence do you have in the way that the courts are doing the following?'

ent functions of the courts. It reveals considerable variance in public confidence levels for specific functions of the courts. Fully four out of five respondents are confident that the courts respect the rights of the accused, yet only about two in five think that sentencers get the sentences right.[1] This variability surely reflects the broader perception that the justice system goes too far in protecting the rights of suspects, and not far enough in dispensing tough justice. Another interesting feature of this table is the low percentages of respondents who respond 'don't know'. Even for a relatively technical question such as whether the courts function expeditiously, fully 95 per cent feel capable of expressing an opinion.[2]

Considering Tables 4.1 and 4.2 together reveals the challenge for the justice system: the importance of a function is inversely related to the level of confidence that this function is being achieved. Imposing the 'right' sentence is rated very high in terms of importance (Table 4.1), but the public have the least amount of confidence that this objective is being achieved (Table 4.2). Conversely, the highest proportion of the public has confidence that the courts respect the rights of the accused (Table 4.2), yet this is the function of the courts to which the public assign the least importance (Table 4.1). This inversion of assigned importance and confidence levels needs to be redressed if the image of the courts is to improve.

Expeditious justice?

A common theme in public reactions to courts around the world involves the protracted nature of judicial proceedings. Indeed, this issue has probably been around for longer than any other – at least since the seventeenth century when Hamlet fulminated against 'the law's delay' in his famous soliloquy. As Table 4.2 shows, dealing promptly with cases was one of the functions of courts in which the public expressed least confidence. A 1978 survey of US residents also found that court delay was a major source of dissatisfaction. A generation later, almost half the respondents to a nationwide survey 'strongly agreed' that cases were not resolved in a timely manner (National Centre for State Courts 1999). This perception of justice has emerged from every poll in the USA that has addressed the issue (e.g. American Bar Association 1999). Elsewhere the story is the same: Canadians also complain about the inability of the court system to resolve cases expeditiously. This public reaction reflects the 'penal impatience' theme to which we referred in Chapter 1; court delays often arise as a result of procedural safeguards to ensure a fair trial. The public have long been suspicious of this critical feature of Western judicial systems, attributing lengthy trials to incompetent prosecutors, or obstructionist tactics by defence lawyers.

Perceptions of the judiciary

The public generally have a positive view of the impartiality and integrity of the judiciary. However, perceptions become more negative – and this is reflected in confidence levels and performance ratings – when people are asked to consider the sentences imposed by judges and magistrates. The ONS survey of 2003 found that 54 per cent of respondents were very or fairly confident that judges and magistrates were doing a good job. This is significantly lower than the 76 per cent who held this view of the police.

Comparisons across professions reveal the rather negative public image of judges. We return to the survey of Londoners by Fitzgerald *et al.* (2002) which found that only 11 per cent rated judges as doing a 'very good' job. Three-quarters of the sample held this view of firefighters, 64 per cent of nurses, 39 per cent of teachers, and even social workers, who sometimes suffer from a public image problem, received better ratings, at 20 per cent. Eighteen per cent thought the police did a very good job. The same pattern emerges in other countries, and with other questions. When Canadians were asked how much trust they had in various professions, 48 per cent had a great deal of trust in police officers and doctors; only 27 per cent had this level of trust in judges (Hough and Roberts 2004a; see also Paulin *et al.* 2003). Table 4.3 ranks a number of professions in terms of the level of public satisfaction with their job performance. As can be seen, the public is much less satisfied with judges than with members of the medical profession, such as nurses and doctors.[3] Only politicians fare worse – revealing problems of a totally different magnitude.

Table 4.3 Public satisfaction with different professions (percentages)

	Very satisfied	Fairly satisfied	Very or fairly satisfied
Nurses	58	38	96
Doctors	36	54	90
Teachers	28	56	84
Dentists	26	57	83
Police	14	51	65
Accountant	11	45	56
Lawyers	10	47	57
Judges	10	47	57
Politicians	1	26	27

Source: adapted from MORI (2000). Question: 'How satisfied or dissatisfied are you with the way that the following types of people do their jobs?'

Why do people have this negative view of the judicial function? Later in the chapter we discuss surveys that have explored perceptions of sentencing patterns; these perceptions would appear to colour attitudes to the judiciary. People in Britain believe that sentencers are out of touch with the community that they represent. The 1996 BCS found that more than four out of five respondents thought judges were out of touch to some degree; about half thought they were 'very out of touch' with what ordinary people think (Hough and Roberts 1998). These findings were replicated in the 1998 BCS (Mattinson and Mirrlees-Black 2000) and also in Scotland, where 79 per cent of respondents felt that judges were out of touch (Hutton 2005). What does being 'out of touch' mean? Most probably it means failing to impose sentences that are tough enough.

We can summarize these trends as follows: while the overall ratings of the courts are less positive than those associated with the police, considerable variability exists between different functions of the courts. People have confidence that the courts treat accused persons fairly, and that they can generally determine guilt accurately. However, there is far less confidence that they can impose appropriate punishments. It is to this critical issue that we now turn.

Sentencing: from imprisonment to the community

Several surveys have explored public knowledge of the sentencing process. The general finding is that most people know little about the statutory framework of sentencing, the range of sentencing options or actual sentencing practices. This is perhaps understandable; the sentencing process is one of the most complex areas of the administration of justice, and the interplay between sentencing, parole and other forms of executive release creates complexities that confound the average layperson. However, the misperceptions of sentencing that exist in many countries also tend to be systematic distortions: people tend to assume that the sentencing process is more lenient than is in fact the case. The following research examples derive from surveys conducted over the past 20 years.

- Public estimates of the imprisonment rate for specific offences are significantly lower than the actual rates (e.g. Doob and Roberts 1983; Walker *et al.* 1988; Hough and Roberts 1999; Mattinson and Mirrlees-Black 2000).
- The public in many countries also under-estimate the length of sentences of imprisonment (Hough and Roberts 1998; Home Office 2001; Paulin *et al.* 2003).
- Most people have little accurate idea of the maximum penalties that may be imposed by courts.
- Awareness of the range of sentencing options is very limited. When respondents to the 1996 BCS were asked to identify sentences available to judges other than imprisonment, only probation was identified by a more than one-third of the sample (Hough and Roberts 1998). In Scotland, fewer than one respondent in four could name probation or electronic tagging (Hutton 2005); fewer than 10 per cent of respondents could name drug treatment and testing orders or compensation orders (Hutton 2005).
- Home Office research conducted for the Sentencing Review found that less than one-third of respondents could name three sentences without prompting (Home Office 2001).

Attitudes to sentencing

Purposes of sentencing

A number of polls have given members of the public a list of sentencing objectives and then asked them to state whether a given sentencing purpose is important. The problem with this method is that it is like asking diners in a five-star restaurant to choose an item from the menu: all the options probably sound good. An alternative approach consists of asking people to identify the single most important purpose. This approach also has deficiencies; for example, reparation is very important to people, but it may not be the most important sentencing goal. The consequence is that when people are asked to identify a single goal, objectives such as achieving reparation for the victim will appear unimportant. Reviewing all the polls that have explored public support for different sentencing goals leads to the conclusion that the public, like judges, subscribe to a complex model of sentencing that varies according to a number of factors, the most important of which is the seriousness of the crime. This point can be made by reference to Canadian research in which respondents were asked to identify the most important purpose of sentencing minor offenders and then serious offenders. Table 4.4 provides a ranking of the various sentencing purposes in terms of their importance to the public.

Recent public opinion data from New Zealand summarized in Table 4.5 demonstrate well how public support for sentencing purposes changes according to the nature of the crime being considered. Respondents were provided with a specific crime scenario, and then asked to select the most appropriate sentence. They were then asked to identify the most important purpose of the sentence that they had elected to impose. The purpose varied considerably depending upon the nature of the crime. For example, 39 per cent of the sample favoured rehabilitation in the case of

Table 4.4 Public rankings of the importance of sentencing purposes, Canada

	Minor offenders	Serious offenders
Individual deterrence	1	3
General deterrence	2	6
Provide proportional punishment	3	2
Provide restitution	4	7
Denunciation	5	5
Rehabilitation	6	4
Incapacitation	7	1

Source: adapted from Roberts (1988b).

Table 4.5 Public support for the purposes of punishment for specific offences, New Zealand (percentages)

	Fraud	Assault	Smuggling heroin	Possession of cannabis
Incapacitation	7	14	14	1
Individual deterrence	18	17	20	28
Retribution	17	19	22	9
Rehabilitation	8	31	16	39
General deterrence	8	2	15	6
Denunciation	12	13	12	14
Restitution	30	4	<1	<1

Source: adapted from Paulin *et al.* (2003).

cannabis possession; this purpose was deemed to be the most important aim by only 2 per cent of the respondents in the case involving an assault.

Although the public subscribe to a complex sentencing model, the nature of which changes in response to important case characteristics, including the seriousness of the offence, there appears to be a strong cross-cultural adherence to proportional punishment. For example, Walker *et al.* (1988) reported that the most popular choice of sentencing objective in their sample of British respondents was just deserts sentencing, which emphasizes proportionality rather than deterrence or incapacitation. In the most recent study along these lines, researchers found that 'respondents increased the severity of the punishment as the seriousness of the offense increased, but their sentences were not affected by variations in the likelihood of committing future offences, suggesting that just deserts was the primary sentencing motive' (Darley *et al.* 2000: 659). This study replicates earlier research conducted in Canada (see Roberts and Gebotys 1989).

There are clear parallels with the response of the public in other countries. A 1996 national survey of American respondents asked people to select the most important purpose of sentencing offenders from a list of four options, including deterrence, incapacitation, rehabilitation and retribution (the level of public support for denunciation was therefore not tested). Deterrence attracted the least support, being selected by only 13 per cent of the sample; retribution headed the list, having been identified by 54 per cent of respondents (see Gerber and Engelhardt-Greer 1996: Table 5.1).[4]

Perceptions of severity of current sentencing practices

For decades now (see Roberts 1992; Cullen *et al.* 2000 for earlier trends), pollsters in the USA and Britain have asked the public whether they think the sentences imposed are severe enough, and for decades the response has been the same: most people believe that judges are too lenient towards offenders. This widespread dissatisfaction with the severity of sentencing is probably the most replicated finding in the field. It appears that whenever (and wherever) the public have been asked the question, the majority respond in this way. This is true not only of common law jurisdictions such as England and Wales, Canada and the USA, but also on mainland Europe; for example, Kury *et al.* (2002) report that a very high percentage of German respondents thought that sentences were too lenient. Moreover, this perception is not restricted to Western nations. A survey conducted in South Africa in 1999 found that 58 per cent expressed the opinion that sentences were 'much too lenient' and a further 27 per cent held the view that sentences were 'slightly too lenient' (Schonteich 1999). The only exception to this pattern of dissatisfaction of which we are aware is Singapore, where three-quarters of the public believed that sentences were 'just right'; only 5 per cent held the view that sentencing was too lenient (Subordinate Courts of Singapore 1998). It seems likely that this reflects the more punitive sentencing patterns in that jurisdiction.

The public perception of leniency has persisted for some time. For example, in 1990, the British Attitudes Survey found that four out of five respondents agreed with the statement that 'too many convicted criminals are let off lightly by the courts' (Dowds 1995). Over two-thirds of the British public held this view in 1981. The trend with respect to perceptions of sentencing appears to be improving, however. The percentage of respondents expressing the view that sentences are much too lenient has been declining in recent years, from 51 per cent in the 1996 British Crime Survey to 35 per cent in the 2001 administration. Over this period there was in fact a significant toughening up in sentencing practice (Hough *et al.* 2003). The most recent poll in Britain (2003) found that 60 per cent of respondents were of the opinion that sentences were too lenient; only 29 per cent thought that sentences were about right.[5]

Table 4.6 summarizes perceptions of sentencing emerging from the 2003 MORI survey. As can be seen, most people believe that sentences are too lenient at both the adult and youth court levels. The MORI poll found that 60 per cent of the sample believed that sentences imposed on adult offenders were too lenient, while 29 per cent held the view that sentences were about right. Comparable majorities of the public held these views of youth courts. This widespread public perception has been documented in many other surveys in Britain (and elsewhere) using different formulations of the question (see Roberts and Stalans 1997 for a review).

Table 4.6 Public perceptions of adult and youth court sentencing (percentages)

	Adult courts	Youth courts
Too tough	3	4
About right	29	27
Too lenient	60	61
Don't know	7	9

Source: MORI (2003). Question: 'In general, would you say that sentences handed down by the courts are too tough, about right or too lenient?'

Explaining this relatively invariant, cross-cultural perception requires sophisticated statistical analyses that control for the inter-relationships between variables. A number of such analyses have been conducted (e.g. Hough and Roberts 1999), from which we extract the following explanations. People perceive courts to be too lenient as a result of:

- a tendency to answer the question with the most serious crimes and offenders in mind;
- a tendency to recall sentences reported in the media because they were exceptionally lenient;
- a tendency to overlook (or not know about) important mitigating factors such as an early guilty plea or the absence of previous convictions;
- a tendency to under-estimate actual sentencing trends (see above);
- a tendency to under-estimate the true severity of the sentences imposed, particularly sentences of custody (see Chapter 5);
- a tendency to 'discount' sentences of imprisonment, to assume that most of the sentence will be served in the community without any real supervision (on parole);
- a tendency to see many community penalties as a slap on the wrist, rather than a meaningful sentence (see later sections of this chapter);
- a tendency to believe that offenders often violate conditions of probation or other community sentences with impunity;
- a tendency to think that crime rates are rising, and to infer from this that sentences must be too lenient.

Whatever the cause (or combination of causes), this opinion regarding sentencing creates pressure upon sentencers, and may itself contribute to the failure to reduce the use of custody in many jurisdictions, including England and Wales. For example, several of the judges interviewed in research by Hough *et al.* (2003) noted the existence of public or political pressures for greater severity in sentencing. Political pressure is, at the end of the day, public pressure, for politicians are unlikely to press for harsher sentencing unless they perceive this to be consistent with public attitudes.

Comparing judicial practice and public sentencing preferences

A number of researchers have moved beyond the 'severity' question, and have attempted to compare public sentencing preferences with actual sentencing practices. They have encountered many methodological problems, not the least of which is the difficulty of creating an adequate comparison between the two. Although most sentencing hearings tend to be relatively brief, judges have a considerable amount of information about the crime, as well as the offender's social and criminal history. In many cases, a pre-sentence report contains information about the offender's background and social milieu. Judges obviously also have a comprehensive understanding of the relevant mitigating and aggravating factors to be considered at sentencing. Finally, they also know which sanctions are legally possible, and receive (in most common law jurisdictions) submissions from counsel for the offender and the state. Adequate comparisons between the public and the courts can be made only if a sample of subjects actually sat in court and heard all the information to which judges are exposed.

Many public attitudes studies simply give subjects a brief description of a case to consider, and then ask them to impose a sentence from a limited number of dispositions. The International Crime Victimization Survey, for example, asks participants to consider the case of an offender convicted of burglary for the second time. Respondents are allowed to select only one sentence. This exercise – devoid of information about the offence or consequences for the subject – is a far cry from sentencing in the court system. This important limitation should be borne in mind when considering results from studies that compare public opinion and judicial practice. The following conclusions emerge from this literature:

- Public sentencing preferences are much closer to court practices than would be predicted by an analysis based on the single severity question.
- Many – but by no means all – studies have found that public sentencing preferences are no harsher than sentencing practices of the courts (e.g. Mande and English 1989; Roberts and Doob 1989).
- Differences between public and court sentences remain for the most serious offences. The public generally favour the imposition of harsher sentences than the courts impose for crimes such as rape or sexual offences involving children.
- The gap between public and courts is greatest when respondents have a limited amount of information about the sentencing options that may be imposed, or the background of the offender (e.g. Doob and Roberts 1982; Covell and Howe 1996).

Public sentencing preferences in a specific case of burglary

The 1996 and 1998 administrations of the British Crime Survey contained a test of public sentencing preferences. Respondents were provided with the following brief description of a case and asked to select the sentence that should be imposed:

> A man aged 23 pleaded guilty to the burglary of a cottage belonging to an elderly man while he was out during the day. The offender, who had previous convictions for burglary, took a videoplayer worth £150 and a television that he left damaged near the scene of the crime.

An offender with a profile such as this would generally be sent to prison; in fact this description summarizes an actual case in which the individual had received a three-year term of custody, reduced on appeal to two years.

Figure 4.1 summarizes the responses of people participating in the two BCS surveys. Several conclusions can be drawn. First, there was as much support for compensation as for imprisonment; the public are clearly attracted to sentences that generate some tangible benefit for the crime victim (this issue is explored in more detail in Chapter 7).

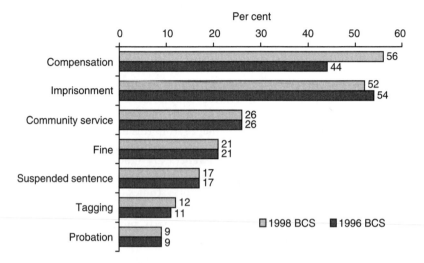

Figure 4.1 Sentencing preferences in a specific case of burglary (*source*: adapted from Mattinson and Mirrlees-Black 2000)

Second, the pattern of responses was remarkably similar across the two independent samples, suggesting considerable stability in response patterns.[6] Third, although as noted this kind of case almost always results in imprisonment, respondents are as likely as not to favour custody. Furthermore, the average length of custody of respondents who choose to impose imprisonment is a year, significantly short of the sentence length actually imposed. This question explored reactions to a single case; before concluding that the public is no more punitive than the courts we would need to make comparisons on a wide range of offences.[7] Finally, it is clear that like judges, the public favour the use of multiple sentences; no single disposition is seen as being sufficient to accomplish the objectives of sentencing.

Mandatory sentencing

Mandatory sentences of imprisonment represent the most punitive (and controversial) sentencing reform of recent years. They have been introduced in many Western nations. Often justified by reference to public opinion, they have proved highly controversial in practice. Where do members of the public stand with respect to the issue? Few studies have addressed public knowledge of statutory minimum penalties. Fortunately, the surveys that exist on this issue have generated the same findings: the general public has little idea of the offences that carry a mandatory minimum penalty, or of the magnitude of the statutory minima.

In 1998, members of the public responding to the British Crime Survey were asked if they were aware of the mandatory minimum prison term of three years for offenders convicted of burglary (this mandatory sentence had been the object of considerable media attention). Fewer than one-quarter of the sample responded affirmatively. This finding is consistent with earlier research in Canada that found that very few members of the public had any idea which offences carried a mandatory sentence (Roberts 1988b).[8]

The limitations of opinion polls as a tool to understanding public opinion are most apparent in the area of mandatory sentencing. A clear bifurcation can be seen with respect to the portrait of public opinion that emerges from standard polls, and other research approaches in which the public are provided with more than a simple question to answer. When simple questions are put to the public, they tend to tap into a vein of punitiveness. For example, when an *Observer* poll asked people in Britain whether they supported or opposed a 'three-strikes' scheme whereby offenders automatically receive a prison sentence if they have been convicted of any three crimes, exactly four out of five respondents expressed their support (*Observer* 2003).

Similarly, when Americans were asked whether their reaction to a 'three-strikes' law for offenders convicted of a third violent felony, almost 90 per cent were in favour (Roberts and Stalans 1997). When questions are phrased in such a way, respondents are not given a chance to think through the consequences (or costs) of such a sentencing policy. Nor are they encouraged to think of the kinds of cases for whom a three-strike sentence of custody may be appropriate.

Attitudes to mandatory sentencing in the USA, Australia and Britain

Applegate *et al.* (1996) explored attitudes to 'three-strikes' laws using a random sample of Ohio residents. First, respondents were asked whether they supported or opposed implementing a three-strikes law in their state. This law would impose a life sentence on anyone convicted of a third serious crime. Fully 88 per cent expressed their support for the proposal. The respondents were then given a series of cases to consider that met the three-strikes criteria, and were asked to select an appropriate sentence. Support for the 'three-strikes' law declined significantly once respondents had to consider individual cases. In fact, on average, only 17 per cent of the sample elected to sentence the offender to this sentence. Additional analyses demonstrated that the public supported making a number of exceptions to the three-strikes law. In other words, they were clearly uncomfortable with the *mandatory* nature of the legislation. Applegate *et al.* (1996: 517) concluded that 'these findings suggest that citizens would endorse three-strikes policies that focus on only the most serious offenders and *that allow for flexible application*' (emphasis added).

Mandatory sentencing exposes the weaknesses of simple poll questions. Thus when the *Observer* poll in 2003 found that four out of five respondents in Britain would support the introduction of a 'three strikes and you're out' law, it simply means that without thinking through the issue, the concept has some appeal to the public. We would argue that the true level of support for mandatory sentencing (or any other complex issue in the area of criminal justice) can only be determined by providing more information and specific examples, in the manner employed by Applegate *et al.* (1997).

Community penalties

All Western countries have attempted to increase the use of community-based penalties in recent years. This has been attempted in a number of ways. For example, in Britain, the Criminal Justice Act 2003 creates a new sanction, 'custody minus' – a form of suspended sentence accompanied by probation supervision – which is served in the community. In 1996, the Canadian Parliament provided judges with a new community-based sentence that has helped to reduce the volume of prison admissions (Roberts and Gabor 2004). In addition, many countries, including England and Wales, New Zealand and Canada, have created statutory directions to judges to use imprisonment as a last resort, only when no community sentence will be sufficient to achieve the objectives of sentencing.[9] These developments have provoked an interest in finding out what the public thinks about sentencing offenders to a community-based sanction. The following conclusions may be drawn from the literature on public attitudes to community sentencing:

- In most countries, judges have a wide range of non-custodial sentences at their disposal. These sanctions clearly do not have the public profile of imprisonment, and this is revealed by surveys in which people are asked to identify spontaneously these penalties: most respondents were unaware of the alternatives to custody (e.g. Hough and Roberts 1998).
- Members of the public tend to associate community alternatives with lenient sentencing. One poll in the USA found that over half the sample believed sentencing alternatives to be evidence of leniency by the courts (University of Arkansas 1999).
- Although support for alternative sanctions varies across jurisdictions, the International Criminal Victimization Survey (ICVS) found strong

support when respondents were asked to choose an appropriate sentence for a case of burglary (see Mayhew and van Kesteren 2002).

- The most popular community sentences are those that require the offender to pay compensation to the victim, or perform work for the community (Maguire and Pastore 1997).
- The least popular community sentences are those such as probation that in the eyes of the public require the offender to do little more than refrain from further offending.
- Making the conditions of a community sentence salient to the public promotes acceptance of these sanctions (e.g. Sanders and Roberts 2000).
- Increasing public awareness of alternative sanctions also promotes public support of these dispositions (e.g. Doble and Klein 1989; Hough and Park 2002).
- Support for the use of community-based sanctions declines as the seriousness of the offence or the number of the offender's previous convictions increases.

Support for Alternative Sanctions as a Substitute for Incarceration

In a later chapter (7) we shall describe research that explores public acceptance of alternative sanctions that have a restorative rather than punitive nature. For the present, we note that public acceptance of alternatives to custody can be demonstrated by studies in which people who have endorsed imprisonment in response to a crime scenario are then asked whether they would find an alternative punishment acceptable. These studies show that large proportions of respondents who initially favour incarcerating an offender nevertheless acknowledge that a non-custodial alternative would be acceptable. Box 4.1 summarizes a test of this 'substitute sanction' hypothesis in the context of sentencing young offenders in Britain.

In a review of the research on public attitudes to community penalties, Maruna and King (2004) argue that the public are ambivalent about the use of non-custodial penalties. We conceive of public attitudes in this area in a rather different way. In our view, public support for community penalties can best be seen in terms of a continuum that maps on to the axis of crime seriousness. For the least serious offences, public support for alternatives is considerable; for the most serious offences, public opposition is equally strong. As the crimes under consideration move from low to high seriousness, support diminishes and opposition increases. Of course this does not tell us *why* the public see community penalties as an inadequate penal response to serious offending; it is more a description than an explanation. Community penalties may be seen as simply too lenient (in which case considerations of proportionality are invoked), or, as some

---

Box 4.1 Substituting community for custody: responses of the British public

A representative sample was divided in half, with respondents being assigned to read about one of two young offender cases. One involved an offender convicted of theft; the other young offender had been convicted of robbery and had three previous (and serious) convictions. After reading one of the cases, respondents were told that the magistrates were considering imposing a term of custody and community supervision. They were asked whether they would find it acceptable if the magistrates imposed instead an alternative sanction. The alternative sanction consisted of a number of elements, including some restorative requirements.

Case history A. Henry is 16 years old and has been convicted of stealing CDs worth about £300 over a two-week period from a local shop. This is the second time that he has been before the courts for stealing. The magistrates are considering sending this young offender to a prison for young offenders, followed by a period of supervision by a probation officer or social worker in the community.

Case history B. Henry is 16 years old and has been convicted of robbery. He punched another 16-year-old several times in the face, and stole his mobile phone. He has three previous convictions, for assault, theft and robbery. The magistrates are considering sending this young offender to a prison for young offenders for 60 days, followed by a term of supervision by a probation officer or social worker in the community.

Question. Would you find it acceptable if the magistrates imposed the following sentence instead of sending the young offender to prison? The young offender would be supervised in the community for three months by a probation officer or social worker. In addition, he would have to write a formal apology to the victim, pay back the money and perform 100 hours of community service.

For the young offender who had stolen compact discs over a protracted period of time, and who had a previous conviction for theft, 79 per cent of respondents found the alternative sanction acceptable. For the other case, just over half the group (52 per cent) found the alternative acceptable. These are striking findings. The second case is a serious one, and following clear guidance from the Court of Appeal it would undoubtedly attract a custodial sentence in the youth court. Despite this, more than half of the sample found the alternative sentence acceptable. Moreover, had the alternative been more severe – perhaps by means of a longer period of community supervision – it would undoubtedly have attracted even more support from the public.

Source: Hough and Roberts (2004b)

---

scholars have argued (e.g. Doob and Marinos 1995), there may be some intrinsic link in the public imagination between prison and serious crime. It may be more the quality rather than the quantity of punishment. But that is a story for another day.

Summary

Members of the public know less about the courts than most other branches of the justice system. This emerges both from surveys that ask respondents to assess how well informed they are and from those that actually test people about their knowledge. What they believe tends to be rather inaccurate, with a systematic tendency to exaggerate the leniency of the courts. Public support for different sentencing purposes varies according to the seriousness of the crime and other legally relevant characteristics. In this sense they resemble judges. Although it is very difficult to make adequate comparisons between public sentencing preferences and the sentences imposed by the courts, careful research in a number of countries suggests that the public are not always or even often harsher. The punitive public reaction springs from simple questions to which people respond while thinking of the worst cases coming before the courts. Support for community sanctions has been increasing. There is now considerable support for alternatives to imprisonment, particularly those that compel or at least encourage the offender to make reparation to the victim or the community. However, the public remain opposed to the use of community penalties for the most serious crimes of violence.

Further reading

Cullen, F., Fisher, B. and Applegate, B. (2000) Public opinion about punishment and corrections, in M. Tonry (ed.) *Crime and Justice: A Review of Research*. Volume 27. Chicago: University of Chicago Press.

Hough, M. and Roberts, J. V. (1999) Sentencing trends in Britain: public knowledge and public opinion, *Punishment and Society. The International Journal of Penology*, 1: 7–22.

Roberts, J. V. (2002) Public opinion and the nature of community penalties: international findings, in J. V. Roberts and M. Hough (eds) *Changing Attitudes to Punishment*. Cullompton: Willan Publishing.

Roberts, J. V. and Stalans, L. S. (2000) Sentencing and parole, Chapter 10 in *Public Opinion, Crime, and Criminal Justice*. Boulder, CO: Westview Press.

Notes

1 These trends are found in other jurisdictions as well, using a slightly different question. Tufts (2000) reports that 41 per cent of respondents in a Canadian poll rated the courts as doing a good job at ensuring a fair trial for the accused; significantly fewer (13 per cent) rated the courts as doing a good job at providing justice quickly. This pattern emerged a decade earlier in another study

(Sacco and Johnson 1990), suggesting that considerable stability exists in public attitudes to the courts.

2 This finding is typical of surveys in the field of criminal justice; few people respond 'don't know' whatever the question. It is unclear whether this is because they really are sure that they have an opinion, or because they did not want to appear 'opinion-less'.

3 The public perception of physicians is not affected by adverse media coverage, although this does appear to influence ratings of criminal justice professionals. In 2000, MORI asked the public to rate the performance of doctors after first having brought to the respondent's attention recent stories in the media that represented doctors in an unfavourable light. Despite this, 89 per cent still rated doctors as doing their job well (MORI 2000).

4 The Halliday Sentencing Review in England and Wales conducted public opinion research in the area of sentencing. When respondents were asked to rank the purposes of sentencing (without any distinction between minor and serious offenders) in terms of their importance, ratings were high for almost all objectives and highest for the goal of 'changing the offender's behaviour' (Home Office 2001). The public clearly see this as a very important purpose of sentencing; however, since the options provided did not include proportional sentencing, it is hard to know how support for these two goals compares.

5 This view of lenient sentencing clearly influences public confidence in the courts. When respondents to the 2003 poll who expressed little confidence in the courts were asked why they had this reaction, the most frequent justification concerned lenient sentencing.

6 When this scenario was presented to a sample of residents of Northern Ireland in 1998, the responses were very similar: 46 per cent elected to impose imprisonment (see Amelin *et al.* 2000).

7 A number of studies have compared public sentencing preferences with actual court practices. The general finding from these studies is that aggregated across all offences, public sentences are not that different from those actually imposed by the courts. Differences do emerge with respect to specific offences; the public tend to be much harsher than the courts for some offences, and more lenient for others. For example, judges react quite punitively to offenders convicted of perjury, whereas the public appear not to regard this as one of the most serious offences (see Walker *et al.* 1988; Roberts and Doob 1989).

8 It should not be surprising that public knowledge of mandatory sentences is poor. Surveys conducted in several jurisdictions have shown that the public know little about maximum sentences, sentencing options, alternatives to imprisonment, sentencing patterns, recidivism rates or any other aspect of the sentencing process.

9 This is known as the principle of *restraint* or *parsimony* in sentencing.

10 Sceptical readers may take the position that these trends reflect social desirability or demand characteristics effects. That is, respondents may have felt that the socially acceptable response was to accept the alternative sanction in place of prison. However, the significant percentage of respondents who rejected the alternative sanction, as well as the variable acceptance rates within any particular study argues against a social desirability interpretation. After all, if 53 per cent of the respondents to one question in the present survey felt that the socially desirable response was to accept the substitute sanction, why

was the acceptance rate so much lower for the other scenario? A social desirability explanation would predict relatively uniform acceptance rates across scenarios. The difference between conditions must reflect respondents' reactions to the acceptability of the sanction, not the social desirability of the response.

Attitudes to prison and parole

Introduction

This chapter explores public opinion about prison and release from prison. As we noted earlier, public ratings of the prison system are more negative than for most other criminal justice agencies. The MORI poll of 2003 found that almost half the sample was not very, or not at all, confident that the prison system was doing a good job. In addition, it appears that public confidence in prisons has been declining in recent years. In 1996, 38 per cent of respondents to the BCS rated the prison system as doing a good job; the proportion holding this view declined progressively to 25 per cent in

2002/3 (Pepper *et al.* 2004). Correctional authorities in other countries attract comparably poor ratings from the public (e.g. Tufts 2000; Roberts 2004).

It is unclear why the public has so little confidence in the prison system. Criticism of the courts can be explained by the fact that judges are seen to be insufficiently harsh; the public sometimes lose sight of the fact that sentencing is about more than just punishment. As for the police, some of the 'lift' in public ratings of the police comes from the fact that their mandate is closer to the public's crime control philosophy – they are seen to be on the public's 'side'.

On both grounds – punishment and crime control – prisons should attract positive ratings from the public, yet this is clearly not the case. The answer may be that the public see prisons as institutions that should punish *and* reform offenders. As we shall see in this chapter, from the perspective of the public, prisons fail on both counts. Prisons do not punish enough – life is thought too easy for prisoners – and as for rehabilitation, the public around the world are very sceptical that this can be accomplished. Insufficient punishment with not much reformation: it is little wonder that prisons fail to inspire much public confidence.

We noted in the previous chapter that the public are generally quite unfamiliar with alternatives to custody; no such lack of awareness exists with respect to the concept of imprisonment. Although detention as a punishment is not the oldest legal penalty,[1] it has acquired an iconic status in public conceptions of legal punishment, at least for the more serious crimes of violence. There is a strong link in the public imagination between violent crime and committal to custody; hence the strong support for custody when people are asked to impose a sentence for serious crimes of violence. As will be seen, however, although the public are well aware of imprisonment as a sanction, this awareness has not resulted in an accurate concept of daily life inside a penal institution.

The very visible public profile of prison as a legal sanction may also help to explain why legislative efforts to reduce the use of imprisonment as a sanction have been relatively unsuccessful; the proportionate use of custody in Britain has not declined in recent years, and this has led to rising prison populations in many Western nations. In England and Wales, for example, the number of people under sentence in prison rose from 36,000 in 1991 to 62,000 in 2003 – an increase of 71 per cent (see Hough *et al.* 2003 for discussion). Judges may well be wedded to the use of imprisonment as a sanction in part because they see no credible alternative in the eyes of the community. Changing public attitudes to custody may therefore have the effect of reducing the use of imprisonment. Although the public see imprisonment as the appropriate sentence for serious crimes, people clearly see both the limitations of imprisonment as a sanction and the advantages of non-custodial sentences, particularly the tougher alternatives (see Chapter 4 of this volume and Roberts 2002b). We begin our analysis of public attitudes to imprisonment with a consideration of public knowledge of the use of imprisonment as a sanction, and then turn to perceptions of prison life.

Prison population statistics

Criminal justice professionals in the UK and the USA are well aware of the rising prison populations in recent years. In the UK, the prison population has risen to a record level. The US prison population exceeded two million inmates for the first time in 2002 (US Bureau of Justice Statistics 2003). Most members of the public were unaware of this costly development. When the British public were asked about changes in the prison population over the period 1992–2002, only one respondent in seven came up with the correct answer, namely that there had been an increase of 50 per cent (Esmée Fairbairn Foundation 2002). This replicates the findings from a British survey conducted in 1966 (reported in Banks *et al.* 1975). Similarly, when Canadians were asked about the use of custody, most people believed that the imprisonment rate was *lower* in Canada than other Western countries, when in reality it is higher (Roberts *et al.* 1999). In addition, research has demonstrated that the public underestimate the costs of incarceration (Jubinville *et al.* 1987). Informing the public about the high numbers of people in prison (as well as the costs of custody) may well represent an effective strategy to promote the use of alternative sanctions. With the exception of serious violent offenders – for whom the public are willing to assume any costs associated with custody – the public are sensitive to the issue of cost savings (see Hough and Roberts 2004b for an example).

Knowledge of prison life and conditions

Most people know little about life in prison and this reflects a lack of direct experience with correctional institutions. In Scotland, Anderson *et al.* (2002) report that almost 90 per cent of a representative sample acknowledged knowing not very much or nothing at all about Scotland's prisons. Glanz (1994) found that many respondents to a South African survey were unable to answer many questions about the nature of prison conditions in that country. For example, when asked to rate the state of conditions in prison, almost 40 per cent responded 'don't know' – an unusually high percentage for criminal justice survey questions, for which most people usually have a response (Glanz 1994). Finally, few members of the public have actually seen the inside of a prison. The 1996 British Crime Survey found that four out of five respondents had never been in a prison in any capacity (Hough and Roberts 1998).

Even those individuals who have visited a prisoner will have been restricted to the public visiting area of the prison, and will have only second-hand insight into daily life on the wings and in the cells. This lack of direct experience explains why most people know little about prison life, prison programmes or the work of prison officers. An early study conducted over 40 years ago in the USA concluded that most people were 'generally ignorant of [prison] programs' (Gibbons 1963: 137). In Britain, Banks *et al.* (1975: 235) found that respondents' 'perceptions of a prisoner's day tended to be quite inaccurate' and concluded that people were 'generally misinformed about conditions in prisons'. The negative image of prison officers is also explained by inaccurate media coverage of the prison (see Bryant and Morris 1998[2]; Freeman 1998). Little appears to have changed over the past 30 years.

Much of what we know about prisons is derived from media stories, television programmes such as *Oz* or films such as *The Birdman of Alcatraz* and more recently *The Shawshank Redemption*.[3] Despite – or perhaps because of – frequent media representations of prison life, the public probably know less about imprisonment than any other stage of the justice system. Many news stories focus on aspects of prison life likely to pique the viewer's interest – this usually means outbreaks of violence, sexual aggression or elements of prison life that will outrage the public.

The pains of imprisonment

Members of the public are probably aware that violence is a daily feature of many prisons, but it seems unlikely that they will know about the elevated risks in terms of assault, sexual assault, homicide and suicide to which many prisoners are exposed (see Walker 1983; Roberts and Jackson 1991; Liebling 1994).[4] They fail to appreciate the problems caused by penal sequestration, or the difficulties associated with re-entry into society, sometimes after many years 'inside'. Nor are they likely to consider the problems that imprisonment creates for innocent third parties, such as offenders' families, who suffer both emotionally and financially (see Ferraro *et al.* 1983). Members of the general public seldom stop to consider the possibility of discrimination against visible minority prisoners in custody, although research in Britain, Canada and other countries has found evidence of such behaviour (e.g. Commission on Systemic Racism in the Ontario Criminal Justice System 1995; Edgar and Martin 2004).

Issues such as these are seldom covered in media accounts of life in prison. Prison conditions usually come to the attention of the public through the media only when there is an 'event' such as the prison riots in Strangeways Prison in Manchester and in Attica Prison in New York state, or the misconduct of correctional officers in Canada's 'Prison for Women' (Arbour 1996). As a result of their dramatic nature (and the loss of life involved), events such as these attract worldwide attention. Otherwise, prison conditions and the workings of the institutions come to attention only under special circumstances, such as when the prisoner happens to be a celebrity. For example, when Jeffery Archer, the former MP and member of the House of Lords, was sent to prison, his progress through the system was the object of numerous media stories, the volume of which intensified upon his release.

A good illustration of the influence of the news media upon public knowledge of correctional issues comes from the USA. Respondents to a survey in Florida were asked to identify the most important problem facing the state's correctional system. The problem identified by most people was prison overcrowding. Coincidentally (or not), a content analysis of news media stories about corrections in Florida found that the most frequent subject was prison overcrowding. The irony is that at the time this survey and content analysis were conducted, there was no problem of overcrowding in Florida's prisons. The news media had created public concern about a correctional 'problem' that simply did not exist (see Bryant and Morris 1998).

Prison as 'easy street'

In Chapter 4 we noted that most people fail to appreciate the severity of the sentencing process; they under-estimate the incarceration rate for most offences, as well as average sentence lengths. It seems that the public also under-estimate the severity of life inside. Prison stories in the news often dwell upon the 'extensive' facilities to which prisoners have access, such as television or computers. Such stories are one cause of a widespread perception among members of the public of various countries that prison life is easy. Several studies conducted in different countries have sustained this curiously upbeat perspective on penal institutions. This view is in part based upon a lack of knowledge about prison life and programmes. Almost 90 per cent of respondents to a survey in Florida believed that inmates were housed in air-conditioned facilities, although for the vast majority of prisoners this is not the case (Bryant and Morris 1998).

Similarly, Doble Research Associates (1994; 1995a, b) conducted research on Americans' knowledge of the correctional system and found that two-thirds of the sample wrongly believed that most prison inmates are idle all day instead of working productively at a job. Farkas (1997: 269) reports a comparable finding: 60 per cent of his respondents in Pennsylvania and Oregon thought that inmates 'spend most of their time watching television, playing cards and not having to work'. Finally, in Canada, surveys have shown that most people assume that computers, televisions and stereos are provided without charge to prisoners, when in fact these amenities have to be paid for by the prisoner, usually out of low prison wages (Roberts 1995).

All surveys that have explored perceptions of prison life have found that the public think that daily life in prison is easy. For example, half the Scottish respondents in a survey reported by Anderson et al. (2002) agreed that life was too easy in Scottish prisons; only 15 per cent disagreed with this view. The comments of participants in qualitative research conducted in the USA are representative of this perspective: '[prisoners] don't do anything except sit around all day, watching TV, listening to the radio and playing cards' (Doble 1987: 27).[5] Some members of the public seem positively envious of prisoners: one participant in a study conducted by Doble Research Associates said that: 'They [prisoners] have it better than some of us. Weights, cable TV, phones, field trips – it's not prison, it's summer camp.'

This perception of cushy prison conditions would appear to be relatively recent. In 1984, when people were asked to agree or disagree that 'prisons today are like hotels', the sample was evenly split (Brillon *et al.* 1984). By 1994, however, around two-thirds of the British public agreed with the statement that: 'prisoners have much too easy a time' (Dowds 1995). The view that prison life is easy helps to explain the low levels of public confidence in the prison system. Needless to say, although members of the public may see prison as a somewhat more austere version of a college residence, prisoners (and their families) do not see matters the same way (see Adams 1992 for a review of research).

Consequences of public perceptions of prison life

A number of negative consequences ensue from the misperception that prison life is not particularly unpleasant. First, people are going to be less likely to see prison as the punishment that it clearly is: the 1996 BCS found that barely half the sample agreed with the statement that 'being put in prison punishes offenders' (Hough and Roberts 1998). Clearly, these people have not had to slop out the cells in Barlinnie Prison. A recent national survey in the USA found that six respondents out of ten agreed that 'criminals don't mind being sent to prison' (Belden Russonello and Stewart 2001). Second, the perception that prison is easy is going to fuel public calls for longer prison terms. After all, if doing time is 'a piece of cake', and if prisoners are released after having served only a small proportion of the sentence (see below), a year or so inside cannot be a severe punishment. The association between the perception of prisons as easy and the attitude that sentences should be longer emerges repeatedly from surveys conducted in many countries. Research in Canada and South Africa has shown that people who think that prisons are 'too soft' also tend to favour longer terms of custody (see Brillon *et al.* 1984; Glanz 1994). This relationship can be illustrated by data from the British Crime Survey. Table 5.1 presents a cross-tabulation between responses to two questions: whether prison serves as a punishment, and whether sentences are too harsh or too lenient. As can be seen, people who believe prison does not punish offenders were significantly more likely to consider sentencing to be too lenient.

Views of prison conditions therefore become a source of *penal*

Table 5.1 Relationship between perceptions of sentencing and whether prison serves as a punishment (percentages)

	Sentences are too lenient	Sentences are about right
Prison punishes	48	65
No opinion	20	18
Prison does not punish	32	17

Source: Hough and Roberts (1998). Questions: 'In general, would you say that the sentences handed down are too tough, about right or too lenient?' 'Please state how much you agree or disagree with the statement "Being put in prison punishes offenders".'

escalation; public pressure for longer sentences may have an impact on judges, particularly in jurisdictions in which judges are elected, not appointed. Further, this public view of a congenial prison environment may encourage politicians and correctional officials to restrict further the amenities available to prisoners. It is critically important, therefore, that the public have a more realistic idea of the nature of life in prison.

Little support for 'penal austerity'

These findings may be taken by some people to indicate that the public want prison conditions to be made much tougher. This would appear to be an over-simplification. Although many people think that prison life is easy (or easier than it should be), there is in fact little support for taking away the amenities available in prison. Politicians in a number of countries have attempted to exploit public dissatisfaction with the 'relative ease' of prison life by advocating harsher conditions.[6] This is a classic case of penal populism: demanding tougher prisons is seen as a good strategy for attracting political support (see Roberts *et al.* 2003). However, there may be less support among the public for this 'get tough with prisoners' line than politicians would appear to believe.

Applegate (2001) found little support among the public in Florida for a policy of making prison life more aversive. For example, only 21 per cent supported eliminating air conditioning in correctional facilities, and only around a third wanted to get rid of televisions. Applegate (2001: 265) concluded that his findings 'question the assumption that harsh public opinion is driving the trend to eliminate prison amenities'. John Doble's research in a number of states found the same result. Participants were in favour of providing more structure: they wanted prisoners to have access to meaningful and remunerated work. However, there was no public support for bans on television or physical exercise, and outright public opposition to 'chain gangs composed of inmates breaking rocks' (see Doble Research Associates 1995a). Support for amenities in prison is particularly strong if prisoners are paying for, or at least contributing to, the costs of these facilities.

This apparent paradox – people see prison life as being too easy but don't necessarily want to make it more aversive – was noted by John Doble in 1987. He found that the participants in his research did not want to make life worse for prisoners, merely to see them suffer: 'Most respondents who said that prison should be "harder" were *not* interested in punishment per se. Rather they wanted to reduce idleness and felt that work is therapeutic and beneficial to society and prisoners' (Doble 1987: 34). This view of public opinion is consistent with the public desire to see change in prisoners. This reflects interest in what might be termed a 'reformation script', not mere punitiveness: people want to see prisoners change themselves for the better.

The purpose of prisons: to punish or rehabilitate?

What purpose do the public ascribe to prisons? Public reaction to the purpose of prisons is strongly influenced by the construction of the question. When people are asked to identify a single purpose – the most important or primary function – punishment or incapacitation generally garners the most support. However, the abiding public interest in the rehabilitative function of prisons emerges clearly when people are asked to identify multiple purposes.

The 2003 MORI survey in Britain provided respondents with a list of functions of the prison service and then asked people to assign a number from one to ten, where one meant that this task was not at all important and ten indicated that this function was absolutely essential. The results provide insight into the British public's views of the function of prisons. The function that received the highest score (73 per cent of respondents assigned a ten) was keeping prisoners securely and preventing escapes. Treating prisoners humanely was identified as absolutely essential by less than half the sample. The public appear to see prisoners as a dangerous group of people. However, as will be seen, there is also strong support for rehabilitation: 60 per cent of the sample assigned a maximum importance score of ten to the function of 'helping to prepare those sent to prison to lead law-abiding lives on release'.

It is clear that the public around the world still see an important role for rehabilitation in prison. Cullen (2002: 288) summarizes the research on public attitudes in the following way: 'the public will is not only to punish offenders but also to rehabilitate them'. Applegate *et al.* (1997) provide ample empirical support for what they term the 'continuing appeal of the rehabilitative ideal'. The level of support for rehabilitation in prison varies across jurisdictions, but is strong everywhere, as the following findings reveal:

• A survey conducted in Britain in 1994 found that over three-quarters of the sample agreed with the statement that 'prisons should reform prisoners' (Dowds 1995).[7]

- When a Gallup survey in the USA asked respondents, 'In dealing with those in prison, do you think it is more important to punish them for their crimes, or more important to rehabilitate them?', 48 per cent supported rehabilitation, 38 per cent punishment (14 per cent were undecided; Sourcebook of Criminal Justice Statistics 1990: Table 2.50).
- When asked to identify the most important goal of prison, the following hierarchy emerged from another nationwide poll: rehabilitation, 48 per cent; deterrence, 33 per cent; punishment, 15 per cent (Sourcebook of Criminal Justice Statistics 1997: Table 2.51).
- The most recent poll conducted on this question in the USA found that 40 per cent of the sample endorsed rehabilitation as the main purpose of sending a person to prison. The options 'to punish' and 'to protect society' each attracted half as much support (Belden Russonello and Stewart 2001).
- Given a choice between 'helping offenders rehabilitate themselves' and 'punishing offenders for their crimes', a sample of Canadians chose the former over the latter, in a six to four ratio (Roberts et al. 1999).
- When a sample of South Africans was asked whether prison should punish or reform prisoners, over 60 per cent chose reformation (Monograph 2000)

The strong public support for rehabilitation in prison (and for parole, see below) is clearly a manifestation of a deeper desire to see offenders improve themselves. This echoes the theme of 'redeemability' that Maruna and King (2004) find in their research on community penalties in Britain. The public are powerfully attracted to cases in which offenders have turned their lives around.[8] This explains the strong public support for legislation that permits ex-offenders to obtain a pardon (see Burbidge 1982). Finally, there is also evidence that the public are willing to pay more tax to support setting up halfway houses for prisoners and job creation programmes for ex-prisoners. One survey found that two-thirds of the public supported increasing taxes for both purposes (Brillon et al. 1984).

Public perceptions of the effectiveness of prison

Although the public endorse the use of imprisonment in order to protect society from dangerous offenders (and believe that imprisonment offers this protection; see below), there has been a collapse of faith in recent years regarding the other functions of the prison. Politicians periodically trumpet the benefits of imprisonment and affirm that prison is an effective punishment. For example, in Britain, a former Home Secretary was closely associated with the slogan that 'prison works', and one of the government's claims in the mid-1990s echoed this rather implausible position (see Baker 1996 for discussion). The public, however, have a different (and more realistic) view of matters. Thus, in 2000, a nationwide survey conducted in Britain found that a significant majority of the public *dis*agreed with the statement that 'prison works' (MORI 2000). Similarly, only 2 per cent of British respondents to another MORI poll in 2002 identified prisons as an agency that can affect the level of crime in society (Ames 2003).

Prisons as schools for crime

Another near universal theme in the countries included in this review is that prisons are regarded as 'schools for crime'. Many people see prisons as as much a cause of as a response to crime. Around half the sample in a survey conducted in the USA agreed that 'prisons are really schools for criminals that turn new inmates into hardened criminals' (Doble Research Associates 1998; see also Farkas 1997). In Britain, more than four out of five respondents to the 1996 BCS agreed with the statement that 'In prison, offenders learn new ways to commit crime' (Hough and Roberts 1998). Research conducted for the Home Office Sentencing Review found the same result (Home Office 2001).

When South Africans were asked to respond to the same statement, almost three-quarters of the sample agreed (Monograph 2000). A MORI poll in 2001 found that over half the sample agreed that 'most people come out of prison worse than they go in', and only 14 per cent disagreed. The words of one participant in a focus group discussing prisons in Canada sums up this theme: 'I've never known anyone come out of prison a better person' (Environics Research 1989). Doble Research Associates (1995b) asked respondents whether inmates leave prison more or less dangerous than when they entered: some two-thirds of respondents believed prisoners became more dangerous, and less than one-fifth held the view that prisoners became less dangerous.

This public disenchantment with prisons may explain why, when asked to choose a strategy to reduce prison overcrowding, respondents in all Western nations place 'building more prisons' at the bottom of the list. After all, why build more prisons if they don't work? According to the 1996 British Crime Survey, constructing more prisons was the least favoured solution to prison overcrowding (endorsed by fewer than one respondent in five; see Hough and Roberts 1998). Six years later, another national poll generated the same result (Esmée Fairbairn Foundation 2002). Flanagan (1996a) reports a similar finding from a national survey in the USA.

More time means more crime

In the light of the widespread perception of prison as a school for crime, it would not be surprising if the public held pessimistic views of the recidivism rate of prisoners. A survey conducted in Florida found that 58 per cent of respondents believed that inmates released from prison would be 'more likely to commit crimes than before they served their time' (Florida Department of Corrections 1997). This view of prisoners is overly pessimistic. In the state of Florida, only 18 per cent of ex-prisoners were reconvicted of another crime within two years of release from prison[9] (Florida Department of Corrections 1997). Recidivism rates of ex-inmates are often higher than this rate, but it seems clear that this is another issue on which the public have an overly pessimistic opinion. Once again, there is support for this finding in other jurisdictions (Roberts and Stalans 1997).

Public scepticism about rehabilitation in prison

One major reason why people have lost faith in prison is that it is perceived to be ineffective in helping prisoners to reform themselves. The same MORI poll found that respondents were far more likely to agree than disagree with the statement that 'most people come out of prison worse than they went in'. In fact, only 14 per cent disagreed with the statement (MORI 2000). In a Home Office survey in 2001, over half of a British sample agreed that prison restricted an offender's opportunities to re-offend; only a quarter, however, believed that prison would change the offender's behaviour (Home Office 2001). In surveys conducted in the USA by John Doble, half the samples approved of the job being done by the state's prison system when asked to rate it 'in a general sense'. However, the proportion holding this view dropped to less than one-quarter when asked to rate the system 'in terms of rehabilitation' (Doble Research Associates 1994, 1998). This perception also emerges from qualitative research involving focus groups in Canada and Scotland (e.g. Solicitor General Canada 1989; Hutton 2005).

While people would like to think that prison rehabilitates offenders, the public around the world have little faith in the power of the prison to reform prisoners. Less than half the polled public in South Africa believed that prison helped prisoners to become law-abiding citizens (Monograph 2000). The 2003 MORI poll in Britain asked people to identify the functions of imprisonment that they felt were important, and then to give their opinion as to whether these functions were being accomplished by the prison system. 'Helping prisoners to live law-abiding lives on release' was the second most important function in the eyes of the public. At the same time, they had less confidence that this objective was being achieved than any other. Americans and Canadians share this view of prisons. A poll conducted in Florida asked respondents to rate the prison system on a number of critical functions. While most respondents thought that the state correctional system did a good job in preventing escapes, very few rated the system as doing a good job in rehabilitating criminals (Florida Department of Corrections 1997). Most recently, a nationwide survey in the USA found over half the sample rated prisons as doing a very poor job of rehabilitating prisoners (Belden Russonello and Stewart 2001; see also Doble Research Associates 1995a).

Table 5.2 summarizes findings from recent surveys in the two principal countries explored in this book. As can be seen, in the USA, over two-thirds of the sample gave the prison system a good rating for maintaining security, but only 14 per cent assigned such a positive rating when asked about promoting rehabilitation. Surveys in other countries confirm these trends: 91 per cent of Canadians were very or fairly confident that the prison system maintained security, but less than half had this level of confidence in the rehabilitative function (Tufts 2000).

An indication of the British public's lack of faith in the effectiveness of prison as a crime prevention tool comes from a survey conducted in 2001, in which respondents were asked to identify the two or three strategies that in their view would be most effective in reducing crime in Britain. Table 5.3 summarizes the pattern of findings. As can be seen, increasing the number of offenders in prison came in last, having been chosen by only 8 per cent of the sample. The public sees prison as a necessary form of social protection from dangerous offenders, but not as an effective way to prevent crime or rehabilitate offenders.

Finally, a number of polls have demonstrated that when they are given a range of policy options, building more prisons holds little attraction for the public. A MORI poll conducted in 2004 first informed people of the fact that the number of women in prison had increased by 180 per cent over the previous decade. Respondents were asked to choose a solution from among a list of options provided. There was significantly more support for

Table 5.2 Ratings of prison system regarding security and rehabilitation, USA and UK (percentages)

	USA			
	Excellent	Good	Fair	Poor
Maintaining security	18	49	23	8
Promoting rehabilitation	2	12	34	48

	UK			
	Very confident	Fairly confident	Not very confident	Not at all confident
Maintaining security	25	64	7	1
Promoting rehabilitation	5	39	40	9

Source: adapted from US Sourcebook of Criminal Justice Statistics; MORI (2003).

Table 5.3 British attitudes to strategies to reduce crime (percentages)

Better parenting	55
More police on the beat	53
Better discipline in schools	49
Constructive activities for the young	40
Introduction of a national identity card	29
Programmes to change offenders' behaviour	21
Capital punishment for murder	20
More offenders in prison	8

Source: Esmée Fairburn Foundation (2002). Question: 'Which two or three of the following do you think would most reduce crime in Britain?'

increasing the use of community sentences and community treatment centres than for building more prisons (MORI 2004b).

Knowledge of parole and life after prison

The prison systems in most industrialized countries have some form of executive release. The systems vary in detail from country to country; usually prisoners serving long prison terms are subject to some form of community supervision after their release. No single term accurately captures the diverse range of executive release systems in Western countries. In this section, we use the term 'parole' as a shorthand to refer to all forms of release from prison prior to the end of the sentence. Most parole systems involve:

- discretionary decisions made about individual prisoners;
- the imposition of conditions, including supervision by parole officers;
- powers to recall parolees to prison if they breach the conditions of their parole.

Only the small minority of very serious offenders serving life sentences in England and Wales are eligible for parole as such. At the time of writing, the majority of prisoners were subject to Automatic Conditional Release (leaving prison after serving half their term if they were serving less than four years) or Discretionary Conditional Release (where release of prisoners serving four years or more is allowed at the discretion of the parole board).[10] Those serving sentences of less than a year are not subject to any supervision following release, but those serving longer sentences are released under licence, and are supervised by probation officers. Additional to the ACR and DCR systems, prisoners can be released early, subject to electronic monitoring.

Public evaluations of parole reflect perceptions of life under supervision in the community, as well as estimates of the proportion of time served in prison. Parole is seen by many people as simply 'time off' a sentence of imprisonment, rather than a community-based portion of the sentence.[11] When parole cuts very deeply into the sentence of custody – for example, if prisoners are granted release after having served one-third (or less) of the sentence in custody – this leads people to see parole as yet another example of unprincipled leniency in the criminal justice system. When a higher proportion of the sentence is served in the community than in prison, this will be seen to violate the general concept of 'truth in sentencing'.[12] Systematic research has demonstrated that the public have distorted views of many parole statistics that go hand in hand with the public misperceptions of sentencing patterns reviewed in Chapter 4:

- most people over-estimate the parole grant rate (Jubinville *et al.* 1987; Roberts *et al.* 1999);[13]
- most people assume that prisoners obtain parole at the first application and under-estimate the proportion of sentences served in prison (Roberts *et al.* 1998);
- a survey in Florida found that more than four out of five respondents believed that inmates serve less than half their sentences 'inside'; in reality prisoners in Florida must serve at least 85 per cent of their sentences in prison;
- two-thirds of the sample held the view that prisoners served less time in prison than five years' previously; in reality the average percentage of prison sentences served had not only increased, but almost doubled (Florida Department of Corrections 1997);
- half the sample believed that life prisoners would eventually be released on parole; in reality, life means life in Florida (Florida Department of Corrections 1997);
- most people see prisoners released on parole to constitute a threat; public estimates of the recidivism rate of prisoners on parole exceed the actual rate by a considerable margin (Jubinville *et al.* 1987; Roberts *et al.* 1998);
- the public over-estimate the failure rate of prisoners on parole (Solicitor General Canada 1981);
- most people assume that when a parolee has his or her parole revoked, it is for a serious offence rather than a technical violation[14] (Roberts *et al.* 1998).

Knowledge of resettlement problems

If the public under-estimate the severity of daily life in institutions, it seems likely that they know little about the many problems confronting ex-prisoners as they make the transition from custody to community. Research over the past few decades has documented the difficulties that ex-prisoners encounter with respect to employment and housing.

Recent research in both the UK and the USA has demonstrated that both homelessness and reincarceration are substantial problems among released prisoners (Metraux and Culhane 2004).

Evidence of distrust of people with criminal records comes from a major survey of over 30 European nations conducted in 2001 (Halman 2001). Respondents were provided with a list of various groups and asked to identify those that they would prefer not to have as neighbours. Averaged across all jurisdictions, just over half identified people with criminal records. To the general public, ex-offenders are less desirable neighbours than right- or left-wing extremists – identified by approximately one-third of the sample as undesirable.[15] Since no description was provided of the kind of individual, respondents were probably thinking of ex-offenders convicted of the most serious crimes. As noted earlier in this book, people tend to think of the 'worst case scenario' when asked general questions about 'offenders' or 'inmates'; nevertheless, the finding suggests that suspicion of, if not prejudice against, ex-offenders is alive and well and living in Europe. These reintegration difficulties are part of the pains of imprisonment, yet seldom come to the attention of the general public.

Finally, research in the USA has also demonstrated that the public have little concrete idea of the problems created for ex-prisoners by legislation that prevents them from participating in all aspects of civil life. Many ex-prisoners cannot vote in the USA, although the public were surprised to learn this fact (Immerwahr and Johnson 2002). The researchers, who conducted a study on public attitudes to the resettlement of offenders, concluded that 'many [members of the public] were surprised, even dumbfounded, to learn about some of the barriers and constraints [applicable to ex-prisoners] existing in some states' (Immerwahr and Johnson 2002: 9).

Public support for parole

Although parole has been abolished or curtailed in scope in some jurisdictions, most Western nations retain some form of discretionary release from prison. On this issue too, the public are somewhat ambivalent. A frequent complaint from members of the public in a number of countries is that too many prisoners are released on parole. However, this observation is made by people who have no concrete idea of how many prisoners are actually released in this way, and who over-estimate the grant rate by a considerable margin. There appears to be far more support for parole than for 'flat-time' sentencing, where prisoners serve the full term of their sentence in prison. At the same time, parole authorities come under constant criticism from members of the public, usually when the media report that an offender released on parole has committed a serious crime of violence.

When asked a general question such as 'Are you satisfied with the way that the parole system is working?', most people respond negatively (e.g. Cumberland and Zamble 1992). As will be seen, however, when asked whether specific prisoners should be granted parole, people tend to be more liberal (Box 5.1).

Part of the problem is that people usually consider parole only when the issue is brought to their attention by the news media, and this generally happens when a person on parole commits a violent crime. A survey conducted in Canada some years ago found that most respondents believed that too many prisoners were being released on parole (Jubinville *et al.* 1987). When people holding this view were then asked to specify the particular offender that they had in mind, over two-thirds were thinking of violent offenders (Jubinville *et al.* 1987). It is not surprising, then, that most people's first reaction to the issue of parole is negative.

When people are asked to make a specific policy decision, however (rather than provide performance ratings of the parole system), matters are quite different, as can be seen in the following examples. Although there is a lot of public criticism of parole, few surveys have asked respondents to make a clear choice between a prison system with parole and one with flat-time sentences. Those that have done so have found support for parole:

Box 5.1 Effects of information on public reactions to parole

Respondents were assigned at random to make a decision about a parole application.

Subjects in Group A were simply asked the following: 'John Smith is currently serving a three-year sentence for breaking into people's homes. He has already served one year in prison, and is now applying for release on parole. Should he be released on parole?'

Subjects in Group B were given a little more information about the case: 'Parole is a programme by which some inmates are allowed to spend part of their sentence in the community. If the parole board is convinced that the offender is not a risk to the community, parole is granted. This means that for the remainder of the sentence, the offender has to report to a parole officer and follow rules imposed by the parole board. If he breaks these rules, he can be returned to prison. John Smith is currently serving a three-year sentence for breaking into people's homes. He has already served one year in prison, and is now applying for release on parole to help him adjust to life once his sentence is completed. Smith will be supporting his family when he leaves prison. Should he be released on parole?'

The reactions to the parole 'application' were quite different: three-quarters of the respondents who read the more comprehensive description, but less than half of the other group, favoured granting parole (Roberts *et al.* 1999). This survey experiment suggests that explaining the nature of controversial programmes such as parole will increase public acceptance.

- A nationwide survey in the USA asked respondents about their position on parole for non-violent crimes. They were asked whether they agreed that 'we should allow parole for people who commit non-violent crimes and spend more tax dollars on training and education programs to help them become productive citizens' or the position that 'we should do away with parole for people who commit non-violent crimes and spend more tax dollars to keep them in prison for longer'. Accepting the limitation on 'non-violent offenders' and the somewhat leading nature of this question, support for parole was strong: almost nine out of ten respondents favoured the parole option (Belden Russonello and Stewart 2001).[16]
- Gottfredson *et al.* (1988) asked a sample of US respondents whether abolishing parole was a good idea, and only one respondent in four agreed.[17]
- In a Canadian survey reported by Roberts *et al.* (1999) respondents were asked which system they preferred: 'A prison system which keeps inmates in prison right to the end of their sentence' or 'A system which releases some inmates into the community under supervision before their sentence ends'. Given this clear choice, the public favoured the parole option by a ratio of three to one. A comparable level of support for parole emerged from a poll that asked this same question in 1985 (Roberts 1988a), suggesting stability in public support for parole, in that jurisdiction at least. Moreover, this finding is all the more impressive since the poll did not ask respondents to consider only non-violent offenders. In all probability they were considering prisoners serving time for serious crimes of violence.[18]

Can we generalize from these results to the UK? It might be argued that since support for rehabilitation is strong in Canada (as appears to be the case), this is likely to result in high levels of support for parole as well. Perhaps, but it is important to note that polls in Canada also routinely reveal negative attitudes to parole authorities; in fact, the Canadian public have less confidence in the parole system than any other branch of criminal justice (Tufts 2000). In addition, the Canadian public subscribe to the same misperceptions about parole that we identified earlier in this chapter,[19] namely that parole is easy to get and is granted to every prisoner who applies, and that parolees are often convicted of further offences while on parole. We are therefore inclined to the view that although the public in various countries are critical of parole (or the way they perceive the parole system to be working), there is nevertheless a strong core of support for allowing some prisoners to serve part of their sentence in the community.

The public want prisoners to earn the right to spend part of their prison sentence in the community. The public appear opposed to correctional systems in which prisoners are allowed to serve a large proportion of their prison sentences in the community without having to take any steps at self-improvement.[20] Skovron *et al.* (1988) provide a good illustration. When asked whether they favoured or opposed allowing prisoners to earn early release through good behaviour and participation in rehabilitation programmes in prison, 80 per cent were in favour. However, only one-quarter were in favour of expanding the discretionary power of the parole authorities. Cullen *et al.* (2000: 37) note that in the USA, residents support parole 'for offenders who have taken steps to improve themselves and whose prospects for community reintegration thus appear promising', and this appears true for the public in other countries as well. Cumberland and Zamble (1992) asked subjects to make parole decisions in individual case scenarios, and found that the public were far more supportive of granting early release if the prisoner had been participating in rehabilitation programmes while in prison.

When do the public oppose the granting of parole? People are less supportive of parole for offenders convicted of the most serious crimes of violence (e.g. Glanz 1994), and, as noted, when the community portion of the total sentence exceeds by a large margin the custodial period.[21] Offenders convicted of murder represent the extreme exception to the general support for parole among members of the public. A number of studies have demonstrated clear public opposition to parole for this category of offending. In 2003, for example, the *Observer* poll found that almost nine out of ten respondents supported the concept of detaining life prisoners in prison for the rest of their lives (*Observer* 2003; see also Roberts 1988b).[22]

In Chapter 1 of this volume, we drew attention to a very robust finding in the area of public attitudes to criminal justice: when people are given an adequate amount of information to consider, they tend to be less punitive in their responses to criminal justice issues. Box 5.1 provides an illustration of this finding with respect to public reactions to parole.

Disenfranchisement of prisoners and ex-prisoners

We conclude this chapter with consideration of what is arguably one of the more punitive prisoner-related policies: disenfranchisement. In the USA – as in many other jurisdictions – most prisoners are denied the right to vote while they are actually in prison. However, in some US states this disenfranchisement continues to apply after release for many categories of prisoner. Uggen and Manza (2002) estimate that almost five million Americans have been denied the vote as a result of a past or current criminal conviction. No survey has recently explored public awareness of these laws; however, a study published in 1972 found quite limited public knowledge of the civil deprivations visited upon ex-prisoners (Reed and Nance 1972). How do the public react to this policy of disenfranchisement? The American public appear to favour disenfranchisement for imprisoned offenders, but oppose extending this denial of civil liberties to ex-prisoners serving their sentences in the community on parole (Immerwahr and

Johnson 2002; Manza *et al.* 2004). Ethnic minorities are particularly opposed to taking the right to vote away from former prisoners: three-quarters of African-Americans opposed this policy in a recent poll (Bendixen and Associates 2004).[23]

Summary

Most people know little about prison conditions, or statistics relating to the parole process. This reflects their lack of direct experience with prisons. Media depictions of prison life reflect a paradoxical image of violence and relative ease; the result is that many people believe that prison life is an easy existence. Further, there is no evidence that the public understand the health and safety risks confronting prisoners, or the problems that they encounter in re-adjusting to life 'on the outside'. Although people see incapacitation and punishment as the most important goal of prisons, there is nevertheless strong support for rehabilitation as well. Not surprisingly, the public expect the prison system to protect society from dangerous offenders, but also to help prisoners to become law-abiding citizens upon their release from prison. There is widespread scepticism among members of the public regarding the ability of prisons to achieve or promote rehabilitation. Prison is more likely to be seen as a school for crime. Misperceptions abound with respect to the parole system. People over-estimate the proportion of offenders that get parole, and under-estimate the percentage of the sentence that is served in custody (rather than the community). Despite these erroneous perceptions, and the fact that the parole system attracts very low confidence ratings, the public in the USA and Canada appear to support the concept of parole, except for prisoners serving time for the most serious crimes of violence.

Further reading

Cullen, F., Fisher, B. and Applegate, B. (2000) Public opinion about punishment and corrections, in M. Tonry (ed.) *Crime and Justice: A Review of Research*. Volume 27. Chicago: University of Chicago Press.

Flanagan, T. (1996) Reform or punish? Americans' views of the correctional system, in T. Flanagan and D. Longmire (eds) *Americans View Crime and Justice*. Thousand Oaks, CA: Sage, Chapter 6.

Roberts, J. V. and Stalans, L. S. (1997) Sentencing and parole, in *Public Opinion, Crime, and Criminal Justice*, Chapter 10. Boulder, CO: Westview Press.

Notes

1 The use of imprisonment as a punishment did not emerge until the late Middle Ages. Until then it was used to ensure the accused's attendance at trial, or to encourage compliance with other penalties. For example, a felon ordered to pay a fine would be imprisoned until the fine was paid (Bellamy 1973).

2 Bryant and Morris (1998) found that over two-thirds of the public and over half a sample of news reporters believed that prison guards working inside the prison were armed, when this in fact is not the case. Such a misperception presumably reflects the emphasis in the media on prison violence.

3 When MORI asked a sample of the British public to identify the broadcasts that most influenced their views in this area, 'news programmes' headed the list (cited by 48 per cent of respondents). Only 6 per cent cited TV detective series such as *Inspector Morse*, while 6 per cent cited films such as *Shawshank Redemption*. We cannot discount the influence of the latter, however, since millions more people watch fictional shows and films than news programmes such as *Panorama*.

4 There is some limited evidence to suggest a quite callous attitude on the part of the public with respect to rape in prison. One American survey found that half the respondents agreed with the statement that 'society accepts inmate sexual assault as part of the price criminals pay for committing crimes' (see Stop Prisoner Rape 2004).

5 Living next to these establishments does not seem to result in a more knowledgeable populace. Kingston in Canada is small town that contains a number of large prisons, yet a study of Kingston residents' attitudes found that 'There is a prevalent belief that prison conditions are too good . . . respondents feel prisoners enjoy excellent food . . . big screen TVs in their cells. There is a perception that prisoners lead a better life than some people who are not in prison' (Environics Research Group 2000: 18).

6 For example, in Canada some politicians have argued (in the absence of any supporting evidence, as is their wont) that making prison life more unpleasant will result in lower re-offending rates. In the USA, politicians have promoted a return to prison features such as striped uniforms and chain gangs (see Flanagan 1996b: 91–2).

7 Additional evidence comes from reactions to prisoners' rights: 89 per cent of the public supported giving prisoners 'as many books as they wish', presumably in the belief that this would promote rehabilitation.

8 Of course, this powerful theme can be seen in literature (*Les Miserables*) as well as in films (*The Birdman of Alacatraz*).

9 Two-year conviction rates of offenders serving prison sentences in England are much higher than this, averaging between 50 and 60 per cent. We cannot say whether the differences reflect methods of computing reconvictions, or real differences.

10 At the time of writing, legislation was in hand to extend the scope of ACR at the expense of DCR.

11 In some countries, supervision of parolees is fairly minimal and there is therefore an element of reality to this public perception. In England and Wales, those sentenced to less than 12 months are not subject to supervision, and the supervision of the remainder is by no means intensive.

12 Truth in sentencing is usually invoked to justify 'flat-time', no parole sentencing, but it has a broader application as well. The sentence served by the offender should be relatively close to the sentence imposed in court. If a judge imposes a nine-year sentence of imprisonment and the offender is living at home after three years, many people will see this as a violation of truth in sentencing.

13 For example, when asked to estimate the parole grant rate, two-thirds of a sample of Canadian respondents over-estimated this statistic. When asked to estimate the percentage of prisoners released on parole who re-offend, 86 per cent provided a response in excess of the true rate (Roberts *et al.* 1999).

14 Most parole revocations are for technical violations, rather than allegations of fresh offending.

15 There was a considerable degree of variation in response to this question. In Slovakia and Hungary, more than four out of five respondents fingered people with a record as undesirable neighbours; in France, only 21 per cent took this view of ex-offenders.

16 A survey reported by Davis (1997) asked respondents the following question: 'Should a person convicted of a crime serve the full sentence with no parole even if there is evidence that he or she has changed or has been rehabilitated?' Slightly over half said yes to this inappropriately worded question. Prisoners are (or should be) granted parole when there is evidence that they have taken steps towards rehabilitation.

17 This study is a good illustration of the periodic misperception of public views. When criminal justice professionals were asked how the public would respond to this question, three-quarters of these individuals assumed that the public would support the abolition of parole (see Gottfredson *et al.* 1988).

18 A number of studies have demonstrated that when people are asked about offenders or prisoners in general, they tend to think about violent offenders (see Roberts and Stalans 1997 for a review).

19 In fact, almost all the surveys that have demonstrated the extent of public misperceptions of parole statistics have been conducted in Canada (e.g. Roberts 1988a).

20 For example, in Canada, federal prisoners benefit from release from prison after having served two-thirds of their sentence, regardless of their progress towards rehabilitation. This is a statutory entitlement; prisoners are entitled to release at this point, unless correctional authorities can demonstrate why they should be detained in prison until the end of the sentence.

21 In Canada, most prisoners become eligible for full parole after having served one-third of the sentence; they may apply for day parole even earlier, after having served one-sixth of the total sentence in custody.

22 There is nevertheless some evidence that jurors can put aside this implacable opposition to parole for murderers. An analysis of jury reviews of parole eligibility dates in Canada found that in most cases jurors granted offenders convicted of murder the right to make an application for parole, in some cases years ahead of their statutory eligibility date (see Roberts 2002a).

23 Manza *et al.* (2004) note that support for enfranchisement varied according to the category of offender under consideration: lower proportions of the public supported giving former sex offenders the right to vote. This finding is important, for, as the researchers note, it undermines the criticism that could be levelled at many surveys, namely that people are responding to the survey in the way

that they believe will make them 'look good' in the eyes of the researcher. Had this been the case, levels of support would have been relatively constant across all offender scenarios.

chapter six

Attitudes to youth justice

Introduction

In this chapter we explore public attitudes to the youth justice system. To what extent do the public view youth and adult crime as requiring a different response from the justice system? As will be seen, members of the public subscribe to different models of youth and adult justice, although there are important common elements. In Chapter 2 we noted that the British public has less confidence in the youth justice system than any other branch of justice. International parallels exist in this respect: prior to the introduction of a new youth justice law in Canada (in 2003), Canadians held their youth justice system in very low esteem. Part of the explanation for the low levels of public confidence in the youth justice system can be found in youth crime rates, and public perceptions of those rates. During much of the second half of the twentieth century violent crime by young people increased significantly in a number of countries. Despite recent reversals in this trend, the public have retained the view that youth crime rates are constantly on the rise.

Concern about youth crime – particularly violent crime – focuses public and political attention upon the youth justice system designed to address the problem. In the USA, this has led to calls to abolish the separate juvenile court system, and to impose the same penalties on juvenile and adult offenders. Most jurisdictions have significantly amended their youth justice legislation over the past decade, and Britain is no exception to this trend (see Bottoms and Dignan 2004 for an overview of developments in juvenile justice). This chapter pays particular attention to public knowledge and opinion of youth justice in Britain. We draw upon the first[1] systematic examination of British attitudes to youth crime and youth justice, conducted for us in 2003 by the Office of National Statistics (for more information, see Hough and Roberts 2004b; for discussion of public opinion in other jurisdictions, see Roberts 2004).

Recent reforms in juvenile justice

In the light of the high levels of public concern about youth crime, it comes as no surprise that many countries have recently reformed their youth justice systems (see Tonry and Doob 2004 for a review of recent developments). The youth justice system in England and Wales has been subject to significant reform over the past five years. The Crime and Disorder Act 1998 created a system of Youth Offending Teams (YOTs), and set up the Youth Justice Board to oversee YOTs (see Bottoms and Dignan 2004 for further information). The YOTs are multidisciplinary teams comprising social workers, probation officers, police officers and health authority staff. These professionals pool their skills and draw upon their common experience to devise an appropriate response to youth offending.

Numerous legislative and administrative changes have been introduced since the 1998 Crime and Disorder Act. The new court disposals include curfew orders, electronic tagging, secure remands for offenders aged 12–15 and Intensive Supervision and Surveillance Programmes (ISSPs) for persistent young offenders. The Youth Justice Board has always espoused a clear preventive philosophy, and there is general agreement within the youth justice system that young offenders should be imprisoned only as a last resort, a goal shared by the youth justice systems of other countries, such as Canada and New Zealand (see Roberts and Bala 2003). The belief is widely held among sentencers, youth justice workers and academics that imprisonment is particularly damaging to young people and has more negative consequences for young persons than adults (e.g. National Audit Office, cited in Audit Commission 2004).

Despite this, the imprisoned juvenile offender population has continued to grow; as of 2004 it stands at almost double the figure of a decade ago, and well over half of the Youth Justice Board budget is now consumed by the costs of imprisonment for young offenders (Audit Commission 2004). One explanation for this state of affairs is that judges, magistrates and those responsible for youth justice policy believe that public opinion is highly intolerant of less punitive but more constructive responses to youth crime. Given this perception of public opinion, sentencers may feel constrained about their ability to employ more constructive and cost-effective – if less punitive – ways of dealing with young offenders. The Audit Commission report lends some weight to this view. Its survey of magistrates found that almost half said that they took account of public opinion when sentencing young offenders (National Audit Office, cited in Audit Commission 2004).

Public knowledge of youth crime and youth justice

This chapter addresses public reaction to the justice system (rather than youth crime trends). However, since the British public's knowledge of youth crime has not been systematically explored before, we summarize some findings from the 2003 survey that shed light on this issue (see Hough and Roberts 2004b for more details). Many of the misperceptions of crime by adults also apply to crime by young offenders, as the following examples reveal:

- Most people (three-quarters of the sample) believed that the number of young offenders increased over the period 2001–3. In fact, statistics suggest that youth crime rates in Britain over this period have been stable or declining, with the exception of certain offences. This pattern of findings is consistent with results of surveys in the USA and Canada (see Roberts 2004: Table 1). We asked respondents who held this view to cite their source for the belief that the number of young offenders is on the increase: almost two-thirds of respondents cited the media as the source of their information.[2] Direct or indirect experience was cited by a much smaller percentage of the sample.
- Most respondents over-estimated the proportion of crime for which young offenders are responsible. While it is hard to be precise about this statistic, the best estimate is that young offenders account for somewhere between 10 and 20 per cent of all recorded crime in Britain. Respondents generated estimates significantly in excess of this figure (see Hough and Roberts 2004b). Mattinson and Mirrlees-Black (2000) found that almost a third of the BCS sample believed that crime was committed 'mainly by juveniles' – a patent over-estimate of the volume of crime for which young people are responsible. An additional 55 per cent believed that adults and juveniles accounted for similar proportions

of recorded crime – also incorrect. Only about 15 per cent of respondents were correct in their estimate of the amount of crime by young offenders. Surveys in the USA have produced similar findings (see Roberts 2004).

- Most respondents over-estimated the proportion of crime by young offenders involving violence: over two-thirds of the sample placed the estimate for youth crime at over 40 per cent. While there is no indisputable 'right answer' to this question, around a fifth of all recorded crimes involving a young person involve some form of violence.
- The public also over-estimated the likelihood of recidivism by young offenders. Respondents were asked to estimate the proportion of first-time offenders who would be reconvicted of another offence within a year. Recent Home Office statistics show that of all *first-time* young offenders for a cohort of 2000, 12 per cent were reconvicted within a year.[3] Most respondents estimated the recidivism rate to be significantly higher. Again, the views of the British public mirror those of people in other countries, such as Spain and Canada (Roberts 1988a; Redondo *et al.* 1996; Doob *et al.* 1998).

Researchers have yet to explore public knowledge of the changes to youth justice in Britain. As noted earlier, the Crime and Disorder Act 1998 introduced a new organizational structure for youth justice, and a range of new ways of dealing with young offenders. The new youth justice framework contains a number of components consistent with a restorative justice approach to juvenile offending. Two questions were included in the 2003 survey to test knowledge about the YOTs. We first asked respondents whether they had heard about this particular youth justice reform. Fully three-quarters of the sample (76 per cent) had not heard about YOTs. Those respondents who had heard about YOTs were asked: 'What do these teams mainly do?' A bare majority – or one in eight of the total sample – correctly identified the purpose of Youth Offending Teams.[4] If this relatively high profile initiative is so poorly understood, a greater effort needs to be made to educate the public about recent criminal justice reforms in the area of youth justice.

Attitudes to young people in general

These public misperceptions about specific criminal justice statistics reflect a more general attitude to young people. There is a widespread perception – held by more than four out of five respondents in Britain – that teenagers today are less respectful of authority than their predecessors.[5] The British public were asked whether teenagers today were more, less or about the same as previous generations in this regard. If we exclude the 4 per cent of the respondents who classified themselves as being too young to express an opinion or held no opinion on the issue, the percentage of respondents holding the view that teenagers today are less respectful rises to 88 per cent. The perception that youth today are different from – and worse than – their predecessors is by no means restricted to the British public. Over three-quarters of respondents in a Canadian survey agreed that 'Youth crime is worse than it was when I was young' (Earnscliffe Research and Communications 2000).[6] This fairly negative view of the younger generation may well influence perceptions of youth crime.

Confidence in the functions of the youth justice system

In Chapter 2 we noted that the youth justice system inspires less confidence than any other branch of the criminal justice system in Britain – only 46 per cent of respondents to the 2003 MORI poll were very or fairly confident in the work of youth courts (compared to 76 per cent of the sample who had this level of confidence in the police, and 59 per cent in the probation service). Which aspects of the youth justice system are particularly problematic from the perspective of the public? Table 6.1 reveals the strong public interest in a youth justice system that prevents re-offending. This is consistent with a more general desire to prevent re-offending by all types of offenders. Less predictably, Table 6.1 clearly shows dissatisfaction with the extent to which the youth justice system incorporates parents into the disciplining of their children: over half of the sample lacked confidence that this was being accomplished by the youth justice system.

The importance of parents and schools

This finding illuminates an important theme in the practice of youth justice, as well as popular conceptions of the appropriate response to young

Table 6.1 Public confidence in functions of the youth justice system in Britain

	Percentage very or fairly confident	Percentage not very or not at all confident
Dealing promptly with young people who commit crimes	48	40
Preventing offending by children and young people	40	49
Preventing re-offending by children and young people	35	54
Providing effective punishments that help young people behave more responsibly	35	55
Helping parents be more responsible for their children	32	57

Source: MORI (2003). Question: 'How confident are you in the way that the youth justice system is doing each of the following?' Excludes 'don't know' responses (between 10 and 12 per cent for all options).

offenders. Most juvenile justice systems try to involve the parents of the young accused or offender in the sentence imposed. Sometimes this is accomplished by means of a family group conference, on other occasions parents attend court and provide input into the disposition that will be imposed on their son or daughter. The public see considerable merit in this interaction between the state and the family,[7] and to a lesser extent schools. This perspective emerges from a number of recent surveys:

- A MORI poll in 2001 asked people to identify the strategy that would do most to reduce crime in Britain. The most popular solution, supported by 55 per cent of the sample, was 'better parenting'. Better discipline in schools was cited by almost as many (49 per cent). In contrast, putting more offenders in prison was supported by only 8 per cent, further demonstrating the public lack of faith in prisons (see Chapter 5). This emphasis on parenting seems to be common to all the countries that have addressed the issue. For example, a survey of residents of Barbados found that better parenting was by far the most frequently cited strategy for reducing crime among young people (Nuttall *et al.* 2003).
- In 2003, another survey asked the same question, with slightly different response options. Once again, 'better parenting' headed the list, supported on this occasion by 59 per cent of the sample (better discipline in schools was identified as the most effective crime reduction strategy by 45 per cent, 'putting more people in prison' was cited by only 10 per cent; Esmée Fairbairn Foundation 2003).
- The most popular way of reducing crime according to a survey of residents of Northern Ireland was to increase discipline in the family (Amelin *et al.* 2000).
- The 1998 BCS asked respondents to identify the best way of dealing with young offenders. The most popular solution was to increase parental responsibility[8] (Mattinson and Mirrlees-Black 2000).
- The 1998 BCS contained a question about the causes of crime in general, and the cause cited by the highest percentage of respondents was 'lack of discipline from parents' (Mattinson and Mirrlees-Black 2000: Table A4.7).
- The public want to involve parents more in large measure because the home environment is seen as the source of crime. When a sample of Canadians was asked to identify the causes of crime, 'poor parenting' was the option cited by most respondents (69 per cent; see Environics Research Group 1998).
- The 2003 MORI poll provided people with a list of different functions of the youth justice system, and asked respondents to rate the importance of each function on a ten-point scale. The function that was described as 'helping parents be more responsible for their children' was identified as 'absolutely essential' (ten on the scale) by the highest percentage of respondents (63 per cent).

Attitudes to youth crime and justice

The first evidence that people see youth justice as being different from the adult system can be seen from the responses to a question asking about the best way to respond to offending. Half the respondents in our ONS survey were asked the following question with respect to adults, and half were asked about young offenders: 'Which of the following is the best way to reduce crime?' Comparisons between adults and young offenders are complicated somewhat by the fact that not all options are relevant to both groups. Nevertheless, Table 6.2 suggests that people think that quite different strategies are needed for tackling youth and adult offending – although there were also some important commonalities. For young offenders, 'more discipline in schools' was by far the most popular crime prevention strategy, endorsed by 42 per cent of the sample. Tougher sentences and increasing the number of police officers on the street were the next most popular options, although they attracted significantly less support from the public.

The public appear to recognize clear limitations to the capacity of the criminal justice system to prevent crime by young offenders. Taken together, the policing and the courts options still fall significantly short of the 41 per cent of the sample who identified 'more discipline in schools' as the most effective way of preventing youth crime. This echoes the public

Table 6.2 Public perceptions of the best way to reduce crime by young and adult offenders

	Young offenders	Adult offenders
More discipline in schools	42	Not a response option
Tougher sentences	17	31
More police officers on streets	15	25
More funding for job-training programmes for adults	Not a response option	7
More support for parents	7	Not a response option
More funding for schools and after-school programmes	6	Not a response option
Treatment for drug, alcohol and mental health problems	4	14
More jobs	8	8
More surveillance cameras in public places	2	4
More support to help offenders become law-abiding citizens	Not a response option	11

Source: Hough and Roberts (2004b). Questions: 'In your view, which of the following is the best way to reduce crime by [adult/young] offenders?'

emphasis on parental and academic discipline to which we have already referred.

The findings summarized in Table 6.2 demonstrate that tougher sentencing is not top of the public's mind when people are asked to identify strategies to counter youth crime. This trend is not restricted to Britain. Figure 6.1 summarizes public opinion data from 15 European nations. Respondents were asked to agree or disagree with a series of statements regarding youth crime. When members of the public are asked to agree with a list of statements in this way, there is a tendency for respondents to agree with all statements offered to them. What is important, therefore, is the ranking that emerges; the absolute levels of agreement may well represent inflated values. As can be seen, the public saw far less utility in tougher sentences than in reducing poverty.

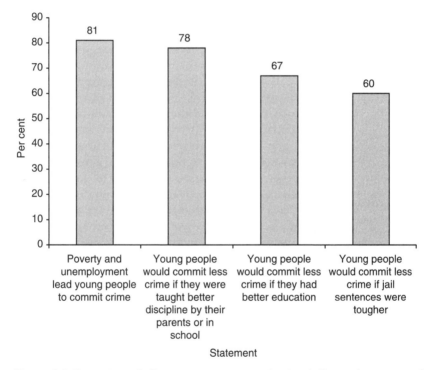

Figure 6.1 Perceptions of effective responses to youth crime in Europe (percentage of all respondents agreeing; *source*: European Opinion Research Group 2003)

Performance ratings of youth courts

Public reaction to youth courts has been explored in several administrations of the BCS; accordingly we can place the results from our ONS in the context of the past six years. Successive sweeps of the British Crime Survey have found that most people hold a negative view of youth courts. Indeed, perceptions of the youth courts are more negative than for any other component of the criminal justice system. The first time this question was asked in the British Crime Survey, in 1998, only 14 per cent of the sample rated juvenile courts as doing a good or excellent job (Mattinson and Mirrlees-Black 2000). This question was repeated in our ONS survey conducted in 2003, and Table 6.3 shows that these negative public perceptions of the courts persist today. Only about one respondent in ten rated the youth courts as doing a good or excellent job. American views of youth courts are also more likely to be negative than positive (Roberts 2004). However, comparison between the two countries suggests that people in Britain are more critical of youth courts: over a third of the US respondents rated the youth courts as good or excellent (Hough and Roberts 2004b).

Purposes of sentencing

Which purposes do the public believe that the sentencing of young offenders should serve? Survey researchers have often tried to determine the purposes that attract most support from the public. The aim has usually been to assess the relative weight people attach to deterrence, rehabilitation, incapacitation and retribution (the traditional sentencing objectives found in common law countries). There has often been a degree of artificiality in these questions. Respondents have been asked either to identify the most important aim, or to rank-order the aims. The difficulty with this approach is that people ascribe a high level of importance to most of the main sentencing goals (Roberts and Stalans 1997). In part this is because, like judges, members of the public are *eclectic* sentencers: no single purpose is regarded as significantly more important than any other: each case demands a particular balance of aims, and this balance varies from case to case.

In the youth justice survey we adopted a comparative approach. We asked respondents to choose the single sentencing goal that was most important. Half the sample was asked about the sentencing of young

Table 6.3 Public ratings of youth courts

	1998 BCS	2000 BCS	2001/2 BCS	2003 ONS
Excellent	>1	>1	1	1
Good	12	10	13	10
Fair	36	36	36	42
Poor	33	33	28	28
Very poor	11	11	9	8
Don't know	7	9	13	12

Question: 'How good a job do you think the youth courts are doing?' Percentages do not sum to 100 due to rounding error.

Table 6.4 Perceptions of the most important purpose of sentencing young offenders and adults in Britain

	Young offenders	Adult offenders
Deterring the offender and other people from committing crimes in the future	34	31
Imposing a just sentence that reflects the seriousness of the crime	33	46
Helping to rehabilitate offenders	20	12
Showing society's disapproval of the crime	5	3
Keeping offenders out of circulation	4	5
Compensating crime victims for their losses or injury	4	3

Source: Hough and Roberts (2004b). Question: 'Choosing from this list, what do you think should be the most important aim when sentencing [young/adult] offenders?'

offenders, half about adult offenders. The results can be seen in Table 6.4, which reveals some important commonalities between the purposes seen as relevant to adults and juveniles, but also a critical difference. For young offenders, two sentencing purposes received equal levels of support, and together accounted for two-thirds of the responses. Thus 34 per cent of respondents chose deterrence, and 33 per cent identified 'just deserts' or imposing proportional sanctions[9] as the most important sentencing aim.[10]

These same two goals were also seen as being the most important sentencing purposes for adult offenders. However, there was more support for proportional sentencing for adults, 46 per cent of the sub-sample endorsed proportionality for adults, compared to only 33 per cent for young offenders.[11] Another important difference between the two levels of offender concerns rehabilitation, which was seen to be more important when sentencing young offenders (20 per cent chose this aim, compared to only 12 per cent when considering adult offenders). Compensating victims was cited as being the most important aim by less than 5 per cent of both samples. This should not be interpreted to mean that people regard victim compensation as unimportant, however; respondents simply do not regard it as the overriding purpose of sentencing. Previous research has revealed that compensating the victim is central to public views of sentencing for both adults and young offenders (Roberts and Stalans 2003). The low level of support for compensation is a consequence of the nature of the question that required respondents to identify only one purpose.

Sentencing preferences and expectations of sentencing practices

Before we examine public perceptions of sentencing practices in response to some specific cases, it is worth noting that the perception of leniency in

Table 6.5 Perceptions of leniency/severity of youth justice system (percentages)

	1998 BCS	2000 BCS	2001/2 BCS	2003 ONS
Much too lenient	39	30	36	25
A little too lenient	35	33	34	46
About right	22	22	22	20
A little too tough	1	2	2	2
Much too tough	1	1	1	1
Don't know/no opinion	2	4	6	5

Question: 'In general, would you say that the way the police and courts deal with young offenders, that is people aged 10 to 17, is too tough, too lenient or about right?'

adult courts also applies to youth courts. As can be seen in Table 6.5, most people perceive youth court sentencing to be excessively lenient. This pattern of findings emerges whenever and wherever the question is posed. In 2000, over three-quarters of respondents to a Canadian survey endorsed the view that sentencing in youth courts was too lenient (Earnscliffe Research and Communications 2000). Amelin *et al.* (2000) also reported that most respondents to a survey in Northern Ireland expressed the opinion that the youth courts were too lenient.

The ONS survey posed a set of questions designed to explore the gap between people's *expectations* of sentencing practices and their sentencing *preferences*. Respondents were presented with a case involving a young offender, and then asked two questions. First, they were given a list of possible sentences and asked to state the sentence that this young offender *would be likely* to receive. Then, with the same list of dispositions in front of them, they were asked to select the sentence that they thought he *should* receive.

The survey sample was divided into three, with each group considering a different case. The three cases were selected to include different crimes as well as a range of seriousness:

1 A 16-year-old has been convicted of burglary and has stolen £250 worth of property. He has no previous convictions.
2 A 16-year-old has been convicted of selling cannabis near his school. He has previous convictions for possession of drugs and assault.
3 A 16-year-old has been convicted of assault. He has two previous convictions for assault and selling stolen property.

Although multiple sentences are permitted in youth courts, in order to keep the question easily comprehensible respondents were asked to select a single sentence from the following list. Some of the sanctions represent simplified versions of those actually available in youth court:

• a fine;
• community service (unpaid work);

- a period of community supervision by a probation officer or social worker;
- a curfew order with tagging;
- a period of detention in a prison for young offenders followed by a period of community supervision.

Table 6.6 reveals that there is a considerable gap between expected and desired sentencing outcomes. For all three scenarios, there is a significant difference between the sentence that respondents *expected* the offender to receive, and the sentence that they believed he *should* receive. In general, the 'expected' sentence was much more lenient than the 'favoured' sentence. This point can be clearly seen in responses regarding detention. For all three offenders, respondents favoured the use of custody at a much higher rate than they thought would be imposed. Thus, only 4 per cent of the respondents who sentenced the burglary case *expected* the offender to receive a sentence of detention; however, over one-quarter of this group *favoured* imposition of a term of custody. Similarly, only 28 per cent of the assault group expected the offender to be imprisoned, but almost two-thirds (62 per cent) favoured custody as a sentencing option. Finally, for the young offender convicted of drug dealing, 21 per cent of respondents expected him to be imprisoned, while 53 per cent wanted to see him imprisoned.

This finding is consistent with previous research on attitudes to the sentencing of adults: Hough and Roberts (1998) report that the most common response from respondents in the 1996 British Crime Survey was that the courts would deal less severely with the offender than they desired. Finally,

Table 6.6 Public sentencing preferences, three 16-year-old offenders (percentages)

	Burglary, no previous convictions		Assault, two previous convictions		Selling cannabis, previous convictions	
	Young offender *would get*	Young offender *should get*	Young offender *would get*	Young offender *should get*	Young offender *would get*	Young offender *should get*
Community service	44	20	25	7	27	10
Fine	16	4	5	1	8	1
Community supervision plus probation	26	32	31	13	31	18
Curfew with tagging	4	13	9	14	11	14
Detention followed by community supervision	4	26	28	62	21	53

Source: Hough and Roberts (2004b). Question: 'Choosing your answer from this card, what sentence do you think he is likely to receive? What sentence do you think he should receive?'

it should be recalled that respondents in our survey were allowed to choose only a single sentence. Had they been free to impose multiple dispositions, it is likely that support for imprisonment, particularly for case 1, would have been lower, as some of the respondents who chose custody would instead have chosen a combination of different sanctions.

The purpose of prison for young and adult offenders

To date, no survey has explored public expectations of the use of imprisonment for adults and young offenders. As with previous questions on this survey, the sample was divided in half to explore adult/young offender differences. Figure 6.2 shows strong support for education, treatment and work programmes for young offenders in prison. Providing educational or employment training clearly emerged as the most important function of imprisonment for young prisoners, attracting almost double (38 per cent) the support of the next most popular alternative (drug/alcohol/mental health treatment, 22 per cent). These functions of the prison

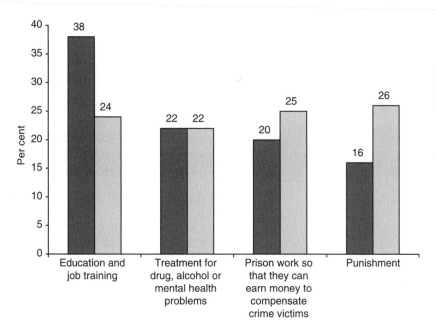

■ Perceptions of the purpose of prison for young offenders

☐ Perceptions of the purpose of prison for adult offenders

Figure 6.2 Perceptions of the purpose of prison for young offenders and adult offenders. Question: 'When [young/adult] offenders are sent to prison, do you think that the emphasis should be on . . .?' 'Other' responses omitted (3 per cent for both age levels) (*source:* Hough and Roberts 2004b)

were also seen to be important for adult prisoners, although there was understandably less emphasis on education and job training. Another difference between the two age levels involves punishment, which was viewed by more respondents as being appropriate for adults than for young offenders (26 per cent compared to 16 per cent). Although they appear under no illusion about what prison does for prisoners (see Chapter 5), the public clearly want prison to do something positive for young prisoners – simply punishing them is insufficient. As with the goals of sentencing, the public make a distinction between young and adult offenders.

Finally, the importance of compensating the victim emerges clearly from responses to this question: thus one-quarter of the adult question group and one-fifth of the young offender group identified this as the function of prison that should be emphasized. Once again it is worth noting that respondents were allowed to choose a single option; had they been allowed to choose multiple responses, support for providing prisoners with an opportunity to earn money to make compensation would undoubtedly have been higher.

Restorative sentencing and young offenders

The next chapter explores public attitudes to restorative justice in greater detail. Here we note the importance of restorative justice to public attitudes to sentencing young offenders. A key goal of the 1999 Crime and Disorder Act in England and Wales was to promote the use of restorative responses to juvenile offending (Crawford and Newburn 2003). Indeed, restorative justice has had a great impact upon the youth justice systems of many Western nations, especially New Zealand and Australia (see Morris 2004). At the sentencing stage of the criminal process, restorative justice attempts to promote the interests of the victim by encouraging the offender to apologize and, if possible, to make reparation. In this survey we explored the impact that such restorative gestures may have upon public responses to the sentencing of young offenders. Does it make a difference to the public if the young offender has taken, or intends to take, some restorative steps to repair the harm inflicted?

We created an experimental test of this question in our ONS survey. Three scenarios were created, although the offence was the same in all three versions. In version A, respondents were simply provided with a description of a case involving a young offender. Version B contained some social history information to flesh out the description of the individual. This information includes what might be termed mitigating factors (e.g. the offender recently lost his job), as well as aggravating ones (e.g. he has been playing truant from school and has been warned by the police).[12]

Version C can be considered the experimental condition. This version contained all of the information available in the second version. However, respondents in this group were also informed that the offender was described as having taken a number of steps that may be described as 'restorative', including expressing remorse, accepting responsibility and indicating a clear intention to make reparation to the victim of the crime (see Box 6.1).

Table 6.7 shows that the inclusion of information that the young offender had undertaken some steps towards reparation had a powerful effect upon public sentencing preferences. When the offender takes restorative steps, public support for imposing custody declines. One-third of respondents in the 'offence only' condition (version A) favoured imposing a term of custody; this fell to 13 per cent in the group who had read about the restorative steps taken by the offender.

The level of support for incarceration in the 'social history' condition was between these two, at 21 per cent. This finding suggests that some, but by no means all, of the mitigating effect of restorative steps is attributable to the impact of simply hearing a little more about the offender. When people know nothing more about the case than simply the offence of conviction, they tend to be quite punitive. It is clearly easier to be punitive to abstract 'offenders' than to specific individuals. Doob *et al.* (1998: 39) provide data to explain this finding: when members of the public are given no details about the offender, he is seen 'as more dangerous, less mature,

---

Box 6.1 Scenarios used in youth sentencing question

Version A (offence alone)
A young offender aged 17 has admitted to breaking into someone's home and stealing property worth £500.

Version B (offence plus description of offender's circumstances)
A young offender aged 17 has admitted to breaking into someone's home and stealing property worth £500. John lives at home with his parents and two brothers. His father has been unemployed for the past 18 months. John has been repeatedly missing school. Although he has not appeared before a youth court before, he has been warned by the police in the past. John says that he stole the property because he wanted the money, having just lost his part-time job at the local supermarket.

Version C (with reparation)
A young offender aged 17 has admitted to breaking into someone's home and stealing property worth £500. John lives at home with his parents and two brothers. His father has been unemployed for the past 18 months. John has been repeatedly missing school. Although he has not appeared before a youth court before, he has been warned by the police in the past. John says that he stole the property because he wanted the money, having just lost his part-time job at the local supermarket. John has expressed remorse for having committed the crime. In addition, he has written a letter of apology to the victims, and has promised to pay them back over the next three months.

Table 6.7 Effect of restorative steps on public sentencing preferences (percentages)

	Version A: offence only	B: offence plus case history information	C: offence plus case history information and restoration
Fine	4	2	3
Community service	20	23	25
Community supervision	29	43	48
Curfew plus tagging	14	11	10
Detention followed by community supervision	33	21	13

Source: Hough and Roberts (2004b). Question: 'Which of the following sentences is most appropriate in this case?'

less employable and more likely to re-offend than a young offender described in any of four different ways'. As well, when people have little or no information about the offender to consider, they naturally focus on the seriousness of the crime. Since this offence is very serious, considering the crime in the absence of any other information results in stronger support for the most severe sanction.

If public support for imprisonment declined when the offender made restoration, which other sanctions increased in popularity? As can be seen in Table 6.7, public support for community supervision was much higher in the condition in which restoration was made: 48 per cent of respondents favoured this option, compared to 29 per cent in the condition containing little information and 43 per cent in the condition with social history information alone.

The impact of the inclusion of restorative gestures on preferences in our scenarios is all the more striking when one considers how mild they were. The young offender had not actually paid back the victim, but merely signalled his intention to do so. A small (but important) gesture of good faith nevertheless had an important impact upon public sentencing preferences. This experiment therefore represents a conservative test of the power of restoration to mitigate the public desire for punishment.

Summary

In this chapter we have seen that the perceptions of youth crime and justice are subject to the same errors associated with knowledge of adult offending. Widespread concern over youth crime has led people to exaggerate the volume of crime for which young people are responsible. The public clearly view youth crime as different from adult crime. This is apparent whenever questions explore issues such as the best way to reduce crime. Different strategies are seen to be applicable to young people in conflict with the law. The public also see different purposes in sentencing offenders. Ratings of youth courts are as negative as ratings of adult courts, and once again public criticism focuses on lenient sentencing. The gap between sentences that the public want to impose and the sentences that they believe will be imposed is as great for youth courts as for adult courts. The public apply a different model of justice to young offenders, one that places more emphasis on rehabilitation and less on proportional punishment. Although the public appear to favour harsher sentencing for young offenders, when asked about the most effective way to prevent crime, or re-offending by young people, better parenting and better discipline in homes and schools head the list.

Further reading

Hough, M. and Roberts, J. V. (2004b) *Youth Crime and Youth Justice: Public Opinion in England and Wales*. Bristol: Policy Press.

Mattinson, J. and Mirrlees-Black, C. (2000) *Attitudes to Crime and Criminal Justice: Findings from the 1998 British Crime Survey*. Home Office Research Study 200. London: Home Office, Research and Development Directorate, Chapters 2 and 3.

Roberts, J. V. (2004) Public opinion and the evolution of juvenile justice policy in Western nations, in M. Tonry and A. Doob (eds) *Youth Crime and Youth Justice. Comparative and Cross-National Perspectives*. Crime and Justice, Volume 31. Chicago: University of Chicago Press.

Triplett, R. (1996) The growing threat: gangs and juvenile offenders, in T. Flanagan and D. Longmire (eds) *Americans View Crime and Justice*. Thousand Oaks, CA: Sage, Chapter 10.

Notes

1 Mattinson and Mirrlees-Black (2000) provide some limited data based upon responses to the 1998 British Crime Survey.

2 It is interesting to note in this context that an American study of news media has shown that the volume of crime coverage in the news media does not reflect actual crime trends (cited in Dorfman and Schiraldi 2001).

3 For repeat offenders the re-offending rate was significantly higher (see Jennings 2003).

4 There is no single purpose ascribed to YOTs. They are intended to serve a number of functions, including some that were not offered to respondents in this survey. For example, YOTs may help to deliver various youth justice services and reduce delays in the youth justice system. However, we see crime prevention as being central to the work of YOTs, and this is why we have

provided it as the 'correct' response to this question. The other alternatives considered by respondents are clearly outside the remit of YOTs.

5 It may well be true that young people today are less respectful of authority, and less law-abiding than preceding generations. We suspect, however, that the public's view is always that this is the case, and is not based on any systematic evidence. Adults have tended over the years to assume that the moral standards of young people are declining.

6 These negative perceptions of young people, combined with the perception that youth crime rates have been rising, may explain why people are quite pessimistic about future trends in juvenile crime. A survey of US respondents conducted in 2002 found that half the sample expected the number of crimes by juveniles to rise during the next five years; only 7 per cent expected a decline (Centre for Opinion Research 2002).

7 The public's position on this issue is supported by research involving young people. A sample of young people, both in and out of school, was asked what had the greatest effect on stopping young people from committing crimes. Parental reaction was cited by the same proportion as 'fear of being caught', the latter presumably referring to the justice system (Youth Justice Board 2002).

8 There is a punitive side to this opinion. A number of surveys in different countries have shown that the public is quite supportive of legislation that makes parents financially responsible for the criminal acts of their children. A decade ago the British Social Attitudes Survey found that almost two-thirds of the public supported making parents responsible for fines imposed on their children (Dowds 1995). Surveys in the USA have shown that almost two-thirds of the public supported legislation that makes parents financially responsible for loss and damage caused by their children (Belden Russonello and Stewart 1997).

9 According to the principle of proportionality in sentencing, sentences should get progressively more severe in response to increases in the seriousness of crimes for which they are imposed.

10 The Canadian survey of attitudes to youth crime conducted by Doob *et al.* (1998) also found that deterrence was rated as the most important purpose of youth court sentencing, although just deserts or proportional sentencing was not one of the options offered to respondents.

11 It is interesting to note that the most popular sentencing aim for adults was just deserts. This finding has also emerged from earlier polls in Britain. For example, findings from a 1986 poll reported by Walker *et al.* (1988b) found that 44 per cent of the public supported this option.

12 This balance was sought because we did not wish simply to make the offender more sympathetic to respondents, which would obviously have resulted in more lenient sentencing recommendations.

chapter seven

Attitudes to restorative justice

With Loretta J. Stalans[1]

Introduction

Previous chapters in this book have addressed public attitudes to what might be termed the 'traditional' criminal justice system. In this chapter our focus is upon reactions to a relatively new paradigm that has changed the face of criminal justice in many nations. Within the past decade, restorative justice has emerged as a truly global phenomenon. Restorative programmes and policies have been created in most industrialized and many developing nations. Restorative initiatives exist at all stages of the criminal process, from policing to prisons and community-based corrections (e.g. Braithwaite 1999; Johnstone 2002; Dignan 2005). Restorative justice encompasses a very broad range of programmes and policies, from initial contact with a suspect (restorative cautioning by the police), through to diversionary programmes for accused persons that involve victim–offender meetings, and restorative sentencing options. In some countries, such as Belgium, restorative justice has even permeated the correctional and post-release stage of the criminal process, with victim–offender meetings involving prisoners or parolees and their victims, or panels of other crime victims.

Restorative versus traditional responses to crime

A number of features distinguish restorative justice from more conventional criminal justice processing. First, restorative programmes attempt to promote the interests of the victim to a greater degree – there is a strong emphasis on reparation. Second, offenders are encouraged to accept responsibility and issue an apology to the victim – steps that many crime victims appreciate (if the expressions of remorse are genuine). Further, restorative initiatives attempt, wherever possible and appropriate, to reconcile the victim with the offender. Third, these programmes also strive to reconcile the offender with the community, often by imposing a term of community service.

This chapter explores the nature of public reaction to the elements of restorative justice. At first glance, we might expect the public to be opposed to restorative justice programmes and sentencing options. After all, most people think the system is too lenient, and that prison should be used for a wide range of offenders. However, the research that we review here suggests otherwise; in many contexts the public actually prefer a 'restorative' to a 'punitive' response such as imprisoning the offender. In this chapter, we attempt to uncover the reasons why laypersons may oppose or support particular restorative initiatives. What factors explain the appeal of, or resistance to, restorative justice programmes? We focus on restorative initiatives at sentencing (rather than at earlier stages of the criminal process) for two reasons. First, the sentencing stage of the justice system represents the apex of the criminal process, and thereby attracts more public and media attention than earlier stages of the justice system. Second, there is far more research on reactions to restorative sentencing, than, say, restorative cautioning by the police. At present we know little about public reaction to restorative initiatives at the stage of policing or corrections.

Knowledge of restorative justice

The state of public *attitudes* must be considered in the context of public *knowledge* of restorative justice. Although restorative justice has deep historical roots (see Johnstone 2002), it is unlikely that most members of the public are familiar with more recent restorative programmes such as victim–offender mediation, restorative conferencing or sentencing circles. When most people in Western nations consider criminal justice, they tend to think about police, courts and prisons – components of an adversarial criminal justice model with punitive and deterrent aims. Alternatives to incarceration – dispositions much more closely associated with restorative than with punitive justice – tend to be poorly understood by the public (see Roberts 2002b).

Restorative justice programmes are often local rather than national in scope, and do not attract much media attention. For this reason, few members of the public are aware of them, a finding that emerges from the empirical explorations of public knowledge of restorative justice programming. For example, Doble and Greene (2000) asked Vermont residents whether they had heard of three restorative justice programmes in their state: diversion, reparative boards and prison furloughs. Public awareness levels were quite variable: 61 per cent were aware of the furloughs and diversion programmes, but only 11 per cent reported knowing about the reparative boards.

The 1996 administration of the British Crime Survey sheds additional light on public awareness of restorative sanctions. Respondents were asked to identify the sentencing options available to courts in England and Wales. The results indicated varying levels of public awareness of the restorative sanctions in that jurisdiction. For example, only 16 per cent of the public identified compensation as a sanction, although over two-thirds of the sample was aware of community service (Hough and Roberts 1998).[2]

The lack of public knowledge of restorative justice processes creates challenges for researchers exploring public attitudes to restorative sanctions. For example, if the public are asked to sentence an offender without having first been given restorative justice options to consider, support for punitive sanctions such as imprisonment may reflect this lack of knowledge rather than genuine support for custody. Members of the public may well support restorative justice sanctions if they are made aware of the availability of these sanctions; a later section of this chapter reviews research that supports this hypothesis. With these cautions in mind, we turn to examining the empirical research on public attitudes to specific restorative justice programmes and then to restorative justice sanctions.

Attitudes to restorative justice

Reaction to the concept of restorative justice

Before we examine public reaction to specific restorative initiatives (such as conferencing), it is worth noting public reaction to the concept of restorative justice. Respondents to a nationwide survey in Canada in 1999 were asked whether they were in favor of, or opposed to restorative justice. First, however, they were given the following definition to consider: 'Restorative justice means that the justice system attempts to repair the harm done to the victim and the community as a result of the crime. Judges may follow restorative justice by sentencing the offender to pay some money to the victim, and to do community work without pay. Restorative justice is usually used for crimes that do not involve violence, such as theft and vandalism.' Given this rather narrow definition, 90 per cent of the sample said that they were in favour: 41 per cent were 'strongly in favour' and 49 per cent 'somewhat in favour' (Roberts *et al.* 1999).[3]

Wording the question differently produces the same result: when asked whether restorative justice programmes should receive a great deal, some or little emphasis, over half the sample responded 'a great deal' (Environics Research Group 1998). Doble and Greene (2000) provided participants with information about reparative boards and then asked their views about the appropriateness of sending 'carefully selected, non-violent' offenders to a reparative board instead of prison. Fully 91 per cent were in favour of the restorative option in this context. These findings are the first indication that the public is quite receptive to restorative justice, *if the aims and nature of this response to crime are made clear.*

Victim–offender reconciliation and mediation programmes

Victim–offender reconciliation programmes represent a form of mediation that has been in existence for over 30 years (see Fogel *et al.* 1972; Peachey 1989). Research demonstrates that the public are quite supportive of the concept. Pranis and Umbreit (1992) report a typical finding. Respondents were given a definition of a victim–offender mediation programme, and were then asked the following question: 'Suppose you were the victim of a non-violent property crime. How likely would you be to participate in a programme like this?' Just over half the sample stated that they would be 'very likely'. It is worth noting, however, that the crime they were asked to consider did not involve violence. More recently, a similar question was put to respondents to a survey in Northern Ireland. They were asked: 'If a young person had stolen something from you, would you be prepared to attend a meeting to help decide what should happen to them?' Fully three-quarters of the sample stated that they would be prepared to participate in such a meeting (Amelin *et al.* 2000).

An early survey dealing with victim–offender reconciliation programmes was conducted in Britain in 1983 (see Wright 1989). This poll found that 40 per cent of respondents thought that it was a good idea for offenders to meet their victims, although as Wright points out, 'the question was asked very badly, and the concept was at that time little known in Britain, so perhaps it is noteworthy that as many as 40 per cent supported the idea' (Wright 1989: 267). More recently, Doble and Greene (2000) examined public reaction to a number of restorative programmes in Vermont. Respondents were asked about the state's diversion programme. Specifically, they were asked how they felt about 'sentencing carefully selected, first time offenders to the diversion programme instead of prison'. Given this rather narrow offender profile, 43 per cent of respondents were strongly in favour, and a further 40 per cent 'somewhat' in favour, suggesting that a restorative response enjoyed considerable public support.

Vermont residents were also very positive when asked their opinion of reparative boards. These boards are composed of citizens who meet with offenders to devise a reparation plan that follows restorative objectives. Offenders are required to restore losses incurred by the crime victim, and to make amends to the community. In the first year of operation alone, the reparative probation programme handled 650 cases (Sinkinson and Broderick 1997). Over three-quarters of the public sample who had heard of these boards held a positive view, although as noted earlier, only a very small minority (11 per cent) was aware of the boards (Doble and Greene 2000). This illustrates an important theme in this review: informed members of the public also have a more positive view of restorative justice.

Few studies have examined public support for victim–offender mediation across a wide range of criminal cases. One such study used a number of crime scenarios ranging in seriousness from the trivial to the most serious crimes. Respondents were asked to state whether they would send the offender to victim–offender mediation. Respondents were also asked whether, if they had been victimized, they would have wanted the case mediated (Bilz 2002). For example, participants were less willing to send the offender to victim–offender mediation as the seriousness of the offence increased, as the violence of the offence increased, and as the moral offensiveness of the offence increased. Participants were most willing to send an offender assaulting a man in a bar and property offenders (stealing either a bike or valuable oil drums), but were (understandably) more reluctant to send an offender who had stalked his ex-girlfriend and violated an order of protection or a terrorist who had bombed a bookshop.

Explaining public support for mediation

Why do people support mediation? When asked to state the reasons behind their response, over half who thought that mediation was a good idea believed that it would make the offender think about what he did and regret his actions, while one-quarter believed that it would help change the offender's attitudes and behaviour. Of those who indicated that mediation was a bad idea, one third believed that it would be ineffective, 15 per cent believed that it would upset or not benefit the victim, 15 per cent believed it was a waste of time and effort and 13 per cent believed it was not appropriate because it was not a first offence (Justice 1 Committee 2002).

Conferences

One way of reconciling offenders and victims (or at least getting them to talk to each other) is by means of a 'conference'. In the area of juvenile justice, a conference usually involves family members who meet with criminal justice officials with a view to devising a response to the crime that does not involve going to court. Although most people have little familiarity with family group conferencing, empirical research suggests that there is considerable support for the concept. In New Zealand, slightly more than half of a random community sample agreed that offenders should meet with their victims and, wherever possible, 'put things right' (Lee 1996). Participants in New Zealand focus groups also supported conferencing for a wide range of offences as long as the victim agreed to the conference (MRL Research Group 1995). In research reported by Doob *et al.* (1998) a sample of the Canadian public was given a description of a minor property theft by a juvenile offender, and asked to rate the appropriateness of holding a conference (rather than going to court) to resolve the matter. Before responding, participants were provided with a description of a typical conference. The public responses demonstrated substantial support for the conference option over the traditional court-based approach: 65 per cent of the sample considered the conference approach to be appropriate.

Public support for the victim

Restorative justice models attempt to promote the involvement of the victim. Many studies have found strong public support for this increased level of victim participation in the justice system. The following examples are illustrative:

• in a national survey in the USA, 90 per cent indicated that they would probably or definitely support an amendment to their state's constitution that would increase victim rights (National Victim Center 1991);
• the vast majority (over 80 per cent) of a sample of Alabama residents in 1988 agreed that victims should be notified of, and should have input

into, parole hearings, should be able to sit with the prosecutor at the trial and should be able to influence the sentencing decision (Smith *et al.* 1990);

- a survey of California adult residents found that 87 per cent supported reforming the system to enhance victims' rights in the criminal justice system (California Poll 1982);
- a Colorado survey found that 83 per cent of respondents believed that victims must be listened to 'throughout the process' (Christian 2000);
- focus groups in New Zealand consistently referred to the importance of victims' rights (MRL Research Group 1995).

There is also strong public support for specific victim-oriented programmes and policies. For example, a representative survey of Canadians found that 90 per cent agreed with the use of victim impact statements at sentencing (Department of Justice Canada 1988). From these studies, it is clear that to the extent that restorative justice promotes the interests of victims, it is likely to prove popular with the public.[4]

The impact of apology and the expression of remorse

In everyday life, apologies and expressions of remorse are very important. This is even the case for accidents. If someone steps on your toes, or bumps into you on the underground, your reaction will be quite different depending upon whether they apologize or not. Similarly, when people transgress but in a non-criminal way – when someone is rude, for example – we are far more accepting of their behaviour if they subsequently apologize. So it is with criminal behaviour.

Many restorative justice programmes require, or at least strongly encourage, the offender to make an oral or written apology to the victim. In evaluations of restorative justice programmes, an apology has appeared in the majority of reparation agreements (e.g. Indianapolis Restorative Justice Experiment 2001; Karp 2001). Apologies for reprehensible conduct are expected in most cultures and have an effect on public perceptions of fairness and sentencing preferences. Thus, a representative sample of South Africans believed that a hearing involving a man who killed people with a bomb during apartheid was significantly fairer to the families of the victim when the offender apologized than when he did not apologize (Gibson 2001). South Africans clearly expect and desire an apology, and believe that it is important to assist in the healing of the families of victims.

Research has demonstrated that apologies and the expression of remorse by the offender reduce the severity of punishment assigned to offenders. The public attribute less blame to people who commit minor transgressions of social norms when they apologize (e.g. Darby and Schlenker 1989; Ohbuchi *et al.* 1989). Respondents were more willing to recommend victim offender mediation if the offenders expressed remorse in theft and stalking cases (Bilz 2002). Several experimental studies have found that apologies and the expression of remorse decreased the severity of the recommended sentence. For example, offenders who confessed to vehicular homicide and appeared remorseful received shorter prison sentences from public respondents than offenders who did not appear remorseful (Robinson *et al.* 1994; see also Harrel 1981; Scher and Darley 1997). The expression of remorse also resulted in the imposition of shorter prison sentences in a rape case (Kleinke *et al.* 1992). Similarly, experimental research in Germany has found that apologies influenced the assigned punishment for property and battery crimes (see Hommers 1988, 1991; Hommers and Endres 1991).

Restorative justice dispositions at sentencing

Public reactions to 'restorative' versus 'retributive' sentences

An often-heard critique of restorative justice is that it is (or is perceived by the public to be) a lenient response to offending. Hough and Roberts (2004b) report findings from a MORI survey in Britain that provides a comparison between responses to 'restorative' versus 'retributive' sentences. The sample was divided in half at random. A scenario – involving a 17-year-old offender convicted of burglary – was provided to respondents in both conditions. The groups differed only in the sentence that had been imposed.

Respondents assigned to read about the retributive sanction were told that 'Magistrates have imposed a brief term of custody in a prison for young offenders followed by a period of six months' community supervision.' In the other (restorative sentencing) condition, respondents were told the following: 'The offender admits to the crime and has accepted responsibility for his actions. He has written a letter of apology to the owner of the house, and has agreed to pay the money back over the next three months. In addition, he has agreed to perform 200 hours community work for a local charity.' After receiving this information, all respondents were asked to provide their reaction to the sentence. Table 7.1 shows the results.

As can be seen, a significantly higher proportion of respondents in the restorative condition rated the sentence as being 'about right': 81 compared to 66 per cent. This outcome alone is an interesting finding; it reveals greater public satisfaction with the 'restorative' disposition. However, it is also interesting that the percentage of respondents rating the custodial and restorative sentencing options as 'too lenient' was the same: 15 per cent in both conditions. In other words, the public did not see the restorative sanction as being 'softer' than the custodial alternative. This finding is consistent with research on public views of reparative boards in Vermont: almost three-quarters of the sample held the view that 'the sentences

Table 7.1 Perceptions of appropriateness of custody versus restorative sanction, 17-year-old offender (percentages)

	Custodial disposition	Restorative disposition
This sentence was:		
Much too tough	2	<1
A little too tough	17	4
About right	68	83
A little too lenient	8	7
Much too lenient	5	6

Source: Hough and Roberts (2004b). Question: 'Consider a young offender aged 17 who is convicted of breaking into someone's home and stealing property worth £300. (Magistrates have imposed a term of custody in a prison for young offenders followed by a period of six months' community supervision/ He has written a letter of apology to the owner of the house, and has agreed to pay the money back over the next three months. In addition, he has agreed to perform 200 hours community work for a local charity.) In your view, is this sentence too tough, too lenient or about right?'

handed down by a reparative board are more difficult than a brief stay in prison' (Doble and Greene 2000).

It is clear that of all the alternative sentencing options available to judges in most Western nations, those with a restorative purpose are particularly popular with the public. A typical finding from the literature can be found in research by Doble Research Associates (1998), who asked respondents to express their support for, or opposition to, alternative sanctions, some of which could be described as primarily restorative, others as principally punitive. A higher percentage of respondents supported the restorative sanctions (restitution and community service) than the punitive sanctions (e.g. house arrest, boot camp). For example, fully 79 per cent of the sample was strongly in favour of restitution, compared to only 54 per cent who favoured a 'military-style' boot camp programme (see Table 7.2).

Similar findings emerge from earlier surveys of the public in other countries. When asked to consider a number of alternative sanctions,

Table 7.2 Public support for various sentencing alternatives

Specific sentencing programme	Percentage of respondents 'strongly in favour'
Restitution	79
Community service	78
Probation	59
House arrest	56
Military-style 'boot camp'	54
Halfway house	49

Source: adapted from Doble Research Associates (1998).

Dutch respondents found the reparative options to be more attractive than the non-restorative alternatives. Thus two-thirds of the sample rated compensation as being very appropriate, while far smaller percentages gave this rating to electronic monitoring, intensive probation or training programmes (Junger-Tas and Terlouw 1991). Wright (1989) reported that 85 per cent of a sample of the British public believed that it was a good idea to make some offenders perform community service rather than go to prison. Canadians, too, see more merit in alternatives that involve the offender making restoration to the community; these were significantly more popular than other non-restorative options, such as electronic monitoring or house arrest (Angus Reid 1997). For example, more than four out of five respondents supported community service and compensation.

One of the most convincing demonstrations of the strength of public support for restorative sentencing rather than incarceration comes from a survey conducted in Germany by Boers and Sessar (1989). Respondents were presented with a series of criminal cases to consider, and were asked which of a number of responses was most appropriate. These ranged from purely restorative to purely punitive in nature. The most restorative response option was 'a meeting between victim and offender to arrive at a restitution agreement' and the 'purest' punitive response was 'the offender should be punished. Even if he provides restitution to the victim, the punishment should not be dispensed with or reduced.' Across the 38 cases included for 'sentencing' by the public respondents, there was significant support for what may be termed the restorative justice options. Thus in four-fifths of the cases, respondents favoured a resolution that consisted entirely or partially of a restitution-based agreement between offender and victim.[5]

Doble Research Associates' (1994) research in Vermont also uncovered very strong public support for sentencing by 'community reparations boards'. These boards work with a judge to determine and oversee the sentencing of non-violent offenders. Rather than sending the offender to prison, the boards focus on developing alternative dispositions with a strong restorative component, including the imposition of community work and restitution. When asked their reaction to this concept, 92 per cent of Vermont residents were in favour; only 6 per cent were opposed to the concept. However, once again, the question concerned 'selected, non-violent offenders'. When the residents were asked about the application of these boards in two violent offender scenarios (armed robbery and rape), results changed dramatically: the public were almost unanimous in preferring to imprison these offenders.[6]

Restitution and compensation

Restitution and compensation are central to restorative sentencing, and both attract considerable support from the public. A theme that emerges from almost every study that has investigated public sentencing preferences over the past 30 years concerns the importance of restitution and compensation to public opinion. The following examples reveal the attraction of restitution to the public:

- Shaw (1982) found that two-thirds of a sample of Britons supported a sentence of restitution as a way of reducing the size of the prison population.
- In a 1982 national survey of the Dutch public, 89 per cent believed that requiring the offender to make compensation to the victim was a suitable way of addressing the crime (van Dijk 1984, cited in Wright 1989).
- Doble Research Associates (1994) asked a sample of Vermonters to consider the kinds of changes they would favour with respect to dealing with offenders. Mandatory restitution attracted near unanimity: 96 per cent were in favour. The increased use of community work instead of prison attracted 95 per cent of the sample.
- Fully 98 per cent of respondents to a poll in North Carolina supported restitution (Higgins and Snyder 1996).

In addition to the appeal of restitution at the general level, sanctions that incorporate restitution attract substantial support from the public when asked to sentence individual offenders (e.g. Gandy 1978; Hudson 1992). For example, in a survey in Scotland, 30 per cent favoured victim compensation and 19 per cent favoured community service for theft (Scottish Office 1996). In an early demonstration of the power of restitution, Galaway (1984) conducted a survey of New Zealand citizens and found that across six different crime scenarios, public support for incarcerating the offender declined dramatically when the offender was required to make restitution to the victim. Although the study did not include any crimes of violence, one of the offences was quite serious: the offender had six prior convictions (four for burglary) and was now being sentenced for another burglary. Even for this offender, support for imprisonment declined when he had made restitution (Galaway 1984). This study is 20 years old now, and thus demonstrates that public support for restitution as a component of sentencing is far from new.

Galaway's finding has subsequently been replicated in several other jurisdictions (e.g. Sessar 1999). Bae (1992) found that respondents who were presented with restitution as one of the sentencing options were significantly less likely to choose imprisonment for a range of property offences than were respondents who were not given the option of restitution. As was the case with the earlier study by Galaway, the American respondents in Bae's study were asked to consider only property offenders. More recently, Doble and Greene (2000) asked respondents to rate the importance of a number of components of reparative boards in the state of Vermont. The most important element, rated as being 'very important' by more than 90 per cent of the sample, was making restitution. This strong support for restitution and compensation has been replicated in several other jurisdictions, including Britain (Wright 1989) and Holland (van Dijk 1984, cited in Wright 1989).

One of the clearest demonstrations of the appeal of restitution over incarceration comes from a survey reported by Pranis and Umbreit (1992). Respondents were asked to imagine that their homes had been burgled, with the loss of $1200 worth of property. The offender was described as a recidivist with a previous conviction for burglary. People were asked to choose between two sentences: (a) four months' probation plus four months' jail; or (b) four months' probation plus repayment of the $1200. Three times as many respondents chose repayment over the incarceration of the offender. This finding is interesting because it shows that the punitive response carries little appeal for the public *when placed in contrast to the compensatory alternative*. In addition, it is worth noting that this scenario involved a serious offence by a repeat offender. Thus, the reviewed studies indicate that support for imprisonment declines precipitously when respondents are made aware that the offender has made restitution or restitution is a sanction option.

Another illustration of the attraction of compensation comes from the 1996 and 1998 administrations of the British Crime Survey (Hough and Roberts 1998; Mattinson and Mirrlees-Black 2000). Respondents were asked to choose a sentence in a relatively serious case of burglary (the offender was a repeat offender). Despite the seriousness of the case, more respondents chose compensation than imprisonment.

The appeal of restitution even in cases of murder

Most of the studies on restitution have focused on property crimes. However, evidence has also accumulated that the public support restitution combined with life imprisonment without parole over the death penalty. Several studies have posed the following question to members of the public: 'If convicted first degree murderers could be sentenced to life in prison without parole and also be required to work in prison industries for money that would go to the families of their victims, would you prefer this as an alternative to the death penalty?' (Bowers 1993; McGarrell and Sandys 1996). McGarrell and Sandys (1996) found that 76 per cent of a sample of Indiana residents supported the death penalty when no alternative was presented, 40 per cent supported the death penalty over life imprisonment without parole and 26 per cent supported the death penalty when the alternative of restitution to the family coupled with life imprisonment without parole was presented. Even among those who initially expressed strong support for the death penalty, half of the respondents preferred the restitution and life imprisonment without parole option. These findings have been replicated in six other states (Bowers 1993).

Community service

Community service is another reparative sanction with a clear restorative justice character. The community service sanction sends the message that the offender's crime harmed the community as well as the individual victim. This explains why it often forms part of a 'restorative' response to offending. For example, community service was the most common restorative sanction imposed by reparation boards in Vermont (73 per cent of the reparative contracts containing a community service order; Karp 2001). Although much research suggests that the public knows little about alternatives to prison, community service orders were spontaneously mentioned by almost three-quarters of a representative sample from Scotland (Justice 1 Committee 2002). It is also a sentence that carries strong appeal for the public, at least for offences of low to moderate seriousness.[7]

Public support for community service can also be demonstrated by research that offers respondents a choice between imposing one of two sanctions, community service or imprisonment. Doob and his colleagues (1998) report a typical example of such a study. Respondents were asked how appropriate they felt it would be to substitute community service in a case in which a judge was 'thinking about putting the offender in prison for 30 days'. When given a choice, the vast majority of respondents were willing to substitute community work for a period of imprisonment. For example, when considering an adult offender convicted of a minor assault, 72 per cent of the sample favoured community service over imprisonment. Even for the more serious offence of sexual assault, 76 per cent of the sample believed that it was appropriate to substitute community service for imprisonment (Doob *et al.* 1998).

A frequent method used to explore public sentencing preferences involves providing respondents with a choice between two sanctions, a period of incarceration and one that was more restorative. Alternatively, respondents are sometimes asked to sentence an offender, and if they choose imprisonment, are then subsequently asked if they would find a non-custodial restorative sanction to be equally acceptable. Tufts and Roberts (2002) report an example of this kind of research. Respondents were asked to sentence an adult offender described in a crime scenario. Those who elected to impose a term of custody were then asked to consider the acceptability of a substitute (reparative) sanction. Specifically, they were asked: 'If a judge sentenced the offender to probation and 200 hours of community work, would that be acceptable?'

As can be seen in Figure 7.1, in scenarios involving the offences of assault and burglary (and first offenders and recidivists), almost half the respondents stated that they would find the alternative, restorative sanction acceptable.[8] In fact, fully half the respondents who read the scenario involving a recidivist burglar found the alternative sanction to be acceptable. This finding demonstrates the influence of reparative community work on popular conceptions of punishment, and has been replicated in

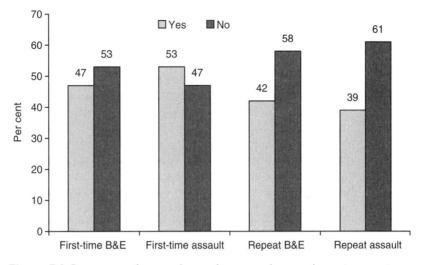

Figure 7.1 Percentage of respondents who agree that an alternative sanction to imprisonment is acceptable. (Adult offenders; *Source*: adapted from Tufts and Roberts 2002)

many surveys over the past 20 years (e.g. Doob and Roberts 1983). Figure 7.2 provides comparable data from respondents who were asked about juvenile offenders convicted of the same offences.

Finally, in this context we return to the survey involving Scottish respondents who were asked to sentence individuals described in detailed cases. Researchers provided participants with eight sentencing options

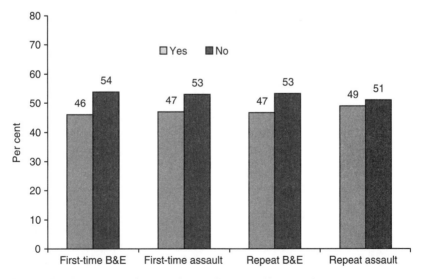

Figure 7.2 Percentage of respondents who agree that an alternative sanction to imprisonment is acceptable (juvenile offenders; *Source*: adapted from Tufts and Roberts 2002)

(community service order, pay compensation to the victim, fine, probation, prison, deferred sentence, electronic tagging and drug treatment and testing order). In sentencing a first-time convicted burglar who stole a video recorder, the most popular sentence was a community service order (selected by 35 per cent), followed by paying compensation to the victim (selected by 29 per cent). When asked the importance of different sentencing aims, over 75 per cent rated making amends to the victim for the harm done as being extremely or very important. In comparison, 57 per cent gave these ratings to incapacitation and 43 per cent to the aim of punishing the offender 'simply because he deserves it' (Justice 1 Committee 2002).

Greater support for restorative sentencing in cases involving juvenile offenders

Although there is widespread public support for restorative sanctions, the public appear to see these options to be particularly appropriate for juvenile offenders. For example, in a 1991 national survey, 81 per cent of United States respondents believed that it was very important to spend government funds on programmes where juveniles can repay their victims or the community, whereas only 36 per cent indicated this response for building more training schools or small group homes and 47 per cent believed it was very important to spend funds on closed supervision of juveniles (Schwartz 1992). When respondents were asked about the appropriate sentences for juveniles, strong support also emerged for restorative sanctions.

For example, in the Tufts and Roberts (2002) study in which respondents favouring imprisonment were asked about the acceptability of alternate restorative sanctions, support for these alternatives was significantly higher when the offender was a juvenile rather than an adult (see also Doob 2000). A review of studies on views of restitution conducted from 1990 and earlier found that the public expressed strong support for restitution to the victim as an alternative to incarcerating juveniles, especially for property offenders (see Hudson 1992). Gandy and Galaway (1980) found that the majority of their survey respondents believed that juvenile offenders (compared to adults) were more appropriate candidates for a sentence of restitution instead of imprisonment (see also Doob et al. 1998).

The role of criminal record

Another theme that has been replicated across studies is that restorative sanctions are seen to be a more plausible option for first offenders (see also Galaway 1984; Bilz 2002; Tufts and Roberts 2002). The same finding emerges from the New Zealand focus group research: restorative justice was seen as being ideal for first offenders, but not for recidivists (New Zealand Department of Justice 1995). However, there is an important qualification: if the current offence is non-violent, the public still view restorative interventions as appropriate. Once again the findings from the

Vermont study of public attitudes are instructive: significant proportions of respondents endorsed the use of community board sentences for a three-time shoplifter (76 per cent favoured the use of the community board); a five-time bad cheque writer (73 per cent) and even a repeat unarmed burglar (66 per cent). However, even a first-time armed robber was regarded as an appropriate case for the community board by only 4 per cent of respondents (Gorczyk and Perry 1997). Gandy (1978) also found that for non-violent offences, the existence of previous convictions made little difference in terms of support for reparative sanctions rather than imprisonment. Previous convictions, then, undermine the case for a restorative response in the eyes of the public, but generally only for crimes involving violence.

The finding that previous convictions significantly reduce public support for restorative justice for less serious violent offenders, but not for property offenders, also applies to juvenile offenders. Research using samples of the British Crime Survey illustrates that criminal history reduces public support for restorative alternatives for juveniles convicted of burglary and violent crimes. The survey compared first-time offenders to persistent offenders described as having committed the crime for the third time. For a juvenile offender convicted of shoplifting, half of the sample chose a caution for a 10-year-old first-time offender, but only 12 per cent supported a caution for a persistent offender. Support for community service rose from 18 per cent for first-time shoplifters to 50 per cent for persistent 10-year-old shoplifters, and similar results were found for 15-year-old shoplifters.

Moreover, for 15-year-old persistent offenders, a higher percentage (44 per cent) of the public preferred community service to imprisonment (36 per cent). For 15-year-old juveniles convicted of burglary, support for community service declined when the public sentenced a persistent offender (29 per cent) compared to a first-time offender (42 per cent). A similar difference between first-time and persistent offenders convicted of a violent attack on a teacher was found for 15-year-old juveniles. The majority of the public preferred imprisonment for persistent 15-year-old juveniles convicted of burglary or violent attack, but not persistent 15-year-old shoplifters (Mattinson and Mirrlees-Black 2000).

Explaining the importance of previous convictions

Why do the public see restorative justice as being inappropriate for repeat offenders? It is possible that the public see restorative justice options as aimed at offenders who have yet to become persistent offenders, and for whom rehabilitation is more likely. Attributions of future offending may also play a role: the public regard persistent offenders as more likely to re-offend, and this may justify the higher levels of public support for a non-restorative sentencing option such as imprisonment.

The appeal of compensatory sentencing options

The idea that the offender has made amends to the individual victim or the larger community clearly carries considerable popular appeal. As noted earlier in this chapter, the public are very supportive of criminal justice initiatives that promote the voice of the victim. It is probable that sympathy with the victim drives much of the public interest in compensatory sentencing options. And this itself may reflect a desire on the part of the public to assist victims of crime, as well as the belief that by making compensation, the offender is taking an important step towards rehabilitation and restoration. In focus group research, the public clearly perceive community service to be serving a dual purpose. The public believe that community service is appropriate for young, first-time burglars because it gives them a warning, keeps them out of prison and allows them to repay their debt to society (Russell and Morgan 2001).

Data from the United Kingdom are relevant to this point. Members of the public were asked to rate the effectiveness of different sentences at reducing crime. Somewhat surprisingly, perhaps, 'offenders compensating and making amends' was rated as very effective by 24 per cent of the sample, approximately the same percentage that rated 'prison and supervision in the community' as being very effective (25 per cent). In fact, making amends and providing compensation were seen to be more effective than fines, electronic monitoring and probation (Chapman *et al.* 2002).

This result echoes findings from the USA: Flanagan (1996a) reports the findings from a poll in which Americans were asked to rate the effectiveness of various alternatives to prison in protecting citizens against crime. Making offenders pay 'so that they can earn money to repay victims' was seen as being the most effective option, far more effective than jail or fines. Thus almost 90 per cent of the sample rated the reparative initiative as being effective, compared to less than half who rated prisons or fines in this way (Flanagan 1996a). Assuming that prisons punish more than court-ordered reparation, and fines involve a comparable deprivation (of money), it is clearly the reparative element of the amends to victims that appealed to respondents.

The importance of proportionality and crime seriousness

Most of the research reviewed in this chapter reveals declining public support for a restorative justice response to crime in the case of the most serious forms of offending, particularly crimes of violence. One explanation for this concerns the sentencing principle of proportionality, to which reference has already been made. Support for proportional sentencing has emerged repeatedly from many studies of public attitudes to sentencing conducted in several countries, and using different research methodologies (e.g. Blumstein and Cohen 1980; Gebotys and Roberts 1987; Darley *et al.* 2000). The general finding is that the severity of punishments favoured by the public rises in direct proportion to the seriousness of the crime, although the relationship is not always perfect (see Rossi *et al.* 1985).

The central role of crime seriousness as a determinant of public support for restorative initiatives also emerges from the Vermont study by Doble and Greene (2000). As noted, there was strong general support for the use of reparative boards. However, when respondents were asked to consider specific offender scenarios, a somewhat different pattern emerged. For the most serious crimes (rape; heroin dealer, repeat offender; armed robbery), there was almost no support for assignment to a reparative board (percentages under 5 per cent). For less serious offences, public support was stronger. For shoplifting, auto theft and theft, over two-thirds of the sample favoured the use of a reparative board over imprisonment.

In research in England and Wales in 2000 conducted for the Sentencing Advisory Panel, proportionality emerges in the context of sentencing for the offence of residential burglary (Russell and Morgan 2001). For example, 81 per cent of respondents chose imprisonment and only 6 per cent chose community service for a serious burglary involving an elderly victim. By contrast, in the case of a 19-year-old who climbed through an open window and was detained without struggle by the victim, three-quarters of the public favoured imposition of a community-based sentence (with 22 per cent choosing a community service order). Most respondents (92 per cent) ordered a community sentence (with 30 per cent choosing community service) for a first-time burglar who stole approximately £500 of goods from an empty house.[9]

Support for proportionality in sentencing may explain public opposition to some restorative programmes. Thus, although there was widespread support for diversion and the use of reparative boards for non-violent offenders, more Vermont residents had a negative than positive view of the state's furlough programme. The explanation for this apparent inconsistency would appear to be the more serious offender population involved in furloughs, a finding confirmed by comments made in focus groups conducted by the same researchers (see Doble and Greene 2000).

Explaining lower levels of support for restorative justice in cases involving violent offenders

As with the issue of offender age and prior record, it still remains to be established why the public see restorative sanctions as being less appropriate, or even inappropriate, for the more serious personal injury offences. One explanation is that compensation – however large – is unable to create a proportional response to the crime, or to be sufficiently onerous to hold the offender accountable. This view, supported by research by Doob and

Marinos (1995), suggests that imprisonment occupies a unique place in public conceptions of sentencing. These researchers found that even when members of the public were able to impose unlimited fines, if the offence involved serious violence, people still favoured incarcerating the offender.

However, the sparse descriptions of crimes in prior research also raise questions about whether public support for restorative sanctions actually decreases for all types of serious or violent crimes. The scenarios did not include violent crimes in which the offender committed the violent act due in part to external circumstances. The public may not blame offenders who commit homicide due to external factors if such circumstances suggest that the offenders have a good character. There are several examples of murders or homicides where offenders may merit restorative sanctions rather than punitive sanctions: battered women killing their abusive partners, battered children killing their abusive parent, physician-assisted suicide, active euthanasia because of the terminally ill victim's pleading requests to die, or a father accused of negligent homicide because he forgot to put a seatbelt on his son and the son died in a car accident.

In these types of homicide cases juries have acquitted defendants even though the prosecutor had enough evidence to prove beyond reasonable doubt that the defendant committed the crime. This is called jury nullification (see discussion in Roberts *et al.* 2003). Juries assessed the character of the offender and victim and concluded that the defendants had a good character and committed unlawful acts due to extenuating external factors. These jury nullification cases illustrate that the public's conception of justice includes mercy and forgiveness. Thus, another reason why the public may support restorative sentencing is that it is consistent with a desire to forgive certain types of offenders. For members of the public, proportionality is based not solely on the seriousness of the offence but also on other background and external characteristics surrounding the crime (see Roberts 1996; Stalans and Lurigio 1996). The public will support restorative justice for offenders who committed violent crimes if there are extenuating circumstances that suggest good character or intention.

Summary

Restorative justice programmes often vary in many ways, but all programmes have three common central components. First, restorative justice programmes require that the offender accept responsibility for the crime and at least strongly encourage the offender to make a sincere apology to the victim. Second, the process provides victims with greater participation and allows victims to express their concerns and desires. Finally, the outcomes often include reparation to the victim and/or to the community so that the offender may be re-integrated into the community as a productive citizen. The popularity of these components may explain why the majority of the public supports restorative justice programmes. Additionally, each component may contribute to public support for restorative sanctions such as restitution and community service.

Although the full extent of public knowledge remains to be determined, it seems clear that there is less familiarity with restorative justice initiatives such as conferences, community boards, sentencing circles and other such programmes. Victim satisfaction and the severity of the criminal justice response to offenders may well be the most important elements of public reaction to restorative justice programmes. Public support for victims' rights – particularly at the stage of sentencing – is very strong, and any response that promises to do more for crime victims will carry great appeal for the public. The public appear willing to forgo a considerable part of the punishment imposed if there are clear benefits to the victim (for example, in terms of restitution). At the same time, if the crime is relatively serious, the public seem opposed to the use of a restorative solution. The lesson would appear clear: restorative justice advocates need to ensure that the restorative response carries meaningful consequences for the offender, and that the public are aware of this fact.[10]

Further reading

Johnstone. G. (2002) *Restorative Justice*. Cullompton: Willan.
Lee, A. (1996) Public attitudes toward restorative justice, in B. Galaway and J. Hudson (eds) *Restorative Justice: International Perspectives*. Monsey, NY: Criminal Justice Press.
Sessar, K. (1999) Punitive attitudes of the public: reality and myth, in G. Bazemore and L. Walgrave (eds) *Restorative Juvenile Justice: Repairing the Harm of Youth Crime*. Monsey, NY: Criminal Justice Press.

Notes

1 Department of Criminal Justice, Loyola University, Chicago.
2 The one study of public awareness of a restorative programme in a developing nation also revealed relatively low levels of awareness: less than half the sample of Ugandans had heard of community service (Sita and Edanyu 1999). Thus, as will be seen over the course of this chapter, the public are very supportive of compensatory sentencing options, but *knowledge* of restorative options is fairly poor.
3 This question was repeated in a survey conducted two years later (2001) with little change in the level of support for restorative justice.
4 It is also worth noting that when asked to rate the believability of different

groups with respect to crime and justice, the public rate victims' groups as being the most believable (Environics Research Group 1998), suggesting that victims exercise an important influence over public conceptions of justice.

5 It should be noted, however, that as with most mail surveys, this one had a relatively low (44 per cent) response rate. It is possible that the responses are to some unknown degree less representative of all residents than a telephone or in-person survey with a higher response rate. Nevertheless, the results offer impressive support for restorative considerations in sentencing.

6 Ninety-nine per cent favoured prison (rather than sentencing by community boards) for the rapist, 95 per cent for the offender convicted of armed robbery.

7 Almost all the research on this issue has been conducted in Western countries, but the appeal of community service is not restricted to developed nations: Sita and Edanyu (1999) report that fully 86 per cent of their respondents in Uganda supported the concept.

8 It might be argued that this is a 'leading' question, which may over-estimate the true proportion of respondents who would find the substitute sanction acceptable.

9 Sita and Edanyu (1999) asked their respondents in Uganda to identify offences for which community service would be appropriate. Although respondents identified some offences against the person, these were exclusively minor assaults (Sita and Edanyu 1999: 22).

10 For an empirical demonstration of the effect of making consequences salient to the public, see Sanders and Roberts (2000).

chapter eight

Conclusion

Introduction
Conditions giving rise to punitive responses
    Public support for crime prevention
Effects of information on attitudes
    Reviewing attitude change experiments
    Education or propaganda?
    People talking about crime and justice
The future
Notes

Introduction

In this concluding chapter we first draw some lessons from the vast body of research that has been reviewed throughout the course of this volume. Then we examine the prospects for changing attitudes to criminal justice, by reviewing the findings from experimental studies in the area. One conclusion that we have drawn is that the time scale of all empirical reviews published to date tends to be quite constrained. Reviewers can explore trends in public opinion only since the inception of systematic polling in the 1960s. Yet even within this time frame public attitudes have evolved considerably: we have witnessed a growing acceptance of community-based responses to crime accompanied – and possibly caused by – a corresponding decline in public support for the use of imprisonment. At the same time, some elements of public attitudes have remained fairly constant. Support for the following propositions can be found repeatedly in polls conducted over the past 30 years:

- In the eyes of the public, responding to crime involves far more than simply the agencies of the criminal justice system; people have always seen an important role for schools and parents in preventing youth crime, and employment initiatives in responding to adult offending.

- Sentencing serves a number of different purposes, and the importance of these purposes varies according to the characteristics of the case and the offender before the court. In this respect, members of the public react like judges when sentencing offenders.
- Despite the public support for multiple sentencing goals, a bedrock of support exists for the principle of proportionality in sentencing.
- The public have always found reparative sanctions very attractive, to the point that they are willing to forgo more severe punishments (such as imprisonment) if the offender has paid back the victim.
- Although few studies have explored the issue, there has always been strong support for crime victims; every reform that has promoted victims' rights in the criminal process has met with high public approval ratings.[1]

Forty years or so is a relatively brief period in the tide of time. While we cannot support the argument with quantitative evidence, it is clear that there has been a significant evolution with respect to public attitudes to justice. This can best be illustrated by reference to punishment.

The punishments inflicted in Western societies, and the conditions of penal detention, have evolved considerably over the past 300 years. A century ago, prison conditions imposed constraints on prisoners that would be unthinkable today. Looking further back to the early eighteenth century reveals a criminal justice system that imposed penalties of astonishing severity. This is best illustrated by the profligate application of the death penalty. Capital punishment was the penalty imposed for a wide range of offences, many quite trivial by today's standards (and possibly standards in the eighteenth century as well).[2] Popular accounts of life in those times reveal no widespread opposition to prison conditions, or public executions. Indeed, public executions at Tyburn in central London appear to have been as popular as Saturday afternoon football games are today.[3] Although a majority of the public in most Western nations still supports the use of capital punishment (according to death penalty polls), this support is restricted to a single offence (murder), and only the most serious forms of this crime. Many scholars have explored the reasons for this 'civilizing process'. Here we simply make the point that public attitudes to crime and justice need to be seen in a broader time frame than has been the case to date. Public attitudes have evolved considerably, and will continue to do so in the future.

Conditions giving rise to punitive responses

Throughout this volume we have noted that the public can often respond to crime (and particularly violent crime) in a punitive fashion. Responses tend to be punitive when:

- the offence involves violence, particularly crimes of sexual aggression;
- the victim was particularly vulnerable (for example, if the victim is a child);
- survey respondents' attention is focused on the offence rather than the offender;
- people are not provided with a range of possible responses to the crime;
- the poll requires a fast decision from the respondent.

But we have also pointed out that when questions are put to the public in a more appropriate manner, people are very interested in less punitive responses to crime, particularly when these responses generate some tangible benefit, such as reparation for the crime victim.

Public support for crime prevention

It also seems clear that members of the public in Western nations are as interested in prevention as they are in punishment. Although in this volume we have concentrated on criminal justice responses to crime, particularly police, courts and corrections, a considerable amount of research has been conducted on public attitudes to crime prevention. The findings from this literature reveal the strength of public interest in this response to crime.

One reason why politicians seem reluctant to promote restorative or preventive responses to crime is that they may be seen as being 'soft on crime'. In Chapter 7 we saw that a restorative sentencing option was not necessarily perceived as a more lenient response to crime. In a similar way, the public do not appear to associate crime prevention with a policy of being soft on offenders. Respondents in a Canadian survey were asked to agree or disagree with the statement that 'if Canada puts more emphasis on crime prevention, we will get soft on crime'. Respondents were significantly more likely to *disagree* than agree with this assertion (Department of Justice Canada 2004).

One way of demonstrating the public's support for crime prevention is to provide respondents with a direct choice between punishment and prevention. For example, a poll conducted in Canada asked respondents the following question: 'Do you think there should be more emphasis placed on crime prevention measures or should there be more emphasis on police and correctional services?' In the light of the strong public support for the police, one might expect respondents to select the latter option. However, fully three-quarters of the sample chose prevention over policing (National Crime Prevention Council of Canada 1997).

The same poll revealed evidence that the public are sensitive to the cost-effective nature of crime prevention initiatives. When asked whether law enforcement or crime prevention was the more cost-effective means of reducing crime, almost three-quarters (71 per cent) favoured crime prevention (National Crime Prevention Council of Canada 1997). Even when people are made aware that some crime prevention programmes must be paid for through tax revenues, public support remains strong. Respondents were asked the following question: 'Bearing in mind that most crime prevention programs are funded by tax dollars, what emphasis should governments place on crime prevention?' (The response options included less emphasis; the same emphasis and more emphasis.) Sixty per cent chose 'more emphasis' as their response (National Crime Prevention Council of Canada 2000). Another poll found that approximately two-thirds of the sample supported spending more on crime prevention (Department of Justice Canada 2004).

In a similar vein, when respondents were asked to identify the main goal of the criminal justice system in Canada, twice as many people chose prevention as chose punishment[4] (National Crime Prevention Council of Canada 2000). These recent findings are consistent with earlier research into public opinion regarding crime prevention (see Roberts and Grossman 1990 for a review).

Findings such as these are particularly striking since crime prevention policies and programmes do not have the high visibility of punitive responses to crime. 'Three strikes' mandatory sentencing laws have an eye-catching appeal – this explains, in part, the proliferation of such sentences across Western nations. Prevention programmes are far less visible, and do not generate the kind of material favoured by news media. Accordingly, crime prevention accounts for far fewer media stories. Despite this lack of profile, the public remain supportive.

The positive public response to crime prevention is not restricted to Canadians. Americans also share this perspective. A number of polls over the past decade have posed the following question to respondents: 'Which of the following approaches to lowering the crime rate comes closer to your own view – do you think that more money and effort should go to attacking the social and economic problems that lead to crime through better education and job training, or more money and effort should go to deterring crime by improving law enforcement with more prisons, police and judges?' As can be seen in Table 8.1, addressing crime through social development has consistently attracted more support from respondents.

The British public are often more supportive of efforts at prevention than of policies that punish. When asked 'If you could spend £10 million on dealing with crime, what would you do with it?', the option of creating teams to work with children emerged as the most popular option. Hiring more police constables – another preventive solution – was the second most popular option. The most punitive response option of putting offenders in prison was supported by only 2 per cent of the sample (Esmée Fairbairn Foundation 2004).

Table 8.1 Attitudes to approaches to lower the crime rate (percentages)

	Attack social problems	More law enforcement
1989	61	32
1990	57	36
1992	67	25
1994	57	39
2000	68	27

Source: adapted from Sourcebook of Criminal Justice Statistics (2004). Question: 'Which of the following approaches to lowering the crime rate comes closer to your own view? Do you think that more money and effort should go to attacking the social and economic problems that lead to crime through better education and job training or more money and effort should go to deterring crime by improving law enforcement with more prisons, police and judges?'

Effects of information on attitudes

We have noted throughout this volume that there is a clear link between public knowledge and public attitudes to criminal justice. In general, the most misinformed members of the public tend also to be the most critical.[5] A good example of this association is found in research reported by Mattinson and Mirrlees-Black (2000), who measured knowledge of crime rates and attitudes to sentencing in youth court. These researchers found that one-quarter of the most informed respondents but over half of the least knowledgeable respondents held the view that sentencing was too lenient. As noted earlier, however, this finding is a simple association; establishing whether levels of knowledge determine the direction of opinions requires an experimental design, or a statistical analysis, such as logistic regression, that permits causal inferences to be drawn from essentially correlational data.

In the light of the limits on public knowledge of criminal justice – and in particular in the critical area of sentencing – an obvious strategy to ameliorate public attitudes involves some form of public legal education. A number of researchers have explored the effects of increasing public awareness of the justice system using experimental designs. The general hypothesis being tested is that public opinion is influenced by, and accordingly will reflect, the amount of information available to respondents. No study has attempted to correct all the misperceptions to which the public subscribe, or to fill all the gaps in public knowledge. Each study therefore represents a partial test of the hypothesis. Nevertheless, taken together, these studies comprise an important element of the public opinion picture.

The general finding is that public attitudes to the sentencing of offenders become less punitive when participants are provided with more information about the sentencing process, the offence or the offender. The following examples illustrate this phenomenon.

• A number of researchers have provided sub-groups of respondents with differing levels of information about the same case (e.g. Doob and Roberts 1983; Covell and Howe 1996). The general finding is that the respondents tend to be more punitive when they are told little about a case. Support for incarceration is high when people are simply informed about the crime of which he has been convicted, and are then asked to impose sentence.

• Researchers have provided detailed information about the sentence that is imposed. For example, Sanders and Roberts (2000) specified the specific conditions of the community-based sentencing option imposed, with the result that respondents were significantly less inclined to incarcerate the offender.

• Researchers such as Doble and Klein (1989), Hough and Roberts (1998) and others have provided respondents with more information on the sentencing options available – rather than simply asking for a sentence without specifying the options – and found that support for imprisonment declined.[6]

Reviewing attitude change experiments

Perhaps the most compelling demonstrations of the impact of information upon attitudes come from Britain. The first, conducted a decade ago, involved the technique known as a 'deliberative poll'. As noted in Chapter 1, this method of exploring public attitudes combines the large poll's power to generalize from a sample to a population, with the ability of the focus group to provide participants with a considerable degree of information. In Chapter 1 we described the deliberative poll on crime and justice that was conducted in Britain in 1994. It will be recalled that subjects attended a weekend seminar on the issues and their attitudes were measured before and after the experience.

The results were encouraging for the 'information leads to attitude change' hypothesis. Hough and Park (2002) analysed the data from the deliberative poll and concluded that 'there were significant and enduring shifts in attitudes'. These changes were all in the same direction, involving reduced support for tough measures such as imprisonment as a response to crime and greater support for rehabilitation. It is not really surprising that there was a measurable shift in attitudes *immediately* after the weekend seminar. More striking is the fact that the change was enduring. Participants were interviewed a third time ten months after the seminar, and the shift in attitudes was still evident.

For example, people were more likely to agree with the statement that 'the courts should send fewer people to prison' and less likely to agree that 'all murderers should be given a life sentence'; support for imprisoning juvenile burglars declined significantly as a result of the weekend experience, and remained lower after ten months (see Hough and Park 2002). Table 8.2 summarizes attitude change data. As can be seen, while significant minorities did not change their views – or shifted in a less liberal direction – the net change was in a more liberal direction.

Chapman *et al.* (2002) report findings from a smaller-scale experiment. In their study, a randomly selected sample of the British public answered a questionnaire about knowledge of sentencing and related issues. Sub-samples of respondents were then asked to participate in one of three 'knowledge improvement' experiments. One group received a booklet about the sentencing process, a second group attended a seminar and a third watched a videotaped presentation. All participants were exposed to the same information. Knowledge of criminal justice was measured before and after the respondents had participated in one of the three conditions. Results indicated that knowledge scores improved in all three groups.[7] It is worth examining this study in a little more detail, focusing on the condition that carries most potential as a vehicle for attitude change: the videotaped presentation.

The participants in the video group revealed the largest increases in knowledge. Some examples of the shifts observed are the following:

- the percentage knowing about post-release supervision from prison rose from 42 to 70 per cent;
- the percentage correctly identifying crime trends over the previous two years rose from 12 to 41 per cent;
- the percentage knowing that in a magistrates' court a jury decides whether someone is guilty rose from 68 to 81 per cent.

Clearly, exposure to a brief 30-minute video can increase the viewer's level of knowledge of crime and justice – it would be surprising if this was not

Table 8.2 Change over time in attitudes before and ten months after deliberative poll experience (percentages)

	Direction of attitude change			
	More liberal	Attitude unchanged	Less liberal	Net liberal shift
Support for imprisoning first time burglars	51	33	17	+34
Reducing crime through better discipline and firmer punishment	44	41	16	+28
Using more reparative/community punishments	44	21	35	+9
Toughening up court sentences and prison regimes	28	52	20	+8

Source: Hough and Park (2002).

the case – but significant shifts in attitudes also emerged. After viewing the programme, people were more confident that the criminal justice system is effective in bringing offenders to justice. The critical question relating to sentencing trends was measured before and after people had watched the video. Most viewers (58 per cent) did not change their opinion about the appropriateness of sentences imposed by the courts. However, over a quarter of the participants became less punitive after watching the programme. In addition, participants themselves acknowledged the effect of information: 44 per cent of respondents said that they had changed their views as a result of the information that they had been given (Chapman *et al.* 2002: 47). For a number of questions no significant effects emerged. However, the modest scale of the project must be considered in evaluating the results. Relative to the deliberative poll, all three educational strategies were brief and low-key.

Salisbury (2004) reports findings from another experimental study conducted in Britain. An informational booklet was given to a sub-sample of people participating in the British Crime Survey. The booklet contained information about crime and sentencing. No financial incentive was provided to respondents, they were not asked to read the booklet and no warning was given that they would be questioned about its contents at a later stage. Two weeks later a follow-up interview was conducted with people who had received the booklet. The responses of people who had received the booklet were compared to those of respondents who had not received the information.

The findings were consistent with other experiments in the field. Salisbury reports modest increases in knowledge levels and confidence in criminal justice. For example, in the second interview, respondents who had received the booklet were more likely to see the criminal justice system as being effective in reducing crime, bringing the guilty to justice and meeting the needs of crime victims (see Salisbury 2004: Figure 5).[8] It is important to note, however, that this was a conservative test of the relationship between knowledge and attitudes or confidence. Since they had not been asked to read the booklet, only 18 per cent of the sub-sample read it in full (a further 19 per cent reported having read certain sections.

Salisbury (2004: 12) concludes that confidence in some aspects of the criminal justice system increased as a result of participation in the British Crime Survey itself. This interesting conclusion is consistent with a general finding in the international literature: one of the central criticisms of the justice system is that it has no contact or engagement with the average member of the public. This criticism manifests itself in the responses to questions about the judiciary: most people see judges as being 'out of touch with what the ordinary person thinks' (Hough and Roberts 1998), which is another way of saying the judiciary has little contact with the public.

It seems likely, therefore, that engaging the public in discussions about criminal justice will have a salutary effect upon public confidence, independent of whether these discussions achieve a significant increase in public knowledge of crime and criminal justice. This finding is consistent with research in a number of areas of the criminal law, which has shown that people often hold more favourable views of the justice system after contact with it. For example, Mathews *et al.* (2004) report that the majority of jurors held more positive views of the jury after having completed their jury service.

The research on the effects of providing information to the public has broadened to field studies that engage participants to a greater degree than is possible with a representative poll or even a focus group. As part of a project of the Magistrates' Association and the Probation Boards' Association in Britain, a diverse collection of people attended presentations made by criminal justice professionals. The researchers who evaluated these seminars found that the presentations had increased both the visibility and the acceptance of community-based sentences (see King and Grimshaw 2003). The participants themselves testified that the sessions had increased their level of knowledge. King and Grimshaw (2003: 11) concluded that 'It is clear that majorities of the audiences felt that the presentations had increased their knowledge about community sentences, the magistracy, the probation service, and sentencing in general.' In other words, the findings from this report mirrored those emerging from the briefer experiments discussed earlier in this chapter.

Finally, although it is not a research study *per se*, it is worth noting a public education website that provides a test of the information–opinion relationship. People who visit www.crimeinfo.org.uk have access to a great deal of information about crime and justice in Britain. In addition, they are also able to participate in an interactive sentencing exercise. This begins by providing participants with a description of a case, at which point they are asked to impose a sentence. The exercise then offers further information about the crime and the offenders, as well as legally relevant material such as the factors that might mitigate or aggravate sentence. At the conclusion, participants are asked whether they stand by their original sentence or whether they would select another disposition. Results tabulated to date[9] confirm the pattern emerging from controlled, randomized experiments: participants are less likely to endorse custody as the appropriate sentence.

Education or propaganda?

Cynics may argue that experiments such as these are little more than exercises in public relations – that is, people change their opinions because they have been fed a biased diet of information. Alternatively, the attitudinal shifts could reflect social desirability considerations associated with the experimental context: participants may change their views towards the position that they believe will make them look more positive in the eyes of the researcher. We feel that neither criticism holds much water in relation to these studies. First, the information provided to participants in the deliberative poll represented a range of views, and did not consist simply of lectures by liberal-minded academics. Second, the fact that attitudes shifted dramatically with respect to some issues in the deliberative poll (for example) and less so, or not at all, for others undermines the social desirability interpretation. If people wanted to 'look good' or confirm what they perceived the researchers expected of them, attitude 'change' would have occurred on all measures.

People talking about crime and justice

What are the implications of these experimental demonstrations? Do they suggest that information can attenuate the ubiquitous perception of leniency and its accompanying demand for harsher punishment? Some scholars are rather sceptical. Maruna and King (2004: 102), for example, argue that 'schemes to educate and inform the public . . . are noble, well-meaning efforts, but unlikely to have any more than marginal impact on either public understanding of crime issues, or punitive, prison-centric attitudes'. We are somewhat more optimistic with respect to the role of information, for several reasons. First, as noted, the attitude change observed in the deliberative poll was clearly lasting and not short term in duration (see Hough and Park 2002).

Second, direct participation in an experience such as this is not necessary for attitude change to occur; people frequently discuss their experiences with family and friends. We should not under-estimate the extent to which people talk about criminal justice issues. Some years ago, a British survey found that fully two-thirds of the sample discussed the crime issue very or fairly often, while almost as many discussed sentencing (Walker *et al.* 1988b). Economic and health issues were rather poor seconds in the ranking of social issues discussed by members of the public. Seventy per cent of the sample said that crime had come up in conversation with family or friends within the previous week.

The 2003 MORI poll found that over two-thirds of the sample cited 'relatives' or friends' experiences' as one of the sources from which they 'receive the most information about the way crime is dealt with'. It seems likely that the deliberative poll reached far more people than the few hundred individuals who actually attended the event.[10] We also know that people who participated in the Home Office study designed to improve public attitudes by improving public knowledge clearly passed some of their information on to others. For example, 80 per cent of the participants who attended the seminar on criminal justice subsequently discussed the session with family and friends (Chapman *et al.* 2002).

In addition, respondents to the 2003 MORI poll were asked whether they trusted different sources of information about criminal justice. Nine respondents out of ten rated the experience of relatives and friends as trustworthy – the highest percentage in the list. In contrast, fewer than one-quarter admitted that they trusted tabloid newspapers, and fewer than one-third trusted the Internet as a source of information (MORI 2003).

Thus, although the media often present a distorted view of criminal justice, the public appear quite sceptical of what they see, hear and read about crime and criminal justice.

The third reason for seeing potential in attitude change following the provision of information concerns the origin of negative attitudes and low confidence ratings. The public have acquired their attitudes to criminal justice as a result of reading about the failures of the system, whether in terms of failed prosecutions or lenient sentences. Direct experience is not generally the explanation for public attitudes to the justice system. If distorted information can create a perception of a justice system that is not 'working', surely there is scope for improving attitudes by providing more accurate information, or information about the many success stories in the area of criminal justice?

The public desire to punish offenders severely is usually attenuated by the provision of information, as we have demonstrated on a number of occasions in this book. Much offending – even of a relatively serious nature – is spontaneous, and results from intoxication. In addition, many offenders have a number of mitigating factors that are brought to the attention of courts at the time of sentencing. The challenge, therefore, is to make the public aware of these factors, and to encourage people to see crime as more than simply a product of 'motiveless malignity', to quote Coleridge's famous description of Iago.

Our final reason for seeing considerable utility in attitude change experiments is more strategic than substantive. Demonstrations of this kind can play an important role in impeding the advance of punitive legislation. They can be used to respond to politicians who call for punitive reforms and cite the responses to simplistic polls in support of their proposals (see discussion in Roberts *et al.* 2003).

Our optimism is somewhat tempered, however. In the first place, governments may be reluctant to make the sort of long-term investment in public education about criminal justice that may pay dividends only after some years. And it should also be recognized that the news values of commercial media organizations are such that, regardless of reality, people will continue to be exposed to coverage about criminal justice that is over-dramatic and over-sensational. Stories about growing crime threats and incompetent responses from the police make better copy than the dull reality of everyday policing (which nevertheless may be quite successful). Leaving the logic of commercial news values to one side, it should also be recognized that the owners and editors of some influential newspapers pursue their own – usually tough-minded – agendas in relation to criminal policy. The media clearly play an important part in shaping public attitudes to crime and justice, and any initiative designed to improve public knowledge will have to take full account of the opportunities and obstacles presented by the press, television and radio programmes. In short, then, it will be a long, hard struggle to achieve a better-informed public debate about crime and its control. The fact that gains may be slow and that there are substantial countervailing pressures is hardly a reason for inaction, however.

The future

What does the future hold for public opinion research in the area of criminal justice? We see a number of important trends emerging. First, research is becoming more international, less parochial. Reviewing public opinion polls conducted in the 1980s and earlier is an exercise in cobbling together a picture of public views based upon surveys conducted in single jurisdictions, with no or little overlap in terms of the issues explored; and the wording of questions used in different countries is rarely comparable. This makes it hard to draw general conclusions about a subject such as public attitudes to the purposes of sentencing, for example.

More recently, there have been signs of some convergence. Researchers in different countries have been exploring the same issues – and have sometimes used comparable questions. This has permitted us to understand better the nature of public opinion. One example concerns the extent of public knowledge. Early research into public knowledge of crime and criminal justice trends was conducted in a single country (Canada). We now know that much of the 'knowledge deficit' regarding crime trends or sentencing patterns applies to the public in all Western nations and some developing countries as well.

Second, the increasing sophistication of polling techniques will permit a more refined examination of public attitudes to any specific issue. Our opinions about criminal justice, the economy, the National Health Service – any issue in fact – evolve in response to new information. Public opinion is never static in this respect. A true reading of public opinion can be obtained only by an interactive methodology that permits the researcher to provide the respondent with factual information relevant to the opinion being explored.

Finally, we have argued in this volume that public opinion has played an increasingly important role in the evolution of criminal justice policy. This is likely to continue. The political systems in developed industrialized countries have attached decreasing importance to the voice of 'experts' in most areas of social policy and have become more sensitive to the viewpoints of ordinary people. We have suggested that there are risks inherent in this process, particularly relating to populist exploitation of public ignorance about crime and justice. As greater political weight is attached to public opinion, it becomes correspondingly important to measure public attitudes carefully and to the best professional standards. A good example of the contribution that can be made by properly conducted surveys can be found in the United States. Although the American public tend to favour the use of capital punishment for the most serious forms of murder, a number of states are contemplating a moratorium on executions. Much of the impetus for this movement comes from public opinion research that has revealed that the public are becoming increasingly aware that judicial error has resulted in the ultimate nightmare for any criminal justice system: the wrongful conviction and subsequent execution of innocent people.

Notes

1 For example, when asked about allowing crime victims to submit impact statements prior to sentencing, the overwhelming majority of the public express their approval (Roberts and Erez 2004).

2 A typical example is the case of one of Jeremy Bentham's servants, who in 1780 stole two spoons from his eminent master and was subsequently hanged for his pains (Linebaugh 1992).

3 The last hanging at Tyburn took place in 1783, after which executions were conducted within the confines of a prison.

4 The breakdown was as follows: prevention, 44 per cent; punishment, 22 per cent; deterrence, 19 per cent; rehabilitation, 14 per cent (National Crime Prevention Council of Canada 2000).

5 Although we have not reviewed this material here, there is also a clear link between levels of fear of victimization and punitive attitudes. Unsurprisingly, people become more punitive in response to concerns about personal safety (e.g. Tufts and Roberts 2002). Public punitiveness is therefore in part instrumental in nature. To the extent that fear about crime is exaggerated, communications that allay some of the fears of the public may prove useful in lowering calls for harsher sentencing.

6 Two kinds of experimental designs have been employed. Doble and Klein (1989) used a pre–post design in which subjects were asked to decide on the sentence, and were then given information about the alternative sanctions available. Hough and Roberts used a 'between subjects' design, in which the total sample was split into two, half being asked to sentence the offender without, and half with, a menu of sentencing options. The result was the same, regardless of the design employed: when alternatives to imprisonment are made salient, support for imprisonment declines.

7 Measuring knowledge levels to ensure that participants learned from their participation represents the 'manipulation check' in the experiment.

8 There was some change noted in people who did *not* receive the booklet, suggesting that participating in a study changed public attitudes.

9 As of January 2005.

10 It is also worth noting that an hour-long television programme devoted to the weekend seminars was screened in Britain shortly after the event took place. Unfortunately, we have no public opinion research to test the impact of the programme on viewers' opinions about criminal justice.

References

Adams, K. (1992) Adjusting to prison life, in M. Tonry (ed.) *Crime and Justice. A Review of Research*, Volume 16. Chicago: University of Chicago Press.

Amelin, K., Willis, M., Blair, C. and Donnelly, D. (2000) *Attitudes to Crime, Crime Reduction and Community Safety in Northern Ireland*. Review of the Criminal Justice System in Northern Ireland. Research Report No. 1. Belfast: Northern Ireland Office.

American Bar Association (1999) *Perceptions of the US Justice System*. Chicago: American Bar Association.

American Correctional Association (1968) *The Public Looks at Crime and Corrections*. Report of a survey conducted by Louis Harris. College Park, MD: American Correctional Association.

Ames, A. (2003) Probation in the eyes of the public, *Probation Journal*, 50: 382–5.

Anderson, S., Ingram, D. and Hutton, N. (2002) Attitudes and knowledge about sentencing and punishment in Scotland, Scottish Parliament Paper 357. Available at www.scottish.parliament.uk/business/committees/historic/justice1/reports-02/j1r02-pats-02.htm

Angus Reid Group (1997) *Attitudes to Crime*. Ottawa: Angus Reid Group.

Angus Reid Group (2003) *Report for the Solicitor General*. Ottawa: Angus Reid Group.

Applegate, B. (2001) Penal austerity: perceived utility, desert, and public attitudes toward prison amenities, *American Journal of Criminal Justice*, 25: 253–67.

Applegate, B., Cullen, F. and Fisher, B. (1997) Public support for correctional treatment: the continuing appeal of the rehabilitative ideal, *Prison Journal*, 77: 237–58.

Applegate, B., Cullen, F., Turner, M. and Sundt, J. (1996) Assessing public support for 3-strikes and you're out laws: global versus specific attitudes, *Crime and Delinquency*, 42: 517–34.

Arbour, L. (1996) *Commission of Inquiry into Certain Events at the Prison for Women in Kingston*. Ottawa: Public Works and Government Services Canada.

Asher, H. (2004) *Polling and the Public. What Every Citizen Should Know*. Washington, DC: Congressional Quarterly.

Ashworth, A. (2000) *Sentencing and Criminal Justice*, 3rd edn. London: Butterworth.

Ashworth, A. and Hough, M. (1996) Sentencing and the climate of opinion, *Criminal Law Review*, 776–87.

Audit Commission (2004) *Youth Justice 2004. A Review of the Reformed Youth Justice System*. London: Audit Commission.

Bae, I. (1991) A survey on public acceptance of restitution as an alternative to incarceration for property offenders in Hennepin County, Doctoral dissertation, University of Minnesota.

Bae, I. (1992) A survey on public acceptance of restitution as an alternative to incarceration for property offenders in Hennepin County, Minnesota, USA, in H. Messmer and H.-U. Otto (eds) *Restorative Justice on Trial: Pitfalls and Potentials of Victim–Offender Mediation – International Research Perspective*. Boston: Kluwer Academic.

Baker, E. (1996) From 'making bad people worse' to 'prison works': sentencing policy in England and Wales in the 1990s, *Criminal Law Forum*, 7: 639–71.

Banks, C., Maloney, E. and Willcock, H. (1975) Public attitudes to crime and the penal system, *British Journal of Criminology*, 15: 228–40.

Bazemore, G. (1998) Crime victims and restorative justice in juvenile courts: judges as obstacle or leader, *Western Criminology Review*, 1: 1–36.

BBC (2002) BBC Race Survey. Available at http://news.bbc.co.uk/hi/english/static/in_depth/uk/2002/race/results_full.stm.

Beckett, K. (1997) *Making Crime Pay: Law and Order in Contemporary American Politics*. New York: Oxford University Press.

Belden Russonello and Stewart Research and Communications (1997) *Report of Existing Public Opinion Data on Juvenile Justice Issues*. Washington, DC: Belden Russonello and Stewart.

Belden Russonello and Stewart Research and Communications (2001) *Optimism, Pessimism, and Jailhouse Redemption: American Attitudes on Crime, Punishment, and Over-incarceration*. Washington, DC: Belden Russonello and Stewart.

Belgrave, J. (1995) Public attitudes towards restorative justice, in *Restorative Justice: A Discussion Paper*. Wellington, NZ: Ministry of Justice.

Bellamy, J. (1973) *Crime and Public Order in England in the Late Middle Ages*. London: Routledge and Kegan Paul.

Bendixen and Associates (2004) *Public Opinion Survey of California Ethnic Groups about Criminal Justice Issues*. California: Bendixen and Associates.

Bilz, K. (2002) Restorative justice and victim offender mediation (VOM): a new area for social psychological inquiry. Available at www.princeton.edu/~kbliz/VOM%20study%20writeup.htm.

Bittner, E. (1970) *The Function of the Police in Modern Society*. Chevy Chase, MD: National Institute of Mental Health.

Blumstein, A. and Cohen, J. (1980) Sentencing of convicted offenders: an analysis of the public's view, *Law and Society Review*, 14: 223–61.

Boers, K. and Sessar, K. (1989) Do people really want punishment? On the relationship between acceptance of restitution, needs for punishment, and fear of crime, in K. Sessar and H.-J. Kerner (eds) *Developments in Crime and Crime Control Research*. New York: Springer-Verlag.

Bottoms, A. (1995) The philosophy and politics of punishment and sentencing, in

C. Clarkson and R. Morgan (eds) *The Politics of Sentencing Reform*. Oxford: Clarendon Press.

Bottoms, A. and Dignan, J. (2004) Youth justice in Great Britain, in M. Tonry and A. Doob (eds) *Youth Crime and Youth Justice. Comparative and Cross-national Perspectives*. Chicago: University of Chicago Press.

Bowers, W. J. (1993) Capital punishment and contemporary values: people's misgivings and the court's misperceptions, *Law and Society Review*, 27: 157–75.

Braithwaite, J. (1989) *Crime, Shame, and Reintegration*. Cambridge: Cambridge University Press.

Braithwaite, J. (1999) Restorative justice: assessing optimistic and pessimistic accounts, in M. Tonry (ed.) *Crime and Justice. A Review of Research*. Chicago: University of Chicago Press.

Brillon, Y., Louis-Guerin, C. and Lamarche, M.-C. (1984) *Attitudes of the Canadian Public toward Crime Policies*. Montreal: Centre for Comparative Criminology, University of Montreal.

Brown, D. (2003) How does England incorporate the results of public opinion surveys on the administration of justice? Paper presented to the International Conference on Public Opinion and the Administration of Justice, Leuven, Belgium, September.

Bryant, P. and Morris, E. (1998) What does the public really think?, *Corrections Today*, 10: 26–79.

Burbidge, S. (1982) *Public Attitudes Concerning Pardons*. Ottawa: Ministry of the Solicitor General Canada.

California Poll (1982) North Carolina University Odum Institute, IRSS Study Number NNSP-CA-016. Available at http://cgi.irss.unc.edu/tempdocs/14:29:45:1.htm.

Centre for Opinion Research (2002) *Balanced and Restorative Justice Survey*. Millersville: Centre for Opinion Research.

Chapman, B., Mirrlees-Black, C. and Brawn, C. (2002) *Improving Public Attitudes to the Criminal Justice System: The Impact of Information*. HORS no. 245. London: Home Office.

Christian, P. (2000) Colorado community survey. A pathway to restorative practices, *VOMA Connections*, 6: 5–11.

Clancy, A., Hough, M., Aust, R. and Kershaw, C. (2001) Ethnic minorities' experience of crime and policing: findings from the 2000 British Crime Survey. *Findings*, No. 146. London: Home Office Research, Development and Statistics Directorate.

Clarke, A., Moran-Ellis, J. and Sleney, J. (2002) *Attitudes to Date Rape and Relationship Rape: A Qualitative Study*. Sentencing Advisory Panel. Available at www.sentencing-advisory-panel.gov.uk.

Cole, G. (1991) Thinking about crime: the scope of the problem and shifts in public policy, *The Public Perspective*, 2: 3–6.

Commission on Systemic Racism in the Ontario Criminal Justice System (1995) *Report of the Commission on Systemic Racism in the Ontario Criminal Justice System*. Toronto: Queen's Printer for Ontario.

Covell, K. and Howe, B. (1996) Public attitudes and juvenile justice in Canada, *International Journal of Children's Rights*, 4: 345–55.

Crawford, A. and Newburn, T. (2003) *Youth Offending and Restorative Justice. Implementing Reform in Youth Justice*. Cullompton: Willan Publishing.

Cullen, F. (2002) Rehabilitation and treatment programs, in J. Wilson and J.

Petersilia (eds) *Public Policies for Crime Control*. Oakland, CA: Institute for Contemporary Studies.

Cullen, F., Fisher, B. and Applegate, B. (2000) Public opinion about punishment and corrections, in M. Tonry (ed.) *Crime and Justice. A Review of Research*. Chicago: University of Chicago Press.

Cumberland, J. and Zamble, E. (1992) General and specific measures of attitudes toward early release of criminal offenders, *Canadian Journal of Behavioural Science*, 24: 442–55.

Darby, B. W. and Schlenker, B. R. (1989). Children's reactions to transgressions: effects of the actor's apology, reputation and remorse, *British Journal of Social Psychology*, 28: 353–64.

Darley, J., Carlsmith, K. and Robinson, P. (2000) Incapacitation and just deserts as motives for punishment, *Law and Human Behavior*, 24: 659–83.

Davis, D. (1997) *Attitudes toward Crime and Criminal Justice: What You Find Depends on What You Ask*. MSU State of the State Survey. Available at www.ippsr.msu.edu.

Department of Justice Canada (1988) *Public Attitudes towards Justice-related Issues*. Ottawa: Department of Justice Canada.

Department of Justice Canada (2004) *Canadian Attitudes towards Crime Prevention*. Ottawa: Department of Justice Canada.

Dignan, J. (2005) *Understanding Victims and Restorative Justice*. Maidenhead: Open University Press.

Doble, J. (1987) *Crime and Punishment: The Public's View*. New York: Edna McConnell Clark Foundation.

Doble, J. and Greene, J. (2000) *Attitudes towards Crime and Punishment in Vermont: Public Opinion about an Experiment with Restorative Justice*. Englewood Cliffs, NJ: Doble Research Associates.

Doble, J. and Klein, J. (1989) *Punishing Criminals. The Public's View*. New York: Edna McConnell Clark Foundation.

Doble Research Associates (1994) *Crime and Corrections. The Views of the People of Vermont*. Englewood Cliffs, NJ: Doble Research Associates.

Doble Research Associates (1995a) *Crime and Corrections. The Views of the People of Oaklahoma*. Englewood Cliffs, NJ: Doble Research Associates.

Doble Research Associates (1995b) *Crime and Corrections. The Views of the People of North Carolina*. Englewood Cliffs, NJ: Doble Research Associates.

Doble Research Associates (1998) *Crime and Corrections. The Views of the People of New Hampshire*. Englewood Cliffs, NJ: Doble Research Associates.

Doleschal, E. (1970) Public opinion and correctional reform, *Crime and Delinquency Literature*, 2: 456–76.

Doob, A. N. (2000) Transforming the punishment environment: understanding public views of what should be accomplished at sentencing, *Canadian Journal of Criminology*, 42: 323–40.

Doob, A. N. and Marinos, V. (1995) Reconceptualizing punishment: understanding the limitations on the use of intermediate punishments, *University of Chicago Law School Roundtable*, 2: 413–33.

Doob, A. and Roberts, J. V. (1982) *Crime and Official Response to Crime: The View of the Canadian Public*. Ottawa: Department of Justice Canada.

Doob, A. N. and Roberts, J. V. (1983) *Sentencing: An Analysis of the Public's View*. Ottawa: Department of Justice Canada.

Doob, A. N. and Roberts, J. V. (1988) Public punitiveness and public knowledge of the facts: some Canadian surveys, in N. Walker and M. Hough (eds) *Public Attitudes to Sentencing*. Cambridge Studies in Criminology. Aldershot: Gower.

Doob, A. N., Sprott, J., Marinos, V. and Varma, K. (1998) *An Exploration of Ontario Residents' Views of Crime and the Criminal Justice System*. Toronto: University of Toronto Center of Criminology.

Doob, A. N. and Webster, C. (2004) Sentence severity and crime: accepting the null hypothesis, in M. Tonry (ed.) *Crime and Justice. A Review of Research*. Chicago: University of Chicago Press.

Dorfman, L. and Schiraldi, V. (2001) Off balance: youth, race and crime in the news. Building Blocks for Youth. Available at www.buildingblocks foryouth.org/media/media.html.

Dowds, L. (1995) *The Long-eyed view of Law and Order: A Decade of British Social Attitudes Survey Results*. London: Home Office.

Duffee, D. and Ritti, R. (1977) Correctional policy and public values, *Criminology*, 14: 449–59.

Earnscliffe Research and Communications (2000) *Public Opinion Research into Youth Justice*. Ottawa: Earnscliffe Research and Communications.

Edgar, K. and Martin, C. (2004) *Perceptions of Race and Conflict: Perspectives of Minority Ethnic Prisoners and of Prison Officers*. London: Research, Development and Statistics, Home Office Online Report 11/04.

Environics Research Group (1989) *A Qualitative Investigation of Public Opinion on Sentencing, Corrections and Parole*. Ottawa: Environics Research Group.

Environics Research Group (1998) *Focus on Crime and Justice*. Ottawa: Environics Research Group.

Environics Research Group (2000) *Public Attitudes toward Correctional Issues in Kingston, Ontario*. Ottawa: Correctional Service of Canada.

Esmée Fairbairn Foundation (2002) *What Does the Public Think about Prison?* Available at www.rethinking.org.uk.

Esmée Fairbairn Foundation (2003) *Crime and Prisons Omnibus Survey*. Summary Report. London: Esmée Fairbairn Foundation.

Esmée Fairbairn Foundation (2004) *Rethinking Crime and Punishment: The Report*. London: Esmée Fairbairn Foundation.

European Opinion Research Group (2003) *Public Safety, Exposure to Drug-related Problems and Crime. Public Opinion Survey*. Report for the European Commission. Brussels: EC.

Farkas, S. (1997) Pennsylvanians prefer alternatives to prison, in M. Tonry and K. Hatlestad (eds) *Sentencing Reform in Overcrowded Times*. New York: Oxford.

Ferguson, S. (2000) *Researching the Public Opinion Environment. Theories and Methods*. Thousand Oaks, CA: Sage.

Ferraro, K., Johnson, J., Jorgenson, S. and Bolton, F. (1983) Problems of prisoners' families. The hidden costs of imprisonment, *Journal of Family Issues*, 4: 575–91.

Finney, A. (2004) Perceptions of changing crime levels, in S. Nicholas and A. Walker (eds) *Crime in England and Wales 2002/2003: Supplementary Volume 2: Crime, Disorder and the Criminal Justice System – Public Attitudes and Perceptions*. London: Office of National Statistics.

Fishkin, J. (1995) *The Voice of the People. Public Opinion and Democracy*. New York: Vail-Baillou Press.

Fitzgerald, M., Hough, M., Joseph, I. and Qureshi, T. (2002) *Policing for London*. Cullompton: Willan Publishing.

Flanagan, T. (1996a) Community corrections in the public mind, *Federal Probation*, 60: 3–9.

Flanagan, T. (1996b) Reform or punish? Americans' views of the correctional system, in T. Flanagan and D. Longmire (eds) *Americans View Crime and Criminal Justice. A National Public Opinion Survey*. Thousand Oaks, CA: Sage.

Flanagan, T. and Longmire, D. (eds) (1996) *Americans View Crime and Criminal Justice. A National Public Opinion Survey*. Thousand Oaks, CA: Sage.

Flanagan, T., McGarrell, E. and Brown, E. (1985) Public perceptions of the criminal courts: the role of demographic and related attitudinal variables, *Journal of Research in Crime and Delinquency*, 22: 66–82.

Florida Department of Corrections (1997) *Corrections in Florida: What the Public Thinks. Results of a Survey of Floridians*. Miami: Florida Department of Corrections.

Fogel, D., Galaway, B. and Hudson, J. (1972) Restitution in criminal justice: a Minnesota experiment, *Criminal Law Bulletin*, 8: 681–91.

Freeman, R. (1998) Public perception and corrections: correctional officers as smug hacks, in F. Bailey and D. Hale (eds) *Popular Culture, Crime, and Justice*. Belmont, CA: West/Wadsworth.

Galaway, B. (1984) A survey of public acceptance of restitution as an alternative to imprisonment for property offenders, *Australia and New Zealand Journal of Criminology*, 17: 108–16.

Gallup (2004) *American Attitudes towards the Death Penalty*. Available at www.gallup.com.

Gandy, J. (1978) Attitudes toward the use of restitution, in J. Hudson and B. Galaway (eds) *Offender Restitution in Theory and Action*. Lexington, MA: Lexington Books.

Gandy, J. and Galaway, B. (1980) Restitution as a sanction for offenders: a public's view, in J. Hudson and B. Galaway (eds) *Victims, Offenders, and Alternative Sanctions*. Lexington, MA: Lexington Books.

Garland, D. (2001) *The Culture of Control*. Chicago: University of Chicago Press.

Gebotys, R. and Roberts, J. (1987) Public views of sentencing: the role of offender characteristics, *Canadian Journal of Behavioral Science*, 19: 479–88.

Gehm, J. (1990) Mediated victim–offender restitution agreements: an exploratory analysis of factors related to victim participation, in B. Galaway and J. Hudson (eds) *Criminal Justice, Restitution, and Reconciliation*. Monsey, NY: Willow Tree Press.

Gerber, J. and Engelhardt-Greer, S. (1996) Just and painful: attitudes toward sentencing criminals, in T. Flanagan and D. Longmire (eds) *Americans View Crime and Justice*. Thousand Oaks, CA: Sage.

Giacalone, R. A. and Pollard, H. G. (1989) Comparative effectiveness of impression management tactics on the recommendation of grievant punishment: an exploratory investigation, *Forensics Reports*, 2: 147–60.

Gibbons, D. (1963) Who knows what about corrections?, *Crime and Delinquency*, 9: 137–44.

Gibson, J. L. (2001) Truth, justice, and reconciliation: judging amnesty in South Africa. Paper presented at the annual meeting of the Midwest Political Science Association, Chicago.

Glanz, L. (1994) The South African public's attitudes toward imprisonment and the release of offenders, *Acta Criminologica*, 7: 64–79.

Gorczyk, J. and Perry, J. (1997) What the public wants. Market research finds support for restorative justice, *Corrections Today*, 59: 78–83.

Gottfredson, S., Warner, B. and Taylor, R. (1988) Conflict and consensus about criminal justice in Maryland, in N. Walker and M. Hough (eds) *Public Attitudes to Sentencing. Surveys from Five Countries*. Aldershot: Gower.

Halman, L. (2001) *The European Values Study: A Third Wave. Sourcebook of the 1999/2000 European Values Study*. Tilburg: Tilburg University.

Harrel, W. A. (1981) The effects of alcohol use and offender remorsefulness on sentencing decisions, *Journal of Applied Social Psychology*, 11: 83–91.

Harris, L. (1975) *The Harris Survey. Belief about Major Contributors to Violence in the Country Today*. 27 October.

Hart, Peter D. Research Associates (2001) *The Public's Changing View of Crime*. Survey conducted for the Open Society Institute.

Higgins, D. and Snyder, C. (1996) North Carolinians want alternative sentences for nonviolent offenders, *Overcrowded Times*, 7: 12–15.

Home Office (2001) *Making Punishments Work. Report of a Review of the Sentencing Framework for England and Wales*. London: Home Office.

Hommers, W. (1988) The effects of apology and third party compensation on punishments imposed for two kinds of damages, *Zeitschrift für Sozialpsychologie*, 19: 139–51.

Hommers, W. (1991) The effects of apology, third party compensation, and amount of damage on children's and adults' judgments, *Zeitschrift für Experimentelle und Angewandte Psychologie*, 37: 399–419.

Hommers, W. and Endres, J. (1991) The effects of apology on interrelated judgments concerning restitution and punishment, *Zeitschrift für Experimentelle und Angewandte Psychologie*, 36: 433–52.

Hough, M. (1996) People talking about punishment, *Howard Journal of Criminal Justice*, 35: 191–214.

Hough, M. (1998) *Attitudes to Punishment: Findings from the 1992 British Crime Survey*. Social Science Research Paper No. 7. London: South Bank University.

Hough, M., Jacobson, J. and Millie, A. (2003) *The Decision to Imprison: Sentencing and the Prison Population*. London: Prison Reform Trust.

Hough, M. and Park, A. (2002) How malleable are attitudes to crime and punishment?, in J. V. Roberts and M. Hough (eds) *Changing Attitudes to Punishment. Public Opinion, Crime and Justice*. Cullompton: Willan Publishing.

Hough, M. and Roberts, J. V. (1998) *Attitudes to Punishment: Findings from the British Crime Survey*. Home Office Research Study No. 179. London: Home Office.

Hough, M. and Roberts, J. V. (1999) Sentencing trends in Britain: public knowledge and public opinion, *Punishment and Society: The International Journal of Penology*, 1: 7–22.

Hough, M. and Roberts, J. V. (2002) Public knowledge and public opinion of sentencing, in N. Hutton and C. Tata (eds) *Sentencing and Society: International Perspectives*. Aldershot: Ashgate.

Hough, M. and Roberts, J. V. (2004a) *Confidence in Criminal Justice. An International Review*. ICPR Research Paper No. 3. London: King's College.

Hough, M. and Roberts, J. (2004b) *Youth Crime and Youth Justice: Public Opin-*

ion in England and Wales. Researching Criminal Policy Paper. Bristol: Policy Press.

Huang, W. and Vaughn, M. (1996) Support and confidence: public attitudes toward the police, in T. Flanagan and D. Longmire (eds) *Americans View Crime and Justice. A National Public Opinion Survey*. Thousand Oaks, CA: Sage.

Hudson, J. (1992) A review of research dealing with views on financial restitution, in H. Messmer and H. Otto (eds) *Restorative Justice on Trial: Pitfalls and Potentials of Victim–Offender Mediation – International Research Perspectives*. Boston: Kluwer Academic.

Hutton, N. (2005) Beyond populist punitiveness?, *Punishment and Society*, 7: 243-48.

Immerwahr, J. and Johnson, J. (2002) *The Revolving Door: Exploring Public Attitudes toward Prisoner Reentry*. Discussion Paper for the Urban Institute's Reentry Roundtable. Available at www.urban.org.

Indermaur, D. (1987) Public perception of sentencing in Perth, Western Australia, *Australia and New Zealand Journal of Criminology*, 20: 163–83.

Indermaur, D. (1990) Perceptions of crime seriousness and sentencing: a comparison of court practice and the perceptions of the public and judges, *Report to the Criminology Research Council, Australian Institute of Criminology*, 11: 247–70.

Indianapolis Restorative Justice Experiment (2001) *Juvenile Justice Bulletin*. Available at www.ncjrs.org/html/ojjdp/jjbul2001_8_2/page3.html.

Jennings, D. (2003) One year juvenile reconviction rates: first quarter of 2001 cohort. Home Office Online Report 18/03. Available at www.homeoffice.gov.uk/rds.

Johnstone, G. (2002) *Restorative Justice*. Cullompton: Willan Publishing.

Jones, P. (1994) It's not what you ask, it's the way that you ask it: question form and public opinion on the death penalty, *The Prison Journal*, 73: 32–50.

Jubinville, R., Hatt, K. and Davies, D. (1987) *Attitudes Toward Parole*. Ottawa: Canadian Criminal Justice Association.

Junger-Tas, J. and Terlouw, G. (1991) *The Dutch Public and the Crime Problem*. Bulletin No. 5. The Hague: Ministry of Justice, Research and Documentation Centre.

Justice 1 Committee (2002) *Public Attitudes towards Sentencing and Alternatives to Imprisonment*. Available at: www.scottish.parliament.uk/business/committees/historic/justice1/reports-02/j1r02-pats-02.htm

Karp, D. R. (2001) Harm and repair: observing restorative justice in Vermont, *Justice Quarterly*, 18: 727–57.

Kaukinen, C. and Colavecchia, S. (1999) Public perceptions of the courts: an examination of attitudes toward the treatment of victims and the accused, *Canadian Journal of Criminology*, 41: 365–84.

Kilpatrick, D. G., Beatty, D. and Howley, S. S. (1998) *The Rights of Crime Victims. Does Legal Protection Make a Difference*. Washington, DC: US Department of Justice, National Institute of Justice NCJ 173839.

King, J. and Grimshaw, R. (2003) *Evaluation of the 'Local Crime/Community Sentence' Project. Final Full Report*. London: Centre for Crime and Justice, Law School, King's College.

Kleinke, C., Wallis, R. and Stalder, K. (1992) Evaluation of a rapist as a function of expressed intent and remorse, *Journal of Social Psychology*, 132: 525–37.

Knight, D. (1965) Punishment selection as a function of biographical information, *Journal of Criminal Law, Criminology and Police Science*, 56: 325–7.

Knowles, J. (1985) *Ohio Citizen Attitudes Concerning Crime and Criminal Justice*. Columbus: Ohio Department of Development.

Kotze, H. (2003) Mass and elite attitudes towards the criminal justice system in South Africa: how congruent?, *South African Journal of Criminology*, 16: 38–57.

Kritzer, H. and Voelker, J. (1998) Familiarity breeds respect: how Wisconsin citizens view their courts, *Judicature*, 82: 58–64.

Kury, H. (2002) Introduction to special issue. International comparison of crime and victimization: the ICVS, *International Journal of Comparative Criminology*, 2: 1–9.

Kury, H. and Ferdinand, T. (1999) Public opinion and punitivity, *International Journal of Law and Psychiatry*, 22: 373–92.

Kury, H., Oberfell-Fuchs, J. and Smartt, U. (2002) The evolution of public attitudes to punishment in Western and Eastern Europe, in J. V. Roberts and M. Hough (eds) *Changing Attitudes to Punishment*. Cullompton: Willan Publishing.

Lee, A. (1996) Public attitudes toward restorative justice, in B. Galaway and J. Hudson (eds) *Restorative Justice: International Perspectives*. Monsey, NY: Criminal Justice Press.

Lenz, N. (2002) 'Luxuries' in prison: the relationship between amenity funding and public support, *Crime and Delinquency*, 48: 499–525.

Liebling, A. (1994) Suicide amongst women prisoners, *The Howard Journal*, 33: 1–9.

Linebaugh, P. (1992) *The London Hanged. Crime and Civil Society in the Eighteenth Century*. Cambridge: Cambridge University Press.

Longmire, D. (1996) Americans' attitudes about the ultimate weapon: capital punishment, in T. Flanagan and D. Longmire (eds) *Americans View Crime and Criminal Justice. A National Public Opinion Survey*. Thousand Oaks, CA: Sage.

Maguire, M. and Bennett, T. (1982) *Burglary in a Dwelling: The Offence, the Offender and The Victim*. London: Heinemann.

Maguire, K. and Pastore, A. L. (1997) *United States Department of Justice Sourcebook of Criminal Justice Statistics*. Washington, DC: US Department of Justice.

Mande, M. and English, K. (1989) *The Effect of Public Opinion on Correctional Policy: A Comparison of Opinions and Practices*. Denver: Colorado Department of Public Safety, Division of Criminal Justice.

Manza, J., Brooks, C. and Uggen, C. (2004) *Public Attitudes towards Felony Disenfranchisement in the United States*. Evanston, IL: Department of Sociology, Northwestern University.

Manza, J., Cook, F. and Page, B. (2002) *Navigating Public Opinion*. Oxford: Oxford University Press.

Maruna, S. and King, A. (2004) Public opinion and community penalties, in A. Bottoms, S. Rex and G. Robinson (eds) *Alternatives to Prison. Options for an Insecure Society*. Cullompton: Willan Publishing.

Mathews, R., Hancock, L. and Briggs, D. (2004) Jurors' perceptions, understanding, confidence and satisfaction in the jury system: a study of six courts. *Findings*, No. 227. London: Home Office.

Mattinson, J., and Mirrlees-Black, C. (2000) *Attitudes to Crime and Criminal Justice: Findings from the 1998 British Crime Survey.* Home Office Research Study No. 200. London: Home Office Research, Development and Statistics Directorate.

Mayhew, P. and van Kesteren, J. (2002) Cross-national attitudes to punishment, in J. V. Roberts and M. Hough (eds) *Changing Attitudes to Punishment. Public Opinion, Crime and Justice.* Cullompton: Willan Publishing.

McCold, P. (1996) Restorative justice and the role of the community, in B. Galaway and J. Hudson (eds) *Restorative Justice: International Perspectives.* Monsey, NY: Criminal Justice Press.

McGarrell, E. F. and Sandys, M. (1996) The misperception of public opinion toward capital punishment: examining the spuriousness explanation of death penalty support, *American Behavioral Scientist*, 39: 500–13.

Metraux, S. and Culhane, D. (2004) Homeless shelter use and reincarnation following prison release, *Criminology and Public Policy*, 3: 139–60.

Mirrlees-Black, C. (2001) *Confidence in the Criminal Justice System: Findings from the 2000 British Crime Survey.* RDS Research Findings No. 137. London: Home Office.

Monograph 45 (2000) *Justice versus Retribution: Attitudes to Punishment in the Eastern Cape.* Available at www.iss.co.za/Pubs/Monographs/No45/knowledge.html.

Moore, R. (1985) Reflections of Canadians on the law and the legal system: Legal Research Institute survey of respondents in Montreal, Toronto and Winnipeg, in D. Gibson and J. Baldwin (eds) *Law in a Cynical Society? Opinion and Law in the 1980s.* Calgary: Carswell Legal Publications.

Morgan, R. (2002) Privileging public attitudes to sentencing?, in J. V. Roberts and M. Hough (eds) *Changing Attitudes to Punishment. Public Opinion, Crime and Justice.* Cullompton: Willan Publishing.

MORI (2000) Crime and punishment poll. MORI poll 16 July. Available at www.mori.com/polls/2000/ms000714.shtml.

MORI (2001) Parenting not prison the answer to crime. MORI poll 11 December. Available at www.mori.com/polls/2001/eff_top.shtml.

MORI (2003) *Survey of Public Confidence in Criminal Justice.* London: MORI.

MORI (2004a) Confidence in justice system. MORI poll 14 April. Available at www.mori.com/polls/2004/fawcett.shtml.

MORI (2004b) Public says prison not the answer for women. MORI poll 14 April. Available at www.mori.com/polls/2004/fawcett.shtml.

Morris, A. (2004) Youth justice in New Zealand, in M. Tonry and A. Doob (eds) *Crime and Justice.* Chicago: University of Chicago Press.

MRL Research Group (1995) *Public Attitudes Towards Restorative Justice.* Wellington, NZ: Department of Justice. Available at www.justice.govt.nz/pubs/reports/1996/restorative/chapter4.htm.

National Centre for State Courts (1978) *The Public Image of Courts.* Willamsburg, VA: National Centre for State Courts.

National Centre for State Courts (1999) *How the Public Views the State Courts. A 1999 National Survey.* Willamsburg, VA: National Centre for State Courts.

National Crime Prevention Council of Canada (1997) *Canadian Attitudes toward Crime and Crime Prevention.* Ottawa: National Crime Prevention Council of Canada.

National Crime Prevention Council of Canada (2000) *Canadian Attitudes towards the Prevention of Crime.* Ottawa: National Crime Prevention Council of Canada.

National Institute of Justice (2003) *Factors that Influence Public Opinion of the Police.* Washington, DC: US Department of Justice.

National Victim Centre (1991) *America Speaks Out: Citizens' Attitudes about Victims' Rights and Violence.* New York: National Victim Centre.

Nellis, M. (1988) British prison movies: the case of 'Now Barrabas', *The Howard Journal,* 27: 2–31.

New Zealand Department of Justice (1995) *Public Attitudes towards Restorative Justice.* Wellington: New Zealand Department of Justice.

Nicholas, S. and Walker, A. (2003) *Crime in England and Wales, 2001/02: Supplementary Volume 2. Crime, Disorder and the Criminal Justice System – Public Attitudes and Perceptions.* London: Home Office.

Nicholas, S. and Walker, A. (eds) (2004) *Crime in England and Wales 2002/2003: Supplementary Volume 2. Crime, Disorder and the Criminal Justice System – Public Attitudes and Perceptions.* Home Office Statistical Bulletin 02/04. London: Home Office.

Nuttall, C., Eversley, D., Rudder, I. and Ramsay, J. (2003) *Views and Beliefs about Crime and Criminal Justice.* Bridgetown: Barbados Statistical Department.

Observer (2003) Crime uncovered. A nation under the cosh? The truth about crime in Britain in 2003, *Observer* Magazine, 27 April.

O'Connell, M. (1999) Is Irish public opinion towards crime distorted by media bias?, *European Journal of Communication,* 14: 191–212.

Ohbuchi, K., Kameda, M. and Agarie, N. (1989) Apology as aggression control: its role in mediating appraisal of and response to harm, *Journal of Personality and Social Psychology,* 56: 219–27.

Packer, H. (1968) *The Limits of the Criminal Sanction.* Stanford, CA: Stanford University Press.

Palmer, D. (1990) *Determinants of Canadian Attitudes toward Immigration.* Ottawa: Citizenship and Immigration.

Parmentier, S., Vervaeke, J. Goethals, R., Doutrelepont, R., Kellens, G., Lemaitre, A., Biren, P., Cloet, B., Schloffen, M., Sintobin, M., Vandekeere, M., Vanderhallen, M. and Van Win, T. (2004a) *Une Radiographie de la Justice.* Leuven: Catholic University.

Parmentier, S., Vervaeke, G., Doutrelepont, R. and Kellens, G. (eds) (2004b) *Popular Perceptions and Their Implications for Policy-making in Western Countries.* Brussels: Politeia Press.

Paulin, J., Searle, W. and Knaggs, T. (2003) *Attitudes to Crime and Punishment: A New Zealand Study.* Wellington, NZ: Ministry of Justice.

Peachey, D. (1989) The Kitchener experiment, in M. Wright and B. Galaway (eds) *Mediation and Criminal Justice. Victims, Offenders and Community.* London: Sage.

Pepper, S., Lovbakke, J. and Upson, A. (2004) Confidence and the criminal justice system, in S. Nicholas and A. Walker (eds) *Crime in England and Wales 2002/ 2003: Supplementary Volume 2: Crime, Disorder and the Criminal Justice System – Public Attitudes and Perceptions.* London: Home Office Research, Development and Statistics Directorate.

Pew Research Centre for the People and the Press (2000) *Internet Sapping Broadcast News Audience.* Available at www.people-press.org/media00rpt.htm.

Pranis, K. and Umbreit, M. (1992) *Public Opinion Research Challenges Perception of Widespread Public Demand for Harsh Punishment*. Minneapolis: Citizens' Council.

Pratt, J. and Clark, M. (2005) Penal populism in New Zealand, *Punishment and Society*, 7: 303–22.

Redondo, S., Luque, E. and Funes, J. (1996) Social beliefs about recidivism in crime, in G. Davies, S. Lloyd-Bostock, M. McMurran and C. Wilson (eds) *Psychology, Law, and Criminal Justice. International Developments in Research and Practice*. New York: Walter de Gruyter.

Reed, J. and Nance, D. (1972) Society perpetuates the stigma of a conviction, *Federal Probation*, 2: 27–31.

Reith, C. (1956) *A New Study of Police History*. London: Oliver and Boyd.

Ringham, L. and Salisbury, H. (2004) *Support for Victims of Crime: Findings from the 2002/03 British Crime Survey*. Home Office On-line Report 31/04. London: Home Office.

Roberts, J. V. (1988a) Early release: what do the Canadian public really think?, *Canadian Journal of Criminology*, 30: 231–9.

Roberts, J. V. (1988b) *Public Opinion and Sentencing: The Surveys of the Canadian Sentencing Commission*. Ottawa: Department of Justice Canada.

Roberts, J. V. (1992) Public opinion, crime and criminal justice, in M. Tonry (ed.) *Crime and Justice. A Review of Research*, Volume 16. Chicago: University of Chicago Press.

Roberts, J. V. (1995) *Public Knowledge of Crime and Justice*. Ottawa: Department of Justice Canada.

Roberts, J. V. (1996) Public opinion, criminal record and the sentencing process, *American Behavioral Scientist*, 39: 488–99.

Roberts, J. V. (1997a) American attitudes about punishment, in J. Petersilia (ed.) *Community Corrections*. New York: Oxford University Press.

Roberts, J. V. (1997b) American attitudes towards punishment, in M. Tonry and K. Hatlestad (eds) *Sentencing Reform in Overcrowded Times. A Comparative Perspective*. New York: Oxford University Press.

Roberts, J. V. (2001) Public perceptions of corrections in Canada, in J. Winterdyk (ed.) *Corrections in Canada*. Scarborough: Prentice Hall.

Roberts, J. V. (2002a) Determining parole eligibility dates for life prisoners: lessons from jury hearings in Canada, *Punishment and Society: The International Journal of Penology*, 4: 103–14.

Roberts, J. V. (2002b) Public attitudes to community-based sanctions, in J. V. Roberts and M. Hough (eds) *Changing Attitudes to Punishment. Public Opinion, Crime and Justice*. Cullompton: Willan Publishing.

Roberts, J. V. (2002c) Public opinion and sentencing policy, in S. Rex and M. Tonry (eds) *Reform and Punishment. The Future of Sentencing*. Cullompton: Willan.

Roberts, J. V. (2002d) *Public Perceptions of the Prosecution Function: An International Perspective*. Ottawa: Department of Criminology, University of Ottawa.

Roberts, J. V. (2003a) Public opinion and mandatory sentences of imprisonment: a review of international findings, *Criminal Justice and Behavior*, 20: 1–26.

Roberts, J. V. (2003b) Victim impact statements and the sentencing process: enhancing communication in the courtroom, *Criminal Law Quarterly*, 47: 365–96.

Roberts, J. V. (2004) Public opinion and the evolution of juvenile justice policy in Western nations, in M. Tonry and A. Doob (eds) *Youth Crime and Youth*

Justice. Comparative and Cross-national Perspectives. Chicago: University of Chicago Press.

Roberts, J. V. and Bala, N. (2003) Understanding sentencing under the Youth Criminal Justice Act, *Alberta Law Review*, 41: 395–423.

Roberts, J. V. and Doob, A. N. (1989) Sentencing and public opinion: taking false shadows for true substances, *Osgoode Hall Law Journal*, 27: 491–515.

Roberts, J. V. and Doob, A. N. (1990) News media influences on public views of sentencing, *Law and Human Behavior*, 14: 451–68.

Roberts, J. V. and Erez, E. (2004) Communication in sentencing: exploring the expressive and the impact model of victim impact statements, *International Review of Victimology*, 10: 223–44.

Roberts, J. V. and Gabor, T. (2004) Living in the shadow of prison: lessons from the Canadian experience in decarceration, *British Journal of Criminology*, 39: 92–112.

Roberts, J. V. and Gebotys, R. (1987) Public views of sentencing: the role of offender characteristics, *Canadian Journal of Behavioural Science*, 19: 479–88.

Roberts, J. V. and Gebotys, R. (1989) The purposes of sentencing: public support for competing aims, *Behavioural Sciences and the Law*, 7: 387–402.

Roberts, J. V., Gebotys, R. and DasGupta, B. (1988) News media use and public perceptions of crime seriousness, *Canadian Journal of Criminology*, 30: 3–16.

Roberts, J. V. and Grossman, M. (1990) Crime prevention and public opinion, *Canadian Journal of Criminology*, 32: 75–90.

Roberts, J. V. and Hough, M. (2001) Public opinion, sentencing and parole: international trends, in R. Roesch, R. Corrado and R. Dempster (eds) *Psychology in the Courts: International Advances in Knowledge*. Amsterdam: Harwood Academic.

Roberts, J. V. and Hough, M. (2002a) Changing attitudes to punishment: the context, in J. V. Roberts and M. Hough (eds) *Changing Attitudes to Punishment. Public Opinion, Crime and Justice*. Cullompton: Willan Publishing.

Roberts, J. V. and Hough, M. (eds) (2002b) *Changing Attitudes to Punishment. Public Opinion, Crime and Justice*. Cullompton: Willan Publishing.

Roberts, J. V. and Jackson, M. (1991) Boats against the current: a note on the effects of imprisonment, *Law and Human Behavior*, 15: 557–62.

Roberts, J. V., Nuffield, J. and Hann, R. (1998) *Report of a National Survey on Organized Crime and Corrections in Canada*. Ottawa: Ministry of the Solicitor General.

Roberts, J. V., Nuffield, J. and Hann, R. (2000) Parole and the public: attitudinal and behavioural responses, *Empirical and Applied Criminal Justice Research*, 1: 1–29.

Roberts, J. V., Nuffield, J., Hann, R., Beare, M. and Tremblay, P. (1999) *Public Knowledge and Opinion with respect to Organized Crime and Corrections: Findings from a National Survey*. Ottawa: Ministry of the Solicitor General Canada.

Roberts, J. V. and Stalans, L. (1997) *Public Opinion, Crime, and Criminal Justice*. Boulder, CO: Westview Press.

Roberts, J. V. and Stalans, L. (1998) Crime, criminal justice and public opinion, in M. Tonry (ed.) *The Oxford Handbook of Crime and Punishment*. New York: Oxford University Press.

Roberts, J. V. and Stalans, L. (2003) *Restorative Justice: An Analysis of the Public's View*. Ottawa: Department of Criminology, University of Ottawa.

Roberts, J. V., Stalans, L. S., Indermaur, D. and Hough, M. (2003) *Penal Populism and Public Opinion. Lessons from Five Countries*. Oxford: Oxford University Press.

Roberts, J. V. and White, N. (1986) Public estimates of recidivism rates: consequences of a criminal stereotype, *Canadian Journal of Criminology*, 28: 229–41.

Robinson, D. T., Smith-Lovin, L. and Tsoudis, O. (1994) Heinous crime or unfortunate accident? The effects of remorse on responses to mock criminal confessions, *Social Forces*, 73: 175–90.

Rossi, P. and Berk, R. (1997) *Just Punishments. Federal Guidelines and Public Views Compared*. New York: Aldine de Gruyter.

Rossi, P., Simpson, J. and Miller, J. (1985) Beyond crime seriousness: fitting the punishment to the crime, *Journal of Quantitative Criminology*, 1: 59–90.

Rumsey, M. G. (1976). Effects of defendant background and remorse on sentencing judgments, *Journal of Applied Social Psychology*, 6: 64–8.

Russell, N. and Morgan, R. (2001) *Sentencing of Domestic Burglary*. Research Report, Sentencing Advisory Panel. Available at www.sentencing-advisory-panel.gov.uk/saprr1.htm.

Sacco, V. and Johnson, H. (1990) *Patterns of Criminal Victimization in Canada*. Ottawa: Minister of Supply and Services.

Salisbury, H. (2004) *Public Attitudes to the Criminal Justice System: The Impact of Providing Information to British Crime Survey Respondents*. London: Home Office. Online Report 64/04.

Sanders, T. and Roberts, J. V. (2000) Public attitudes toward conditional sentencing: results of a national survey, *Canadian Journal of Behavioral Science*, 32: 113–25.

Scher, S. and Darley, J. (1997) How effective are the things people say to apologize? Effects of the realization of the apology speech act, *Journal of Psycholinguistics Research*, 26: 127–40.

Schonteich, M. (1999) *Sentencing in South Africa. Public Perception and Judicial Practice*. Occasional Paper No. 43. Cape Town: Institute for Security Studies.

Schwartz, I. (1992) Juvenile crime-fighting policies: what the public really wants, in I. Schwartz (ed.) *Juvenile Justice and Public Policy: Toward a National Agenda*. New York: Lexington Books.

Scott, J. and Al-Thakeb, F. (1977) The public's perceptions of crime: a comparative analysis of Scandinavia, Western Europe, the Middle East and the United States, in C. Huff (ed.) *Contemporary Corrections*. Beverly Hills, CA: Sage.

Scottish Office (1996) Detailed analysis of the 1996 Scottish Crime Survey published today. Available at www.scotland.gov.uk/news/releas96_2/pr1841.htm.

Secretary of State (2002) *Justice for All*. CM 5563. Norwich: The Stationery Office.

Sessar, K. (1990) Tertiary victimization: a case of the politically abused crime victims, in B. Galaway and J. Hudson (eds) *Criminal Justice, Restitution, and Reconciliation*. Monsey, NY: Willow Tree Press.

Sessar, K. (1999) Punitive attitudes of the public: reality and myth, in G. Bazemore and L. Walgrave (eds) *Restorative Juvenile Justice: Repairing the Harm of Youth Crime*. Monsey, NY: Criminal Justice Press.

Shaw, S. (1982) *The People's Justice: A Major Poll of Public Attitudes on Crime and Punishment*. London: Prison Reform Trust.

Sherman, L. (2002) Trust and confidence in criminal justice, *National Institute of Justice Journal*, 248: 22–31.

Silvey, J. (1961) The criminal law and public opinion, *Criminal Law Review*, 349–58.

Simmons, J. (1965) Public stereotypes of deviants, *Social Problems*, 13: 223–32.

Simmons, J. and Dodd, T. (eds) (2003) *Crime in England and Wales, 2002/2003*. London: Home Office.

Sinkinson, H. and Broderick, J. (1997) Restorative justice in Vermont: citizens' reparative boards, *Overcrowded Times*, 8: 1–20.

Sita, N. and Edanyu, G. (1999) Awareness and attitude of the public towards community service. Interim National Committee on Community Service. Available at www.restorativejustice.org.

Skogan, W. G. (forthcoming 2005) Asymmetry in the impact of encounters with the police. *Policing and Society*, in press.

Skovron, S., Scott, J. and Cullen, F. (1988) Prison crowding: public attitudes toward strategies of population control, *Journal of Research in Crime and Delinquency*, 25: 150–69.

Smith, B., Sloan, J. and Ward, R. (1990) Public support for the victims' rights movement: results of a statewide survey, *Crime and Delinquency*, 36: 488–502.

Smith, D. (1983) *Police and People in London. I. A Survey of Londoners*. London: Policy Studies Institute.

Solicitor General Canada (1981) *Solicitor General's Study of Conditional Release*. Ottawa: Solicitor General Canada.

Solicitor General Canada (1989) *A Qualitative Investigation of Public Opinion on Sentencing, Corrections and Parole*. Ottawa: Solicitor General Canada.

Sourcebook of Criminal Justice Statistics (1990) *Table 2.50*. Washington, DC: US Bureau of Justice Statistics.

Sourcebook of Criminal Justice Statistics (1997) *Table 2.51*. Washington, DC: US Bureau of Justice Statistics.

Sourcebook of Criminal Justice Statistics (2003) Washington, DC: US Bureau of Justice Statistics.

Sourcebook of Criminal Justice Statistics (2004) Available at: www.albany.edu/sourcebook.

Stalans, L. S. (2002) Measuring attitudes to sentencing, in J.V. Roberts and M. Hough (eds) *Changing Attitudes to Punishment. Public Opinion, Crime and Justice*. Cullompton: Willan Publishing.

Stalans, L.S. and Lurigio, A. (1996) Public opinion about the creation, enforcement, and punishment of criminal offences. *American Behavioral Scientist*, 39: 435–50.

Stop Prisoner Rape (2004) *Public Attitudes toward Prisoner Rape*. Available at www.spr.org/en/factsheetattitudes.html.

Subordinate Courts of Singapore (1998) Survey on public attitudes and perceptions of the judiciary in Singapore. *Research Bulletin*, 12. Subordinate Courts of Singapore, Research and Statistics Unit.

Sundt, J. (1994) Is there room for change? A review of public attitudes toward crime control and alternatives to incarceration. *Southern Illinois University Law Journal*. Available online at: www.law.siu.edu/lawjour.

Swanton, B., Wilson, P., Walker, J. and Mukherjee, S. (1988) How the public see the police: an Australian survey. *Trends and Issues*, 11. Canberra: Australian Institute of Criminology.

Taylor, H. (1999) How hard it is to communicate good news. Harris Poll 34, 2 June. Available at: www.harrisinteractive.com/harris_poll/.

Taylor, H. (2004) Differing perceptions of the guilt or innocence of Michael Jackson, Kobe Bryant and Martha Stewart. Harris Poll 37, 6 August 2001. Available at www.harrisinteractive.com/harris_poll/.

Tonry, M. and Doob, A. (eds) (2004) *Youth Crime and Youth Justice. Comparative and Cross-national Perspectives*. Chicago: University of Chicago Press.

Triplett, R. (1996) The growing threat: gangs and juvenile offenders, in T. Flanagan and D. Longmire (eds) *Americans View Crime and Justice*. Thousand Oaks, CA: Sage.

Tufts, J. (2000) Public attitudes toward the criminal justice system, *Juristat*, 20(12).

Tufts, J. and Roberts, J. V. (2002) Sentencing juvenile offenders: comparing public preferences and judicial practice, *Criminal Justice Policy Review*, 13: 46–64.

Turner, M., Cullen, F., Sundt, J. and Applegate, B. (1997) Public tolerance for community-based sanctions, *The Prison Journal*, 77: 6–26.

Tyler, T. (1990) *Why People Obey the Law*. New Haven, CT: Yale University Press.

Tyler, T. (2002) *Trust in the Law: Encouraging Public Co-operation with the Police and the Courts*. New York: Russell Sage Foundation.

Uggen, C. and Manza, J. (2002) Democratic reversal? The political consequences of felon disenfranchisement, *American Sociological Review*, 67: 777–803.

Umbreit, M. (1994) *Victim Meets Offender: The Impact of Restorative Justice and Mediation*. Monsey, NY: Criminal Justice Press.

Umbreit, M. and Coates, R. (2001) The impact of victim–offender mediation: two decades of research, *Federal Probation*, 65: 29–35.

University of Arkansas (1999) *Arkansas Crime Poll. Confidence in the Criminal Justice System*. Little Rock, AR: Department of Criminal Justice, University of Arkansas at Little Rock.

Unnever, J., Cullen, F. and Roberts, J. V. (2005) Not everyone strongly supports the death penalty: assessing weakly-held attitudes about capital punishment, *American Journal of Criminal Justice*, in press.

US Bureau of Justice Statistics (2003) Nation's prison and jail population exceeds 2 million inmates for first time. Press release, 6 April. Washington, DC: US Department of Justice, Bureau of Justice Statistics.

van Ness, D. (1990) Restorative justice, in B. Galaway and J. Hudson (eds) *Criminal Justice, Restitution, and Reconciliation*. Monsey, NY: Criminal Justice Press.

van Ness, D. (2002) *Restoring Justice*, 2nd edn. Cincinnati, OH: Anderson Publishing.

von Hirsch, A., Bottoms, A., Burney, E. and Wikstrom, P.-O. (1999) *Criminal Deterrence and Sentence Severity*. Oxford: Hart Publishing.

von Hirsch, A., Roberts, J. V., Bottoms, A. E., Roach, K. and Schiff, M. (eds) (2003) *Restorative and Criminal Justice. Competing or Reconcilable Paradigms?* Oxford: Hart Publishing.

Walgrave, L. (ed.) (2002) *Restorative Justice and the Law*. Cullompton: Willan Publishing.

Walker, J., Collins, M. and Wilson, P. (1988a) How the public sees sentencing: an Australian survey, in N. Walker and M. Hough (eds) *Public Attitudes to Sentencing. Surveys from Five Countries*. Aldershot: Gower.

Walker, N. (1983) Side-effects of incarceration, *British Journal of Criminology*, 23: 61–71.

Walker, N. and Hough, M. (eds) (1988) *Public Attitudes to Sentencing. Surveys from Five Countries*. Aldershot: Gower.

Walker, N., Hough, M. and Lewis, H. (1988b) Tolerance of leniency and severity in England and Wales, in N. Walker and M. Hough (eds) *Public Attitudes to Sentencing. Surveys from Five Countries*. Aldershot: Gower.

Walker, S. (1998) Complaints against the police: a focus group study of citizen perceptions, goals, and expectations, *Criminal Justice Review*, 22: 207–26.

Weatherburn, D. and Indermaur, D. (2004) Public perceptions of crime trends in New South Wales and Western Australia, *Crime and Justice Bulletin*, 80.

Whitehead, E. (2000) *Witness Satisfaction: Findings from the Witness Satisfaction Survey*. London: Home Office.

Whitehead, J., Blankenship, M. and Wright, J. (1999) Elite versus citizen attitudes on capital punishment: incongruity between the public and policy-makers, *Journal of Criminal Justice*, 27: 249–58.

Whitehead, J. and Taylor, J. (2003) Confidence in the criminal justice system, in C. Flood-Page and J. Taylor (eds) *Crime in England and Wales 2001/02: Supplementary Tables*. London: Home Office.

Wood, J. and Viki, G. (2004) Public perceptions of crime and punishment, in J. Adler (ed.) *Forensic Psychology. Concepts, Debates and Practice*. Cullompton: Willan Publishing.

Wortley, S., Macmillan, R. and Hagan, J. (1997) Just des(s)erts: the racial polarization of perceptions of criminal injustice, *Law and Society Review*, 31: 637–76.

Wright, M. (1989) What the public wants, in M. Wright and B. Galaway (eds) *Mediation and Criminal Justice. Victims, Offenders and Community*. London: Sage.

Young, R. and Hoyle, C. (2003) New, improved police-led restorative justice?, in A. von Hirsch, J. V. Roberts, A. Bottoms, K. Roach and M. Schiff (eds) *Restorative and Criminal Justice. Competing or Reconcilable Paradigms?* Oxford: Hart Publishing.

Youth Justice Board for England and Wales (2002) *Summary of the MORI 2002 Youth Survey*. London: Youth Justice Board.

Zamble, E. and Kalm, K. (1990) General and specific measures of public attitudes toward sentencing, *Canadian Journal of Behavioural Science*, 22: 327–37.

Index

Page numbers in *italics* refer to boxes and tables, *passim* indicates numerous scattered mentions within page range.